AMERICANS

AMERICANS

BY

STUART P. SHERMAN, 1881-1926.

AUTHOR OF "MATTHEW ARNOLD," "ON CONTEMPORARY LITERATURE," ETC.

NEW YORK
CHARLES SCRIBNER'S SONS
1922

Republished 1971
Scholarly Press, Inc., 22929 Industrial Drive East
St. Clair Shores, Michigan 48080

40,842

TO
R. M. S.

PREFACE

If this book fulfils in any degree the intention of its author, its tendency will be to encourage readers to keep open the channels of their national traditions and to scrutinize contemporary literature in the light of their national past. I am aware of the current feeling that no national past will bear scrutiny. At the present time, there appears to be no "popular" nation anywhere in the world, and the feelings with which many people regard any encouragement of "nationalistic sentiment," either at home or abroad, are as curiously mixed as those which the ancients entertained towards the daughter of Tyndareus, that beautiful and dangerous woman whose fame has outlasted all their empires.

The old bard Stesichorus, we are told, for reviling Helen was stricken blind; but he afterwards "unsaid all the evil he had sung of her," and accepted a legendary account according to which Helen was never actually in Troy but only her phantasm, while she herself, miraculously transported to Egypt, there awaited the return of her lord. Euripides based his *Helen* upon this story.

Virgil's treatment of the character exhibits the same sense of a perilous impiety in any attempt to

vii

molest her. During the sack of Troy, while Aeneas was wandering desperately among the flaming relics of his city, he espied the seductive cause of all that woe, cowering on the threshold of a temple, a silent, terror-stricken fugitive. To the beauty that had launched a thousand ships his anguish made him blind. The smoke of a world in ruins smarted in his eyes. Hot wrath possessed him. Though he knew there was no glory to be had from slaying a woman, it seemed to him "very stuff of the conscience" to end that hateful life. He clutched his sword. In the instant, his divine mother appeared to him, stayed his hand, and assured him that the real cause of the war was not Helen but the *inclementia divum,* the merciless will of the gods.

Many intellectuals look malignly upon nationalism as the baleful Helen of our recent international disaster. Through the smoke of the conflict they thought they heard an angel with vials of wrath crying: "There shall be no more flags!" As an act of the higher piety, holding nothing sacred which is less than Humanity, they dedicated themselves to the destruction in themselves and in others of all those complex beliefs and emotions which the waving flag of one's land stirs in the heart of the ordinary man. The war multiplied the number of refined young liberals, American, English, Jewish, French, Italian, who in the confidences of the midnight hour, aflame with the "higher piety," conscientiously spit upon what they would call the time-dishonored notion that, in certain circumstances, it is sweet and beautiful to die for one's country. In order to become men, in the higher sense of the word, our disillusioned youth imagine they must slay the thing they loved—they must cease to be Americans.

It was about the year 1917 that I began to meditate rather frequently upon the relation between civilization and the existence of separate nationalities, national traditions, national sentiments, and the national literatures through which the life of vanished generations survives as a living power among the powers of the present day. That sense for Humanity above all nations, which was quickened by certain appeals of the war, it seemed to me that every intelligent man must applaud, and must desire to strengthen. Sentiments which interfered with the growth of this sense, I thought, should be suppressed, and sacrifices which must be made for the extension of it should be courageously offered. An inflamed and egotistical nationalism appeared to me, as to so many others, the prime cause of the world's catastrophe.

And yet if even for a moment it occurred to me that true citizenship in "the country of all intelligent beings" might necessitate the sacrifice of one's essential Americanism and the use of the knife at the root of all fond sentiments related to it, in that instant there came to me, as if in a vision, our "divine mother," the spirit of America as the clear-eyed among our poets and statesmen have seen her, assuring me that the higher piety demands no such immolation. That which we have loved in our country, she declared, that which we have honored in her, that which reveals her to our hearts as proudly beautiful is in no way dangerous to Humanity. On the contrary, the more deeply we loved the true constituent elements of her loveliness, the more clearly we understood her inmost purposes and set ourselves to further them, the more perfectly we should find ourselves in accord with the "friends of mankind" in all nations.

Shall we shun music because we know that barbaric music arouses the cave-man in us and sets the pulses throbbing, the feet dancing, to the "blood-lust song"—forgetting that music of another sort, seizing upon these same impressionable quivering senses of ours, may masteringly attune us to the most harmonious impulses of our nature? Because we fear the tom-toms shall we smash the cathedral organ? All things which have great power are greatly dangerous till they are controlled to right ends; but they are not more dangerous than weak things put in a place where strength is required. At the present moment the isolated individuals and scattered bands of pale-

browed intellectuals striving to realize at once "the
federation of the world" by the renunciation of
their nationalities—these are weak things where
great strength is required.

The most powerful instruments yet existing in the
world for the destruction of international order
are the nations; yet they are still the most powerful
instruments for creating it. The most powerful
agents for the corruption of the world's civilization
are corrupt national civilizations; yet they are still
the most powerful redemptive agents. Power is
the good which the world craves. We cannot
afford to waste it or to turn away from it. The
friends of Humanity will make less progress by
attempting to destroy the national spirit than by
criticizing it and purifying it, and by seizing upon
and fostering those elements in it which are truly
humane. With this program in mind no wise
student of the national past will be an indis-
criminating upholder of traditions. While seeking
to conserve their vital energy, he will steadily
subject their direction to a critical scrutiny in the
best light of his own time.

The studies in this book, though originally published separately as occasion offered, all had their
origin in a fresh interest in American life and letters, which has strengthened side by side with a
strengthening interest in the cause of those young
men to whom the war brought a new vision of the

old *Humanitas*. Some years ago, while preparing a book on Matthew Arnold, I found in his letters a passage which I read with pleasure and envy. It was written when he was putting together the first volume of his *Essays In Criticism*: "I think the moment is, on the whole, favorable for the Essays; and in going through them I am struck with the admirable riches of human nature that are brought to light in the group of persons whom they treat, and the sort of unity that as a book to stimulate the better humanity in us the volume has." The "admirable riches of human nature" are, I am sure, also present in my group of Americans, and something I hope of this unity, may also be found here.

For permission to reprint these revised essays acknowledgments are due as follows: to the *New York Times Book Review* for the *Mr. Mencken And The New Spirit In Letters*; to the *Bookman* for *Tradition*; to G. P. Putnam's Sons for the essay on Franklin from *The Cambridge History Of American Literature*; to Harcourt, Brace, and Co. for the essay on Emerson from my edition of *Essays And Poems Of Emerson*; to Charles Scribner's Sons for the *Hawthorne* and the *Walt Whitman* from my editions of *The Scarlet Letter* and *Leaves Of Grass* in the Modern Student's Library; to G. P. Putnam's Sons for the biographical essay on Joaquin Miller from a forthcoming collective edition of Miller's poems; to the newly erected *Step Ladder* for the *Note on Carl Sandburg*; to *The New York Nation* for the essays on Carnegie, Roosevelt, and the Adamses; and to the *Weekly Review* for *An Imaginary Conversation with Mr. P. E. More.*

S. P. S.

CONTENTS

MR. MENCKEN, THE JEUNE FILLE, AND THE NEW SPIRIT IN LETTERS

A woman whose husband has made money in the war likes to have her portrait painted and her friends coming in to admire it. So a new public, grown conscious of itself, demands a new literature and a new literature demands a new criticism. Fine gentlemen with a touch of frost above the temples, sitting at ease in quiet old clubs under golden-brown portraits of their ancestors, and turning the pages of the *Athenæum* or Mr. More's *Nation*, have seen with disdainful yet apprehensive glance through plate-glass windows the arrival of all three: the formation of a reading public of which they are not a part, the appearance of a literature which they do not care to read, the development of a criticism in which their views are not represented. Since a critic is of no importance except with reference to what he criticizes, you will please bear with me while I bring in the new literature and the new readers. When the stage is properly set, Mr. Mencken will appear.

How shall one indicate the color and spirit of

it?—this new public now swarming up the avenues
of democratic opportunity; becoming prosperous,
self-conscious, voluble; sunning itself in the great
cities; reaching out greedily to realize its "legitimate aspirations." This latest generation of Americans, so vulgar and selfish and good-humored and
sensual and impudent, shows little trace of the once
dominant Puritan stock and nothing of the Puritan
temper. It is curiously and richly composed of the
children of parents who dedicated themselves to
accumulation, and toiling inarticulately in shop and
field, in forest and mine, never fully mastered the
English definite article or the personal pronoun. It
is composed of children whose parents or grand-
parents brought their copper kettles from Russia,
tilled the soil of Hungary, taught the Mosaic law
in Poland, cut Irish turf, ground optical glass in
Germany, dispensed Bavarian beer, or fished for
mackerel around the Skagerrack. The young people laugh at the oddities of their forbears, discard
the old kettles, the Mosaic Law, the provincial dia-
lect, the Lutheran pastor. Into the new society
breaking without cultural inheritance, they derive
all their interests and standards from their immediate environment, and gravitate towards refinement
through more and more expensive gratifications of
the senses.

The prettiest type of this swift civilization—and
I must have something pretty to enliven a discourse
on current criticism—the prettiest type is the *jeune*

fille, who, to modernize the phrase of an old poet, aspires to a soul in silken hosiery and doeskin boots. She springs, this young creature with ankles sheathed and shod like a Virginia deer—ankles whose trimness is, aesthetically speaking, quite the finest thing her family has produced in America— she springs from a grandmother who clumped out in wooden shoes to milk a solitary cow in Sweden. She has no soul, the young thing, but she trusts that the tailor, the milliner, the bootmaker, the manicurist, the hairdresser, and the masseuse can give her an equivalent. Wherever art can work on her surfaces, she is finished. When the car is at the door in the morning—"a distinctive body on a distinguished *chassis*"—and she runs down the steps with somewhat more than a flash of her silken perfections, she is exquisite, what though the voice is a bit hard and shrill with which she calls out, "H'lo, kiddo! Le's go't Brentano's."

She is indeed coming—the new reader! She will bring home an armful of magazines, smelling deliciously of the press, books with exciting yellow jackets, plays newly translated and imported, the latest stories, the most recent ideas, all set forth in the current fashion, and all, as it will seem to her, about herself, her sort of people, her sort of world, and about the effort which her fair young ego is making to emerge from the indiscriminated mass and to acquire physical form and line congruous with that "distinctive body mounted on a distinguished

chassis," which bears her with such smooth speed up
Riverside Drive. She will have no American literature of the "classical period" in her library; for the
New England worthies who produced it wrote before the public of which she is a part began to read
or to be noticed in books. The *jeune fille,* though a
votary of physical form, feels within herself an exhilarating chaos, a fluent welter, which Lowell and
Longfellow and James and Howells do not, but
which her writers must, express.

Therefore, she revels in the English paradoxers
and mountebanks, the Scandinavian misanthropes,
the German egomaniacs, and, above all, in the later
Russian novelists, crazy with war, taxes, hunger,
anarchy, vodka, and German philosophy. She does
enjoy, however, the posthumous pessimism of Mark
Twain—it is "so strong and virile"; and she relishes
his pilot oaths—they are "so sincere and unconven-
tional." She savors Mr. Masters' hard little naturalistic sketches of "passion" on Michigan Boule-
vard; they remind her of her brother. Sherwood
Anderson has a place on her shelves; for by the note
of revolt in *Winesburg, Ohio* she recognizes one
of her own spirit's deserted villages. Lured by a
primitive instinct to the sound of animals roving,
she ventures a curious foot into the fringes of the
Dreiserian wilderness vast and drear; and barbaric
impulses in her blood "answer the wail of the
forest." She is not much "intrigued" by the frosty
fragilities of imagist verse; but at Sandburg's viking

salute to the Hog-Butcher of the World she claps her hands and cries: "Oh, boy, isn't it gorgeous!" This welter of her "culture" she plays, now and then, at organizing on some strictly modern principle, such as her father applies to his business, such as her brother applies to his pleasures—a principle of egotistical combat, a principle of self-indulgence, cynical and luxurious. She is not quite happy with the result. Sometimes, I imagine, she wishes that her personal attendants, those handmen and maidens who have wrought so wonderfully with her surfaces, could be set at work upon her interior, so that her internal furnishing and decoration could be brought into measurable concord with the grace and truth of her contours, the rhythm of her hair.

Imagine a thousand *jeunes filles* thus wistful, and you have the conditions ready for the advent of a new critic. At this point enters at a hard gallop, spattered with mud, H. L. Mencken high in oath— thus justifying the Goethean maxim: *Aller Anfang ist schwer.* He leaps from the saddle with sabre flashing, stables his horse in the church, shoots the priest, hangs the professors, exiles the Academy, burns the library and the university, and, amid the smoking ashes, erects a new school of criticism on modern German principles, which he traces through Spingarn to Goethe, but which I should be inclined to trace rather to Eckermann.

Of my own inability to interpret modern Germany, however, I have recently been painfully reminded by an 86-page pamphlet sent to me from Hamburg, with blue-pencil marks kindly inserted by the author, one Hansen—apparently a German-Schleswigian-American who has studied rhetoric in Mr. Mencken's school—inquiring what the masses can possibly know of the real Germany, "so long as the Shermans squat like toads in the portals of the schools and the Northcliffes send their Niagaras of slime through the souls of the English-speaking peoples." I was amused, of course, to find a great lord of the press so quaintly bracketed with an obscure teacher of literature in a Middle Western university as an effective obstacle between the sunlight and Germany. All the same, my conscience was touched; and I remembered with satisfaction that, on the appearance of Mr. Mencken's *Prefaces,* I made a conscientious effort to tell my countrymen where they should go, namely, to Mr. Mencken, if they desired a really sympathetic presentation of the modern Teutonic point of view with reference to politics, religion, morals, women, beer, and *belles-lettres.*

On the appearance of Mr. Mencken's new volume, *Prejudices*—continuing my humble service as guide to what I am not thoroughly qualified to appreciate—I can only say that here I find again the Nietzschean "artistocrat" of yesteryear, essentially unchanged. He is a little sadder, perhaps, since democracy has unhorsed the autocrats; but his skepticism of democracy is unshaken. He is a shade more cynical since the extension of women's suffrage; but he is as clear as ever that he knows what girls were made for. He is a little more sober since the passage of the national prohibition act, and a bit less lyrical about the Pilsener-motive in the writings of Mr. Huneker; but, come rain come shine, he still points with pride to a digestion ruined by alcohol. In other respects, former patrons of his school for beautifying American letters will find his familiar manners and customs essentially unaltered.

If we are to have a Menckenian academy, Mr. Mencken shows the way to set it up—with vigor and rigor, with fist and foot, with club and axe. The crash of smashed things, the knocking of heads together, the objurgations which accompany his entrance have a high advertising value, fascinating to all the gamins of the press and attractive to our *jeune fille,* who will pay for a copy of *Prejudices* and form her taste upon it. And far be it from me to deny that she may learn something from her heavy-handed disciplinarian. Mr. Mencken, like most men, has his merits, of which it is a pleasure to speak. He is alive; this is a merit in a good man and hardly a defect even in a bad critic. He has a rough, prodding wit, blunted by thrusting at objects which it cannot pierce, but yet a wit. He is passionately addicted to scoffing; and if by chance a sham that is obnoxious to him comes in his way, he will scoff at a sham. He has no inclination to the softer forms of "slush" or to the more diaphanous varieties of "pishposh." He has a style becoming a retired military man—hard, pointed, forcible, cocksure. He likes a sentence stripped of baggage, and groups of sentences that march briskly off at the word of command, wheel, continue to march, and, at word of command, with equal precision, halt. He has the merits of an efficient rhetorical drill-sergeant. By his services in pointing out to our fair barbarian that she need not, after all, read Mr. Veblen, she should acknowledge that he has earned the royalty on her copy of *Prejudices*. He has given her, in short, what she might expect to get from a stiff freshman course in rhetoric.

When he has told her who fits sentences together well and who ill, he has ended the instruction that was helpful to her. He can give her lessons in derision, lessons in cynicism, lessons in contempt; but she was mistress of all these when she entered his school. He can offer to free her from attachment to English and American literary traditions; but she was never attached to these traditions. He will undertake to make her believe that Baptists and Methodists, professors and academicians, prohibition societies and marriage covenants are ridiculous; but she always thought them ridiculous. He is ready to impregnate her mind with the wisdom of "old Friedrich," Stirner, Strindberg, and the rest of the crew; but her mind is already impregnated with that sort of wisdom. "When one has turned away from the false and the soft and the silly," this is the question she is asking, "where does one go to find true and beautiful things?" She has heard somewhere by chance, poor girl, that one who pursues truth and beauty is delivered from the grosser tyrannies of the senses, escapes a little out of the inner welter, and discovers serenity widening like a fair dawn in the mind, with a certain blitheness and amenity. This is æsthetic liberation.

For one seeking æsthetic liberation there is a canon of things to be thought on which the worldliest of sound critics, Sainte-Beuve, pronounced as clearly and insistently as Saint Paul. The Germans, as the great Goethe explained to the saucer-eyed Eckermann, are "weak on the æsthetic side." Aesthetic appreciation is superficially an affair of the palate, and at bottom an affair of the heart, embracing with elation whatsoever things are lovely. Mr. Mencken has no heart; and if he ever had a palate he has lost it in protracted orgies of literary "strong drink." He turns with anguish from the pure and simple flavors that please children as the first gifts of nature, and that delight great critics as the last achievements of art. His appetite craves a fierce stimulation of sauces, a flamboyance and glitter of cheeses, the sophisticated and appalling ripeness of wild duck nine days old.

He devotes, for example, two pages to leading the *jeune fille* away from Emerson as a writer of no influence. He spends several more in showing her that Howells has nothing to say. He warns her that Mr. Garland's *Son of the Middle Border* is amateurish, flat, banal, and repellant. He gives a condescending *coup de pied* to the solider works of Arnold Bennett and singles out for intense admiration a scarlet-lattice scene or so in his pot-boilers. As the author of a work on the American language, over-ambitiously designed as a wedge to split asunder the two great English-speaking peoples, and as an advocate of an "intellectual aristocracy," it has suddenly occurred to him that we have been shamefully neglecting the works of George Ade; accordingly, he strongly commmends to our younger generation the works of Mr. George Ade. But the high light and white flame of his appreciation falls upon three objects as follows: the squalid story of an atrocious German bar-maid by Sudermann; an anonymous autobiographical novel, discovered by Mr. Mencken himself, which exhibits "an eternal blue-nose with every wart and pimple glittering," and is "as devoid of literary sophistication as an operation for gallstones"; and, third and last, the works of Mr. Mencken's partner, Mr. George Jean Nathan, with his divine knack at making phrases "to flabbergast a dolt."

I imagine my bewildered seeker for æsthetic liberation asking her mentor if studying these things will help her to form "the diviner mind." "Don't bother me now," exclaims Mr. Mencken; "don't bother me now. I am just striking out a great phrase. Aesthetic effort tones up the mind with a kind of high

excitement. I shall say in the next number of the
Smart Set that James Harlan was the *damnedest
ass* that America ever produced. If you don't know
him, look him up. In the second edition of my book
on the American language I shall add a new verb—
to *Menckenize*—and perhaps a new noun, *Menckenism*. The definition of these words will clear up
matters for you, and summarize my contribution to
the national *belles-lettres*. It is beginning to take—
the spirit is beginning to spread."

While Mr. Mencken and the *jeune fille* are engaged in this chat on the nature of beauty, I fancy
the horn of a "high-powered" automobile is heard
from the street before the Menckenian school. And
in bursts Mr. Francis Hackett, looking like a man
who has just performed a long and difficult operation under the body of his car, though, as a matter
of fact, he has only just completed a splashing, shirt-
sleeve review for *The New Republic*. "Let's wash
up," cries Mr. Hackett, stripping off his blouse of
blue jeans, "and go out to luncheon."

"Where shall we *fressen?*" says Mr. Mencken.

"At the Loyal Independent Order of United
Hiberno - German -Anti - English -Americans," says
Mr. Hackett. "All the New Critics will be there.
Colum, Lewisohn, Wright, and the rest. I tried
to get Philip Littell to come along. He's too gol
darn refined. But I've got a chap in the car, from
the West, that will please you. Used to run a
column in the World's Greatest. Calls Thomas

Arnold of Rugby 'that thrice-damned boor and noodle.' "

"Good!" Mr. Mencken exclaims. "A Menckenism! A Menckenism! A likely chap!" And out they both bolt.

The *jeune fille,* with a thoughtful backward glance at Mr. Hackett's blouse, goes slowly down into the street, and, strolling up the walk in the crisp early winter air, overtakes Mr. Littell, who is strolling even more slowly. He is reading a book, on which the first snowflake of the year has fallen, and, as it falls, he looks up with such fine delight in his eye that she asks him what has pleased him.

"A thought," he replies gently, "phrased by a subtle writer and set in a charming essay by a famous critic. Listen: *"Où il n'y a point de délicatesse, il n'y a point de littérature."* [1]

"That's a new one on me," says the *jeune fille.*

---

[1] Translated: "When one begins to Menckenize, the spirit of good literature flees in consternation."

II

TRADITION

To lengthen the childhood of the individual, at the same time bringing to bear upon it the influences of tradition, is the obvious way to shorten the childhood of races, nations, classes, and so to quicken the general processes of civilization. Yet in the busy hum of self-approbation which accompanies the critical activities of our young people, perhaps the dominant note is their satisfaction at having emancipated themselves from the fetters of tradition, the oppression of classical precedent, the burden of an inherited culture. By detaching the new literature from its learned past they are confident that they are assuring it a popular future. Turn to any one of half a dozen books which discuss the present movement, and you will learn that people are now discovering, for example, "often to their own surprise," that they can read and enjoy poetry. That is because poetry has been subjected to "democratization." The elder writers, such as Shakespeare, Milton, Emerson, and Longfellow, constantly gravelled them with strange and obsolete phrases, like "multitudinous seas incarnadine," and

13

like "tumultuous privacy of storm." The ancient
writers sent them to out-of-the-way reference books
to look up obscure legends about Troy, not the city
where collars are made, and old stuff about war in
heaven, and the landing at Plymouth Rock. It is
therefore a relief to countless eager young souls that
Mr. Mencken has dismissed all this as "the fossil
literature taught in colleges," and that Mary Austin
insists that native verse rhythms must be "within the
capacity of the democratically bred." It is a joy
to hear from Mr. Untermeyer that modern readers
of poetry may now come out from the "lifeless and
literary storehouse" and use life itself for their
glossary, as indeed they may—or the morning's
newspaper.

Those who encourage us to hope for crops without tillage, learning without study, and literary birth
without gestation or travail are doubtless animated
by a desire to augment the sum of human felicity;
but one recalls Burke's passionate ejaculation: "Oh!
no, sir, no. Those things which are not practicable
are not desirable." To the new mode of procuring
a literary renascence there may be raised one objec-
tion, which, to minds of a certain temper, will seem
rather grave: all experience is against it. Such is
the thesis recently argued by an English critic, Mr.
H. J. Massingham, who reviews with mingled
amusement and alarm the present "self-conscious
rebellion against tradition." In the eyes of our excited young "cosmopolitans," whose culture has a

geographic rather than an historical extension, Mr.
Massingham's opinions will of course appear to be
hopelessly prejudiced by his Oxford breeding, his
acquaintance with the classics, his saturation in
Elizabethan literature, and his avowed passion for
old books in early editions, drilled by the biblio-
maniac worm, "prehistoric" things, like Nares'
Glossary and Camden's *Remains*. But it is not
merely the opinion of our critic that is formidable:
"The restoration of the traditional link with the
art of the past is a conservative and revolutionary
necessity." It is not the supporting opinion of Sir
Joshua Reynolds: "The only food and nourishment
of the mind of an artist is the great works of his
predecessors." Sir Joshua, too, was prejudiced by
his position as a pillar of the robust English classicism of George III's time. It is not even the opinion of Henry James, whom Mr. Massingham pro-
claims the profoundest critic since Coleridge, and
who even our own irreverent youth seem to suspect
should be mentioned respectfully: "It takes an endless amount of history to make even a little tradition
and an endless amount of tradition to make even
a little taste and an endless amount of taste, by the
same token, to make even a little tranquillity."

The formidable arguments against the radical
engineers of renascence are just the notorious facts
of literary history. The fact that a bit of the "fossil
literature taught in colleges," the story of Arthur,
written in Latin by a Welsh monk in the twelfth

century, has flowered and fruited in poetry, paint-
ing, and music generation after generation pretty
much over the civilized world. The fact that Chaucer and his contemporaries, in whom poetry had a
glorious rebirth, had previously devoured everything in what Mr. Untermeyer would call the
"lifeless and literary storehouse" of the Middle
Ages. The fact that the Elizabethans, to quote
Mr. Massingham's vigorous phrase, flung themselves on tradition "like a hungry wolf, not only
upon the classics but upon all the tradition open to
them." The fact that Restoration comedy is simply
a revival of late Caroline in the hands of men who
had studied Molière. The fact that the leaders of
the new movement in the eighteenth century, when
they wished to break from the stereotyped classicism, did not urge young people to slam the door
on the past, but, on the contrary, harked back over
the heads of Pope and Dryden to the elder and
more central tradition of Milton, Shakespeare, and
Spenser; and sluiced into the arid fields of common
sense, grown platitudinous, the long-dammed or
subterranean currents of mediæval romance. The
fact that "Childe Harold," "Adonais," "The Eve
of St. Agnes," "The Cotter's Saturday Night," and
"The Castle of Indolence" were all written by imitators of Spenser or by imitators of his imitators.
The fact, to omit the Victorians, that Mr. W. B.
Yeats, the most skilful living engineer of literary
renascence, set all his collaborators to digging

around the roots of the ancient Celtic tree before we enjoyed the blossoming of the new spring in Ireland. The fact that John Masefield, freshest and most tuneful voice in England, is obviously steeped to the lips in the poetry of Byron, Shakespeare, Spenser, and Chaucer.

Why is it that the great poets, novelists, and critics, with few exceptions, have been, in the more liberal sense of the word, scholars—masters of several languages, students of history and philosophy, antiquarians? First of all because the great writer conceives of his vocation as the most magnificent and the most complex of crafts. He is to be his own architect, master-builder, carpenter, painter, singer, orator, poet and dramatist. His materials, his tools, his methods are, or may be, infinite. To him, then, the written tradition is a school and a museum in which, if he has a critical and inventive mind, he learns, from both the successes and the failures of his predecessors, how to set to work upon his own problems of expression. As Mr. Yeats is fond of pointing out, the young poet may find Herbert and Vaughan more helpful to him than the work of his own contemporaries, because the faults in the elder poets, the purple patches that failed to hold their color, will not attract and mislead him.

But tradition is more than a school of crafts. It is a school of mood and manners. The artist who is also a scholar cannot fail to discover that what distinguishes all the golden periods of art, what constitutes the perpetual appeal of the masters, is a kind of innermost poise and serenity, tragic in Sophocles, heroic in Michelangelo, skeptical in Montaigne, idyllic in Sidney, ironic in Fielding. This enviable tranquillity reigns only in a mind that, looking before and after, feels itself the representative of something outlasting time, some national ideal, some religious faith, some permanent human experience, some endless human quest. Nothing begets this mood and manner, the sovereign mark of good breeding in letters, like habitual association with those who have it, the majority of whom are, in the vulgar sense of the word, dead. Izaak Walton, a minor writer in whose work there is a golden afterglow of the great age, calls, in one of his Angler's Dialogues, for "that smooth song which was made by Kit Marlowe, now at least fifty years ago," and for the answer to it "which was made by Sir Walter Raleigh in his younger days." If some of our modern imitators of the auctioneer and the steam calliope would now and then, instead of reading one another, step into the "lifeless and literary storehouse" and compare these "fossils" conscientiously with their own recent efforts to make verse popular! "They were old-fashioned poetry," says Piscator apologetically, "but choicely good, I think much better than the strong lines that are now in fashion in this critical age."

Out of the tranquillity induced by working in a good literary tradition develops form. The clever

theorists who insist that form alone matters, that
form is the only preservative element in literature,
forget that form is not "self-begotten" but a product of the formative spirit. Mr. Massingham is
a bit fastidious in his use of this word. He denies
form, for example, to Pope and to Swinburne.
Though both have technique, that is another matter.
"Form," he declares, "is a vision contained and
made manifest." He attributes the unproductive-
ness of our age in the field of satire to a vision
without a traditional base, reeling and shifting in
the choppy waters of contemporary opinion. His
remarks on the deficiencies of Gilbert Cannan as a
satirist and novelist further elucidate his idea; and
they may serve also as a comment upon many of
the younger writers in America:

The works of Mr. Cannan seem to say, "That is
what life is—a surge of base and beautiful forces,
intensified in the consciousness of man." But that
is a fallacy. Life is like that to the layman, but it
is the business of the artist to see a clue in it, to
give it shape and order, to weld its particles into
congruity. Here is where his lack of a constructive
or satiric purpose growing out of and controlling
the material tells to his hurt. He knows life in the
raw, but the satirist would put it in the oven and
dish it up. So he wanders in the dark, and we
blunder after him. But we want light, if it be only
from a tallow candle.

Now, many of the young writers in America are
disposed to reject the English tradition as unservice-

able lumber. They scorn equally the greater part of the American tradition as puritanical, effeminate, or over-intellectualized. If they seek foreign allies, it is with those who help them forget our national characteristics, our native bent and purposes, our discovered special American "genius." In what measure is the revolt due to the conduct of the movement by writers whose blood and breeding are as hostile to the English strain as a cat to water? Whatever the answer, I suspect that the young people who are being congratulated right and left on their emancipation from tradition are rather open to condolence than to felicitation. They have broken away from so much that was formative, and they suffer so obviously in consequence of the break. Their poets have lost a skill which Poe had: though they paint a little, and chant a little, and speak a great deal of faintly rhythmical prose, they have not learned how to sing. Their novelists have lost a vision which Howells had: though they have shaken off the "moralistic incubus" and have released their "suppressed desires," they have not learned how to conceive or to present a coherent picture of civilized society. Their leaders have lost a constructiveness which a critic so laden with explosives as Emerson exhibited: though they have blown up the old highways they have not made new roads.

Am I doing the "young people" an injustice? I turn from their anthologies of verse, where I keep searching in vain for such music as the angler's milkmaid sang; and from the novels of Mr. Cabell, in whom I have not discovered that ascending sun heralded by the lookouts; to *A Modern Book of Criticism*, recently collected and put forth by Mr. Ludwig Lewisohn. The editor's desire is to show us that "a group of critics, young men or men who do not grow old, are at work upon the creation of a civilized cultural atmosphere in America." The idea resembles that, does it not? of Mr. Waldo Frank, who recently informed us that literature began in America in 1900—or was it 1910?—at Mr. Stieglitz's place in New York. It is related also to that recent comprehensive indictment edited by Mr. Harold Stearns and ironically entitled *Civilization in the United States*. The implication is clearly that the country which developed Bradford, Franklin, Emerson, Lincoln, Thoreau, Whitman, Mark Twain, here and there in villages and backwoods, had no "civilized cultural atmosphere" worth mentioning. It does not seem quite plausible.

But let us proceed with Mr. Lewisohn. His critics:—"Like a group of shivering young Davids —slim and frail but with a glimpse of morning sunshine on their foreheads—they face an army of Goliaths." The slim and shivering young Davids turn out on investigation to be Mr. Huneker, Mr. Spingarn, Mr. Mencken, Mr. Lewisohn, Mr. Hackett, Mr. Van Wyck Brooks, and Randolph Bourne. It is not a group, taken as a whole, however it may be connected with the house of Jesse, which should be expected to hear any profound murmuring of ancestral voices or to experience any mysterious inflowing of national experience in meditating on the names of Mark Twain, Whitman, Thoreau, Lincoln, Emerson, Franklin, and Bradford. One doesn't blame our Davids for their inability to connect themselves vitally with this line of Americans, for their inability to receive its tradition or to carry it on. But one cannot help asking whether this inability does not largely account for the fact that Mr. Lewisohn's group of critics are restless impressionists, almost destitute of doctrine, and with no discoverable unifying tendency except to let themselves out into a homeless happy land where they may enjoy the "colorful" cosmic weather, untroubled by business men, or middle-class Americans, or Congressmen, or moralists, or humanists, or philosophers, or professors, or Victorians, or Puritans, or New Englanders, or Messrs. Tarkington and Churchill. A jolly lot of Goliaths to slay before we get that "civilized cultural atmosphere."

By faithfully studying the writings of Mr. Mencken, Mr. Lewisohn, and other "shivering young Davids," I have obtained a fairly clear conception of what a "civilized cultural atmosphere" is not. It consists of none of those heart-remembered things—our own revenue officers probing our old shoes for diamond necklaces, our own New York newspapers, and Maryland chicken on the

Albany boat—which cause a native American returning from a year in Europe to exclaim as he sails
up the tranquil bosom of the Hudson and rushes by
a standard steel Pullman, back to the great warm
embrace of his own land, "Thank Heaven, we are
home again." No, it is none of these things. If,
without going to Munich, you wish to know what a
"civilized cultural atmosphere" really is, you must
let Mr. Lewisohn describe it for you as it existed,
till the passage of the Volstead act, in one or two
odd corners of old New York: "The lamps of the
tavern had orange-colored shades, the wainscoting
was black with age. The place was filled with a
soothing dusk and the blended odor of beer and
tobacco and Wiener Schnitzel. *I was, at least, back
in civilization.* That tavern is gone now, swept away
by the barbarism of the Neo-Puritans."

To the book from which this quotation is made,
Mr. Lewisohn's recently published autobiographical
record, *Up Stream,* students of contemporary critical currents and eddies are much indebted. The
author, like many of the other belligerent young
writers who have shown in recent years a grave
concern for the state of civilization in America, has
ostensibly been directing his attack against our national culture from a very elevated position. He
has professed himself one of the enlightened spirits
who from time to time rise above the narrowing
prejudices of nationality into the free air of the
republic of letters, the grand cosmopolis of the true

humanist. From his watch-tower—apparently "in
the skies"—he has launched lightnings of derision
at those who still weave garlands for their Lares
and Penates, at the nationalist with his "selective
sympathies," at the traditionalist with his sentimental fondness for folk-ways. Those who feel
strongly attracted, as I do myself, to the Ciceronian
and Stoic conception of a universal humanity and by
the Christian and Augustinian vision of a universal
City of God, may easily have mistaken Mr. Lewisohn for a "sharpshooter" of the next age, an out-
post from the land of their heart's desire. But in
Up Stream, Mr. Lewisohn drops the mask and reveals himself, for all his Jewish radicalism,[1] as
essentially a sentimental and homesick German,
longing in exile for a Germany which exists only in
his imagination.

Even the purified and liberated mind of a Child
of Light, living according to nature and reason, is
unable to rid itself wholly of "selective sympathies."
It betrays under provocation a merely "traditional

---

[1] In a notably competent article on "The Case of Mr. Lewisohn,"
which appeared in *The Menorah Journal* of June, 1922, Professor
Jacob Zeitlin writes: "Whether entirely just or strongly colored,
it is evident that Mr. Lewisohn's criticism of State Universities
has little relevance to his character as a Jew. It indicates nothing
more than that his sensitive aesthetic organism recoiled in pain
from an environment that was uncongenial. And the same observation holds concerning his reaction toward American life in general. He but adds his voice to a chorus of growing volume, reiterating the now familiar burden of the crudeness and narrowness
of our political and social ideas. There is ample ground for such
a protest as he makes, but it is not a protest that can be identified
with any recognizably Jewish outlook."

emotion" for a cultural atmosphere compounded of the odors of beer, tobacco, and Wiener Schnitzel, with perhaps a whiff of Kant and a strain of Hungarian music floating through it, while two or three high philosophical spirits discuss what a poet can do when his wife grows old and stringy. I do not think it necessary to remonstrate with a man merely because his affective nature responds powerfully to a vision of felicity thus composed; but I think it a bit impractical to ask "a nation of prohibitionists and Puritans" to accept this vision as the goal of cultural efforts in America. It is a help to fruitful controversy, however, when a man abandons his absurdly insincere professions of "universal sympathy"—his purring protestation that he desires "neither to judge nor to condemn"—and frankly admits that he likes the German life, what he knows of it, and that he regards American life, what he knows of it, as "ugly and mean."

The militant hostility of alien-minded critics towards what they conceive to be the dominant traits of the national character is, on the whole, to be welcomed as provocative of reflection and as a corrective to national conceit. But the amendment of that which is really ugly and mean and basely repressive in our contemporary society is less likely to be achieved by listening to the counsels of exiled emancipators from Munich than by harking back to our own liberative tradition, which long antedates the efforts of these bewildered impressionists.

When we grow dull and inadventurous and sloth-
fully content with our present conditions and our
old habits, it is not because we are "traditionalists";
it is, on the contrary, because we have ceased to feel
the formative spirit of our own traditions. It is
not much in the American vein, to be sure, to construct private little anarchies in the haze of a
smoking-room; but practical revolt, on a large scale
and sagaciously conducted, is an American tradition,
which we should continue to view with courage and
the tranquillity which is related to courage. America was born because it revolted. It revolted because it condemned. It condemned because its
sympathies were not universal but selective. Its
sympathies were selective because it had a vision
of a better life, pressing for fulfilment. That vision,
and not a conception of life as a meaningless "surge
of base and beautiful forces" liberated its chief men
of letters. Thence their serenity, in place of that
"gentle but chronic dizziness" which a critic of
Young Germany, Hugo von Hofmannsthal, says
"vibrates among us." Thence, too, their freedom
from ancestor-worship and bondage to the letter.
Listen to Emerson:

> Ask not me, as Muftis can,
> To recite the Alcoran;
> Well I love the meaning sweet;
> I tread the book beneath my feet.

Thence, too, the traditional bent of the American
spirit toward modernity, toward realism. It was

nearly a hundred years ago that our then-leading critic wrote in his journal: "You must exercise your genius in some form that has essential life now; do something which is proper to the hour and cannot but be done." Did he not recognize what was to be done? I quote once more from him a finer sentence than any of our impressionists has ever written: "A wife, a babe, a brother, poverty, and a country, which the Greeks had, I have." The grip and the beauty of that simple sentence are due to a union in it of an Athenian vision with Yankee self-reliance. It is the kind of feeling that comes to a man who has lived in a great tradition.

III

FRANKLIN AND THE AGE OF ENLIGHTENMENT

Americans who desire to know the breadth and humanity of their own traditions should give some days and nights to the study of the eighteenth century, in which the minds of our colonial ancestors definitely turned from the problems of mediæval theology to the assimilation of classical culture and to the practise of a rational philosophy. The civilizing force of even the English eighteenth century has been greatly neglected by English-speaking students, in favor of the excitement and glamour offered by the Romantic Movement. But to the civilizing force of the American eighteenth century the present generation is for assignable reasons singularly inattentive.

Early in the nineteenth century reactionary village clergymen began the practice of referring in the pulpit to conspicuous "liberators" of the preceding age like Franklin, Jefferson, and Paine as "horrible examples," as men of brilliant intellect and patriotic motives, but of "infamous character"; and this clerical tradition is foolishly perpetuated in some metropolitan pulpits to this day. In the second place, German metaphysics and the romantic deluge swept over us quite as devastatingly as over England; and the color and humor and emotion of Scott, Cooper, and then Dickens made the wit and solid sense of our classical period seem flat and unprofitable. Finally, when popular curiosity about our origins is awakened, it is quickly satisfied by a few familiar pictures of the Puritan colonists in the seventeenth century before the dawn of the Age of Enlightenment, here or elsewhere.

It is only by some such considerations as these that one can understand the affrontery of recent critics of civilization in the United States who date the emancipation of the American mind from seventeenth century theology with the introduction of Goethe and Kant to New England. And it is only by assuming the existence of wide general ignorance, the picturesque ignorance of legend, with regard to our own eminent men, that one can explain the friendly condescension with which the average journalist, for example, refers to that "simple," or to that "homespun" fellow, "our honest Franklin."

In a respectful and indeed laudatory notice in the Edinburgh *Review* of July, 1806, Lord Jeffrey employed the case of the "uneducated tradesman of America" to support his contention that "regular education is unfavourable to vigour or originality of understanding." Franklin attained his eminence, so runs the argument, without academical instruction, with only casual reading, without the benefit of association with men of letters, and "in a society where there was no relish and no encouragement for literature." This statement of Franklin's educational opportunities is manifestly inadequate; but it so pleasantly flatters our long-standing pride in our self-made men, that we are loath to challenge it.

The hero presented to the schoolboy and preserved in popular tradition is still an "uneducated tradesman of America": a runaway Boston printer, adorably walking up Market Street in Philadelphia with his three puffy rolls; directing his fellow shopkeepers the way to wealth; sharply enquiring of extravagant neighbours whether they have not paid too much for their whistle; flying his kite in a thunderstorm and by a happy combination of curiosity and luck making important contributions to science; and, to add the last lustre to his name, by a happy combination of industry and frugality making his fortune. This picturesque and racy figure is obviously a product of provincial America,—the first great Yankee with all the strong lineaments of the type: hardness, shrewdness, ingenuity, practical sense, frugality, industry, self-reliance.

The conception is perhaps sound enough so far as it goes, being derived mainly from facts supplied by Franklin himself in the one book through which he has secured an eternal life in literature. But the popular notion of his personality thus derived is incomplete, because the *Autobiography,* ending at the year 1757, contains no record of the thirty-three years which developed a competent provincial into an able, cultivated, and imposing man of the world.

The Franklin now discoverable in the ten volumes of his complete works is one of the most widely and thoroughly cultivated men of his age. He had not, to be sure, a university training, but he had what serves quite as well: sharp appetite and large capacity for learning, abundance of books, extensive travel, important participation in great events, and association through a long term of years with the most eminent men of three nations. The object of our colleges and universities is only to provide a feeble substitute for the advantages which Franklin enjoyed. In touch as printer and publisher with the classic and current literature produced at home and imported from abroad, he becomes in Philadelphia almost as good a "Queen Anne's man" as Swift or Defoe. His scientific investigations bring him into correspondence with fellow workers in England, France, Germany, Italy, Holland, and Spain. Entering upon public life, he is forced into coöperation or conflict with the leading politicians, diplomats, and statesmen of Europe. In his native land he has known men like Cotton Mather, Whitefield, Benjamin Rush, Benjamin West, Ezra Stiles, Noah Webster, Jay, Adams, Jefferson, and Washington. In England, where his affections strike such deep root that he considers establishing there his permanent abode, he is in relationship, more or less intimate, with Mandeville, Paine, Priestley, Price, Adam Smith, Robertson, Hume, Joseph Banks, Bishop Watson, the Bishop of St. Asaph, Lord Kames, Lord Shelburne, Lord Howe, Burke, and Chatham. Among Frenchmen he numbers on his list of admiring friends Vergennes, Lafayette, Mirabeau, Turgot, Quesnay, La Rochefoucauld, Condorcet, Lavoisier, Buffon, D'Alembert, Robespierre, and Voltaire.

It is absurd to speak of one who has been subjected to the molding of such forces as a product of the provinces. All Europe has wrought upon and metamorphosed the Yankee printer. The man whom Voltaire salutes with a fraternal kiss is a statesman, a philosopher, a friend of mankind, and a favorite son of the eighteenth century. With no softening of his patriotic fibre or loss of his Yankee tang, he has acquired all the common culture and most of the master characteristics of the Age of Enlightenment, up to the point where the French Revolution injected into it a drop of madness: its emancipation from unscrutinized tradition and authority, its regard for reason and nature, its social consciousness, its progressiveness, its tolerance, its cosmopolitanism, and its bland philanthropy.

Now this man deserves his large place in our literary history not so much by virtue of his writings, which had little immediate influence upon *belles-lettres,* as by virtue of his acts and ideas, which helped liberate and liberalize America. To describe his most important work is to recite the story of his life.

In reviewing his own career Franklin does not dwell on the fact that he who was to stand before kings had emerged from a tallow chandler's shop. To his retrospective eye there was nothing miraculous nor inexplicable in his origin. On the contrary he saw and indicated very clearly the sources of his talents and the external impulses that gave them direction. Born in Boston on January 6, 1706, he inherited from his long-lived parents, Josiah and Abiah Folger Franklin, a rugged physical and mental constitution which hardly faltered through the hard usage of eighty-four years. He recognized and profited by his father's skill in drawing and music, his "mechanical genius," his "understanding and solid judgment in prudential matters, both in private and publick affairs," his admirable custom of having at his table "as often as he could, some sensible friend or neighbour to converse with," always taking care "to start some ingenious or useful topic for discourse, which might tend to improve the minds of his children." Benjamin's formal schooling was begun when he was eight years old and abandoned when he was ten, together with the design of making him a clergyman. He significantly remarks, however, that he does not remember a time when he could not read; and the subsequent owner of the best private library in America was as a mere child an eager collector of books. For the two years following his removal from school he was employed in his father's business. When he expressed a firm disinclination to become a tallow chandler, his father attempted to discover his natural bent by taking him about to see various artisans at their work. Everything that Franklin touched taught him something; and everything that he learned, he used. Though his tour of the trades failed to win him to any mechanical occupation, "it has ever since been a pleasure to me," he says, "to see good workmen handle their tools; and it has been useful to me, having learnt so much by it as to be able to do little odd jobs myself in my house, . . . and to construct little machines for my experiments, while the intention of making the experiment was fresh and warm in my mind." Throughout his boyhood and youth he apparently devoured every book that he could lay hands upon. He went through his father's shelves of "polemic divinity"; read abundantly in Plutarch's *Lives;* acquired Bunyan's works "in separate little volumes," which he later sold to buy Burton's *Historical Collections;* received an impetus towards practical improvements from Defoe's *Essay on Projects,* and an impetus towards virtue from Mather's *Essays to Do Good.* Before he left Boston he had his mind opened to free speculation and equipped for logical reasoning by Locke's *Essay Concerning Human Understanding,* the Port Royal *Art of Thinking,* Xenophon's *Memorabilia,* and the works of Shaftesbury and Collins.

Franklin found the right avenue for a person of his "bookish inclination" when his brother James, returning from England in 1717 with a press and letters, set up in Boston as a printer, and proceeded to the publication of the *Boston Gazette*, 1719, and the *New England Courant*, 1721. Benjamin, aged twelve, became his apprentice. It can hardly be too much emphasized that this was really an inspiring "job." It made him stand at a very early age full in the wind of local political and theological controversy. It forced him to use all his childish stock of learning and daily stimulated him to new acquisitions. It put him in touch with other persons, young and old, of bookish and literary inclination. They lent him books which kindled his poetic fancy to the pitch of composing occasional ballads in the Grub Street style, which his brother printed, and had him hawk about town. His father discountenanced these effusions, declaring that "verse-makers were generally beggars"; but coming upon his son's private experiments in prose, he applied the right incentive by pointing out where the work "fell short in elegance of expression, in method and in perspicuity." "About this time," says Franklin in a familiar paragraph, "I met with an odd volume of the *Spectator*." Anticipating Dr. Johnson's advice by half a century, he gave his days and nights to painstaking study and imitation of Addison till he had mastered that style —"familiar but not coarse, and elegant but not ostentatious"—which several generations of English essayists have sought to attain. All the world has heard how Franklin's career as a writer began with an anonymous contribution stealthily slipped under the door of his brother's printing-house at night, and in the morning approved for publication by his brother's circle of "writing friends." Professor Smyth is inclined to identify this contribution with the first of fourteen humorous papers with Latin mottoes signed "Silence Dogood," [1] which appeared fortnightly in the *New England Courant* from March to October, 1722. In this year Benjamin was in charge of the *Courant* during his brother's imprisonment for printing matter offensive to the Assembly; and when, on repetition of the offence, the master was forbidden to publish his journal, it was continued in the name of the apprentice. In this situation James became jealous and overbearing, and Benjamin became insubordinate. When it grew evident that there was not room enough in Boston for them both, the younger brother left his indentures behind, and in 1723 made his memorable flight to Philadelphia.

Shortly after his arrival in the Quaker city, he found employment with the second printer in Philadelphia, Samuel Keimer—a curious person who kept the Mosaic law. In 1724, encouraged by the facile

---

[1] *The Writings of Benjamin Franklin.*—Collected and edited by Albert Henry Smyth. New York: 1907. Vol. II, p. 1. The Dogood Papers were claimed by Franklin in the first draft of his *Autobiography*, and they have been long accredited to him; but they were first included in his collected works by Professor Smyth.

promises of Governor Keith, he went to England in
the expectation that letters of credit and recommendation from his patron would enable him to procure
a printing outfit.   Left in the lurch by the governor,
he served for something over a year in two great
London printing houses, kept free-thinking and
rather loose company, and, in refutation of Wollas-
ton's *Religion of Nature* upon which he happened
to be engaged in the composing-room, published in
1725 his suppressed tract *On Liberty and Necessity*.
Returning to Philadelphia in 1726, he reentered the
employ of Keimer; in 1728 formed a brief partner-
ship with Hugh Meredith, and in 1730 married and
set up for himself.   In 1728 he formed the famous
Junto Club for reading, debating, and reforming
the world—an institution which developed into a
powerful organ of political influence.   Shortage of
money in the province prompted him to the composition of his *Modest Inquiry into the Nature and
Necessity of Paper Currency*, 1729; a service for
which his friends in the Assembly rewarded him by
employing him to print the money—"a very profitable job and a great help to me."   Forestalled by
Keimer in a project for launching a newspaper,
Franklin contributed in 1728–9 to the rival journal
published by Bradford a series of sprightly "Busy-
Body" papers in the vein of the periodical essayists.
Keimer was forced to sell out; and Franklin acquired from him the paper known from October 2,
1729, as the *Pennsylvania Gazette*.   To this he con-

tributed, besides much miscellaneous matter, such pieces as the "Dialogue Between Philocles and Horatio Concerning Virtue and Pleasure," the letters of "Anthony Afterwit" and "Alice Addertongue," "A Meditation on a Quart Mug," and "A Witch Trial at Mount Holly." In 1732 he began to issue the almanacs containing the wit and wisdom of "Poor Richard," a homely popular philosopher, who is only the incarnation of common sense, and who is consequently not, as has been carelessly assumed, to be identified with his creator.

By the time he was thirty, Franklin gave promise of becoming by a gradual expansion of his useful activities the leading Pennsylvanian. In 1736 he was chosen clerk of the General Assembly, and in the following year was appointed postmaster of Philadelphia. He made both these offices useful to his printing business and to his newspaper. In compensation, he used his newspaper and his business influence to support his measures for municipal improvements, among the objects of which may be mentioned: street-sweeping, paving, a regular police force, a fire company, a hospital, and a public library. As his business prospered, he expanded it by forming partnerships with his promising workmen, and sending them with printing-presses into other colonies. In 1741 he experimented with a monthly publication, *The General Magazine and Historical Chronicle for All the British Colonies in America;* this monthly, notable as the second issued in America, expired with the sixth number. In 1742 he invented the stove of which he published a description in 1744 as *An Account of the New Invented Pennsylvanian Fire Places*. In 1743 he drew up proposals for an academy which eventually became the University of Pennsylvania, and in 1744 he founded the American Philosophical Society. In 1746 he witnessed Spence's electrical experiments in Boston, bought the apparatus, and repeated the experiments in Philadelphia, where interest in the new science was further stimulated that year by a present of a Leyden jar given to the Library Company by the English experimenter, Peter Collinson. To this English friend Franklin made extended reports of his earlier electrical investigations in the form of letters, which Collinson published in London in 1751 with the title *"Experiments and Observations in Electricity, Made at Philadelphia in America, by Mr. Benjamin Franklin."* In 1752 he showed the identity of lightning and electricity by his kite experiment, and invented the lightning rod. In 1748, being assured of a competency, he had turned over his business to his foreman, David Hall, and purposed devoting the rest of his life to philosophical enquiries. But he had inextricably involved himself in the affairs of his community, which, as soon as it found him at leisure, "laid hold" of him, as he says, for its own purposes—"every part of the civil government, and almost at the same time, imposing some duty upon me." He was made a justice of the peace, member of the common council, alderman, and was chosen burgess to represent the city of Philadelphia in the General Assembly. In 1753 he was appointed jointly with William Hunter to exercise the office of postmaster-general of America. In 1754, as a member of the Pennsylvania commission he laid before the colonial congress at Albany the "Plan of Union," adopted by the commissioners. In 1755 he displayed remarkable energy, ability, and public spirit in providing transportation for General Braddock's ill-fated expedition against the French; and in the following year he himself took command of a volunteer military organization for the protection of the northwest frontier. In 1757 he was sent to England to present the long-standing grievances of the Pennsylvania Assembly against the proprietary for obstructing legislation designed to throw upon them a fair share of the expense of government.

Though Franklin's political mission was not wholly successful, his residence in England from 1757 to 1762 was highly profitable to him. It developed his talent as a negotiator of public business with strangers; it enabled him to consider British colonial policies from English points of view; and it afforded him many opportunities for general self-improvement. After a fruitless effort to obtain satisfaction from the representatives of the Penn family, dismissing as impractical the hope of procuring for Pennsylvania a royal charter, he appealed

to the Crown to exempt the Assembly from the
influence of proprietary instructions and to make
the proprietary estates bear a more equitable proportion of the taxes. To get the Assembly's case
before the public, he collaborated with an unknown
hand on *An Historical Review of the Constitution
and Government of Pennsylvania,* published in
1759. The result was a compromise which in the
circumstances he regarded as a victory. His interest
in the wider questions of imperial policy he exhibited
in 1760 by aspersing the advocates of a hasty and
inconclusive peace with France in his stinging little
skit, *Of the Meanes of Disposing the Enemies to
Peace,* which he presented as an extract from the
work of a Jesuit historian. In 1760, also, he was
joint author with Richard Jackson of a notably influential argument for the retention of Canada, *The
Interest of Great Britain Considered with Regard
to Her Colonies;* to which was appended his *Observations Concerning the Increase of Mankind, Peo-
pling of Countries, etc.* In the intervals of business,
he sat for his portrait, attended the theatre, played
upon the armonica, experimented with electricity
and heat, made a tour of the Low Countries, visited
the principal cities of England and Scotland, received honorary degrees from the universities, and
enjoyed the society of Collinson, Priestley, Price,
Hume, Adam Smith, Robertson, and Kames. He
returned to America in the latter part of 1762. In
1763 he made a 1,600-mile tour of the northern

provinces to inspect the post-offices. In the following year he was again in the thick of Pennsylvania politics, working with the party in the Assembly which sought to have the proprietary government of the province replaced by a royal charter. In support of this movement he published in 1764 his *Cool Thoughts on the Present Situation of our Public Affairs* and his *Preface to the Speech of Joseph Galloway*, a brilliant and blasting indictment of the proprietors, Thomas and Richard Penn.

In the fall of 1764 Franklin was sent again to England by the Assembly to petition for a royal charter and to express the Assembly's views with regard to Grenville's Stamp Act, then impending. On July 11, 1765, after the obnoxious measure had been passed by an overwhelming majority, Franklin wrote to Charles Thomson: "Depend upon it, my good neighbour, I took every step in my power to prevent the passing of the Stamp Act. . . . But the Tide was too strong against us. The nation was provoked by American Claims of Independence, and all Parties joined in resolving by this act to settle the point. We might as well have hindered the sun's setting." This letter and one or two others of about the same date express a patient submission to the inevitable. As soon, however, as Franklin was fully apprised of the fierce flame of opposition which the passage of the act had kindled in the colonies, he caught the spirit of the constituents, and threw himself sternly into the struggle for its repeal.

In 1766 he underwent his famous examination before the House of Commons on the attitude of the Colonies towards the collection of the new taxes. The report of this examination, which was promptly published, is one of the most interesting and impressive pieces of dramatic dialogue produced in the eighteenth century. After the repeal, Franklin received recognition at home in the shape of new duties: in 1768 he was appointed agent for Georgia; in 1769, for New Jersey; in 1770, for Massachusetts. In the summer of 1766 he visited Germany; the following summer he visited Paris; and he was in France again for a month in 1769. His pen in these years was employed mainly in correspondence and in communications to the newspapers, in which he pointedly set forth the causes which threatened a permanent breach between the mother country and the colonies. In 1773 he published in the *Gentleman's Magazine* two little masterpieces of irony which Swift might have been pleased to sign: *An Edict By The King of Prussia* and *Rules By Which A Great Empire May Be Reduced To A Small One*. In 1774, in consequence of his activity in exposing Governor Hutchinson's proposals for the military intimidation of Massachusetts, Franklin was subjected before the Privy Council to virulent and scurrilous abuse from Attorney-General Wedderburn. This onslaught it was, accentuated by his dismissal from the office of Postmaster-General, which began to curdle in Franklin his sincere long-cherished hope of an ultimate reconciliation. It is an ominous coincidence that in this year of his great humiliation he sent with a letter of recommendation to his son-in-law in Philadelphia, Thomas Paine, an obscure Englishman of Whiggish temper, two years later to become the fieriest advocate of American independence. In disgrace with the Court, Franklin lingered in England to exhaust the last possibilities of amicable adjustment; petitioning the king, conferring with Burke and Chatham, and curiously arranging for secret negotiations with the go-betweens of the Ministry over the chess board of Lord Howe's sister. He sailed from England in March, 1775, half-convinced that the Ministry were bent upon provoking an open rebellion. When he arrived in Philadelphia, he heard what had happened at Lexington and Concord. On July 5, 1775, he wrote a letter to an English friend of thirty years standing, William Strahan, then a member of Parliament; it was shortened like a Roman sword and sharpened to this point:

You and I were long Friends:—You are now my Enemy,—and I am

Yours,

B. FRANKLIN.

As Franklin was sixty-nine years old in 1775, he might fairly have retreated to his library, and have left the burden of the future state to younger hands. He had hardly set foot on shore, however, before the Pennsylvania Assembly elected him delegate to the first Continental Congress, where his tried sagacity was enlisted in organizing the country's political, economic, and military resources for the great conflict. On July 7, 1775, the old man wrote to Priestley: "My time was never more fully employed. In the morning at six, I am at the Committee of Safety, appointed by the Assembly to put the province in a state of defence; which committee holds till near nine, when I am at the Congress, and that sits till after four in the afternoon." In the period slightly exceeding a year previous to his departure for France, he served on innumerable committees of the Congress, was made Postmaster General of the Colonies, presided over the Constitutional Convention of Pennsylvania, was sent on a mission to Canada, assisted in drafting the Declaration of Independence, and signed it.

In October, 1776, he sailed for France on a commission of the Congress to negotiate a treaty of alliance, which was concluded in February, 1778, after the surrender of Burgoyne had inspired confidence in the prospects of the American arms. In September, 1778, he was appointed plenipotentiary to the court of France. Clothed with large powers, he transacted in the next few years an almost incredible amount of difficult business for his country. He obtained from the French government the repeated loans which made possible the carrying on of a long war; he made contracts for clothing and ammunitions; he dissuaded or recommended to Congress foreign applicants for commissions in the colonial army; he arranged exchanges of prisoners-of-war; he equipped and to some extent directed the operations of privateers; he supplied information to many Europeans emigrating to America; he made treaties of amity and commerce with Sweden and Prussia. With all this engrossing business on his hands, he found time to achieve an immense personal popularity. He was not merely respected as a masterly diplomat; he was lionized and idolized as the great natural philosopher, the august champion of liberty, and the friend of humanity. In the press of public affairs, never losing interest in scientific matters, he served on a royal French commission to investigate Mesmerism; sent to his foreign correspondents ingenious geological and meteorological conjectures; and transmitted to the Royal Society reports on French experiments in aeronautics. He entertained with a certain lavishness at his house in Passy; and he was a frequent diner-out, adored for his wit and good humor, in the intimate coteries of Mme. Helvetius and Mme. Brillon. He set up for the amusement of himself and his friends a private press in Passy, on which he printed a number of *bagatelles* of an accomplished and charming levity: *The Ephemera*, 1778; *The Morals of Chess*, 1779; *The Whistle*, 1779; *The Dialogue Between Franklin and the Gout*, 1780. In 1784 he resumed work on his unfinished autobiography, and published *Advice to such as would remove to America* and *Remarks Concerning the Savages of North America.* In his residence in France he began seriously to feel the siege of gout, the stone, and old age. In 1781, in reply to repeated supplications for leave to go home and die, Congress had appointed him of the commission to negotiate a treaty of peace between England and the United States. This last great task was completed in 1785. In midsummer of that year he said a regretful farewell to his affectionate French friends, received the king's portrait set in four hundred diamonds, and in one of the royal litters was carried down to his point of embarkation at Havre de Grace.

Franklin arrived in Philadelphia in September, 1785, resolved to set his house in order. He was soon made aware that, like the hero in the *Conquest of Granada,* he had not "leisure yet to die." He was overwhelmed with congratulations; or, as he put it with characteristic modesty of phrase in a letter to his English friend Mrs. Hewson: "I had the happiness of finding my family well, and of being very kindly received by my Country folk." In the month after his arrival he was elected President of the State of Pennsylvania; and the honor was thrust upon him again in 1786 and in 1787. In a letter of November 14, 1785, he says: "I had not firmness enough to resist the unanimous desire of my country folks; and I find myself harnessed again in their service for another year. They engrossed the prime of my life. They have eaten my flesh, and seem resolved now to pick my bones." In 1787 he was chosen a delegate to the convention to frame the Constitution of the United States—an instrument which he deemed not perfect yet as near perfection as the joint wisdom of any numerous body of men could carry it, handicapped by "their prejudices, their passions, their local interests, and their selfish views." In 1789, as President of the Abolition Society, Franklin signed a memorial against slavery which was laid before the House of Representatives; and on March 23, 1790, less than a month before his death, he wrote for the *Federal Gazette,* an ironical justification of the enslaving of Christians by African Mohammedans—quite in the vein of the celebrated *Edict of the King of Prussia.* As the shadows thickened about him, he settled his estate, paid his compliments to his friends, and departed, on the seventeenth day of April, 1790, in his eighty-fifth year.

In the matter of religion Franklin was distinctly a product of the eighteenth century enlightenment. He took his direction in boyhood and early manhood from deistical writers like Pope, Collins, Shaftesbury, and Mandeville. At various periods of his life he drew up articles of belief, which generally included recognition of one God, the providential government of the world, the immortality of the soul, and divine justice. To profess faith in as much religion as this, he found emotionally gratifying, socially expedient, and conformable to the common sense of mankind. He might have sub-scribed without hesitation to both the positive and negative dogmas of the *religion civile* formulated by Rousseau in the *Contrat Social*. In his later years he was in sympathetic relation with Paine, Price, and Priestley. He was, however, of a fortu-nately earlier generation than these English "here-tics," and certain other circumstances enabled him to keep the temper of his heterodoxy sweet, while theirs grew acidulous, and to walk serenely in ways which for them were embittered by the *odium theologicum*. His earlier advent upon the eigh-teenth-century scene made possible the unfolding and comfortable settlement of his religious ideas before deism had clearly allied itself with political radicalism and edged its sword for assault upon in-spired Bible and established church as powers fed-erate with political orthodoxy in upholding the an-cient regime. Among the diverse denominational bodies in Pennsylvania his perfectly genuine toler-ance and his unfailing tact helped him to maintain a friendly neutrality between parties which were far from friendly. Like Lord Chesterfield, he sin-cerely believed in the decency and propriety of going to church; and he went himself when he could en-dure the preachers. He advised his daughter to go constantly, "whoever preaches." He made pecuniary contributions to all the leading denomina-tions in Philadelphia; respectfully acknowledged the good features of each; and undertook to unite in his own creed the common and, as he thought, the essential features of all. Man of the world as he was, he enjoyed the warm friendship of good Quakers, good Presbyterians, Whitefield, the Bishop of St. Asaph, and his French abbés. His abstention from theological controversy was doubtless due in part to a shrewd regard for his own interest and influence as a business man and a public servant; but it was due in perhaps equal measure to his profound indifference to metaphysical questions unrelated to practical conduct. "Emancipated" in childhood and unmolested in the independence of his mind, he reached maturity without that acrimony of free thought incident to those who attain independence late and have revenges to take. He was consistently opposed to the imposition of religious tests by constitutional authority. But in the Constitutional Convention of 1787 he offered a motion in favor of holding daily prayers before the deliberations of the Assembly, for as he declared, "the longer I live, the more convincing proofs I see of this Truth, *that* God *governs in the Affairs of Men.*" With his progress in eminence and years, he seems to have been somewhat strengthened in Cicero's conviction that so puissant a personality as his own could not utterly perish, and he derived a kind of classical satisfaction from the reflection that this feeling was in concurrence with the common opinions of mankind. A few weeks before his death he admitted, in a remarkable letter to Ezra Stiles, a doubt as to the divinity of Jesus; but he remarked with his characteristic tranquillity that he thought it "needless to busy myself with it now, when I expect soon an Opportunity of knowing the Truth with less Trouble." Not elate, like Emerson, yet quite unawed, this imitator of Jesus and Socrates walked in this world and prepared for his ease in Zion.

Franklin set himself in youth to the study of "moral perfection," and the work which only great public business prevented his leaving as his literary monument was to have been a treatise on the "art of virtue." His merits, however, in both the theory and practice of the moral life have been seriously called in question. It is alleged that his standards were low and that he did not live up to them. It must be conceded on the one hand that he had a natural son who became governor of New Jersey, and on the other hand that industry and frugality, which most of us place among the minor, he placed among the major virtues. When one has referred the *"errata"* of his adolescence to animal spirits, "free thinking," and bad company; and when one has explained certain laxities of his maturity by alluding to the indulgent temper of the French society in which he then lived; one may as well candidly admit that St. Francis made chastity a more conspicuous jewel in his crown of virtues than did Dr. Franklin. And when one has pointed out that the prudential philosophy of Poor Richard's Almanac was rather a collection of popular wisdom than an original contribution; and when one has called attention to the special reasons for magnifying economic virtues in a community of impecunious colonists and pioneers; one may as well frankly acknowledge that there is nothing in the precepts of the great printer to shake a man's egotism like the shattering paradoxes of the Beatitudes nor like the *Christian Morals* of Sir Thomas Browne to make his heart elate. Franklin had nothing of what pietists call a "realizing sense" of sin or of the need for mystical regeneration and justification—faculties so richly present in his contemporary Jonathan Edwards. His cool calculating reason, having surveyed the fiery battleground of the Puritan conscience, reported that things are forbidden because hurtful, not hurtful because forbidden. Guided by this utilitarian principle, he simplified his religion and elaborated his morality. His system included, however, much more than maxims of thrift and prudent self-regard, and to assert that he set up wealth as the *summum bonum* is a sheer libel. He commended diligence in business as the means to a competency; he commended a competency as a safeguard to virtue; and he commended virtue as the prerequisite to happiness. The temple that he reared to Moral Perfection was built of thirteen stones: temperance, silence, order, resolution, frugality, industry, sincerity, justice, moderation, cleanliness, tranquillity, chastity, and humility—the last added on the advice of a Quaker. He wrought upon the structure with the method of a monk and he recorded his progress with the regularity of a book-keeper. The presiding spirit in the edifice, which made it something more than a private oratory, was a rational and active benevolence towards his fellow mortals in every quarter of the earth. The wide-reaching friendliness in Franklin may be distinguished in two ways from the roseate humanitarian enthusiasm of the Savoyard Vicar. It was not begotten by a theory of "natural goodness" nor fostered by millennial expectations but was born of sober experience with the utility of good will in establishing satisfactory and fruitful relations among men. It found expression not in rhetorical periods but in numberless practical means and measures for ameliorating the human lot. By no mystical intuition but by the common light of reason the "prudential philosopher" discovered and acted upon the truth, that the greatest happiness that can come to a man in this world is to devote the full strength of body and mind to the service of his fellow men. Judged either by his principles or by his performance, Franklin's moral breadth and moral elevation have been absurdly underestimated.

It is perhaps in the field of politics that Franklin exhibits the most marked development of his power and his vision. A realistic inductive thinker, well versed in the rudiments of his subject long before the revolutionary theorists handled it, he was not rendered by any preconception of abstract rights indocile to the lessons of his immense political experience. He formulated his conceptions in the thick of existing conditions, and always with reference to what was expedient and possible as well as to what was desirable. He served his apprenticeship in the Philadelphia Junto Club, which at its inception was little more than a village improvement society, but which threw out branches till it became a power in the province, and a considerable factor in the affairs of the colonies. In this association he learned the importance of cooperation, mastered the tactics of organization, practiced the art of getting propaganda afoot, and discovered the great secret of converting private desires into public demands. In proposing in 1754 his plan for a union of the colonies he was applying to larger units the principle of cooperative action by which he had built up what we might call today his "machine" in Pennsylvania. He had in too large measure the instincts and the ideas of a leader, and he had too much experience with the conflicting prejudices and the resultant compromises of popular assemblies, to feel any profound reverence for the "collective wisdom" of the people. "If all officers appointed by governors were always men of merit," he wrote in his *Dialogue Concerning the Present State of Affairs in Pennsylvania*, "it would be wrong ever to hazard a popular election." That his belief in

popular representation was due as much to his sense
of its political expediency as to his sense of its political justice is suggested by a passage in his letter on
the imposition of direct taxes addressed to Governor Shirley, December 18, 1754: "In matters of
general concern to the people, and especially where
burthens are to be laid upon them, it is of use to
consider, as well what they will be apt to think and
say, as what they ought to think." His sojourn
in England widened his horizons but not beyond the
bounds of his nationality. As agent, he felt himself essentially a colonial Englishman pleading for
the extension of English laws to British subjects
across the sea, and playing up to the Imperial policy
of crushing out the colonizing and commercial
rivalry of France. The ultimate failure of his mission of reconciliation effected no sudden transformation of his political ideas; it rather overwhelmed
him with disgust at the folly, the obstinacy, and the
corruption rampant among English politicians of
the period. He returned to the arms of his people
because he had been hurled from the arms of his
king, and he embraced their new principles because
he was sure they could not be worse applied than
his old ones. His respect for the popular will was
inevitably heightened by his share in executing it
in the thrilling days when he was helping his fellow
countrymen to declare their independence, and was
earning the superb epigraph of Turgot: *Eripuit ful-
men coelo sceptrumque tyrannis.* His official resi-

dence in France completely dissolved his former antagonism to that country. In the early stages of the conflict his wrath was bitter enough towards England, but long before it was over he had taken the ground of radical pacificism, reiterating his conviction that "there is no good war and no bad peace." He who had financed the Revolution had seen too much non-productive expenditure of moral and physical capital to believe in the appeal to arms. If nations required enlargement of their territories, it was a mere matter of arithmetic, he contended, to show that the cheaper way was to purchase it. "Justice," he declared, "is as strictly due between neighbor nations as between neighbor citizens, . . . and a nation that makes an unjust war is only a *great gang.*" So far as he was able, he mitigated the afflictions of noncombatants. He proposed by international law to exempt from peril fishermen and farmers and the productive workers of the world. He ordered the privateersmen under his control to safeguard the lives and property of explorers and men of science belonging to the enemy country; and he advocated for the future the abolition of the custom of commissioning privateers. In the treaty which he negotiated with Prussia he actually obtained the incorporation of an article so restricting the "zone of war" as to make a war between Prussia and the United States under its terms virtually impossible. His diplomatic intercourse in Europe had opened his eyes to the common interests of all pacific peoples and to the inestimable advantages of a general amity among the nations. His ultimate political ideal included nothing short of the welfare and the commercial federation of the world. To that extent, at least, he was a believer in majority interests! It may be further said that his political development was marked by a growing mastery of the art of dealing with men and by a steady approximation of his political to his personal morality.

For the broad humanity of Franklin's political conceptions undoubtedly his interest in the extension of science was partly responsible. As a scientific investigator he had long been a "citizen of the world," and for him not the least bitter consequence of the war was that it made a break in the intellectual brotherhood of man. If he had not been obliged to supply the army of Washington with guns and ammunition, he might have been engaged in the far more congenial task of supplying the British Academy with food for philosophical discussion. He could not but resent the brutal antagonisms which had rendered intellectual coöperation with his English friends impossible, and which had frustrated his cherished hope of devoting his ripest years to philosophical researches. A natural endowment he certainly possessed which would have qualified him in happier circumstances for even more distinguished service than he actually performed in extending the frontiers of knowledge. He had the powerfully developed curiosity of the explorer and the inventor, ever busily prying into the causes of things, ever speculating upon the consequences of novel combinations. His native inquisitiveness had been stimulated by a young civilization's manifold necessities, mothering manifold inventions, and had been supplemented by a certain moral and idealizing passion for improvement. The practical nature of many of his devices, his absorption in agriculture and navigation, his preoccupation with stoves and chimneys, the image of him firing the gas of ditch water or pouring oil on troubled waves, and the celebrity of the kite incident rather tend to fix an impression that he was but a tactful empiricist and a lucky dilettante of discovery. It is interesting in this connection to note that he confesses his lack of patience for verification. His prime scientific faculty, as he himself felt, was the imagination which bodies forth the shapes and relations of things unknown, which constructs the theory and the hypothesis. His mind was a teeming warren of hints and suggestions. He loved rather to start than to pursue the hare. Happily what he deemed his excessive penchant for forming hypotheses was safeguarded by his perfect readiness to hear all that could be urged against them. He wished not his view but truth to prevail—which explains the winsome cordiality of his demeanor towards other savants. His unflagging correspondence with investigators, his subscription to learned publications, his active membership in philosophical societies and his enterprise in founding schools and academies all betoken his prescience of the wide domain which science had to conquer and of the necessity for co-operation in the task of subduing it. Franklin was so far a Baconian that he sought to avoid unfruitful speculation and to unite contemplation and action in a stricter embrace for the generation of knowledge useful to man. But in refutation of any charge that he was a narrow-minded utilitarian and lacked the liberal views and long faith of the modern scientific spirit may be adduced his stunning retort to a query as to the usefulness of the balloons then on trial in France: "What is the use of a new born baby?"

Of Franklin's style the highest praise is to declare that it reveals the mental and moral qualities of the man himself. It is the flexible style of a writer who has learned the craft of expression by studying and imitating the virtues of many masters: the playful charm of Addison, the trenchancy of Swift, the concreteness of Defoe, the urbanity of Shaftesbury, the homely directness of Bunyan's dialogue, the unadorned vigor of Tillotson, and the epigrammatic force of Pope. His mature manner, however, is imitative of nothing but the thoroughly disciplined movement of a versatile mind which has never known a moment of languor or a moment of uncontrollable excitement. Next to his omnipresent vitality, his most notable characteristic is the clear-

ness which results from complete preliminary vision
of what is to be said, and which in a young hand
demands deliberate preconsideration. To Franklin
the ordering of his matter must have become eventually a light task as, with incessant passing to and
fro in his experience and with the daily habit
of epistolary communication, he grew as familiar
with his intellectual terrains as an old field marshal
with the map of Europe. For the writing of his
later years is marked not merely by clearness and
force but also by the sovereign ease of a man who
has long understood himself and the interrelations
of his ideas and has ceased to make revolutionary
discoveries in any portion of his own nature. His
occasional wrath does not fluster him but rather in-
tensifies his lucidity, clarifies his logic, and brightens
the ironical smile that accompanies the thrust of
his wit. The "decent plainness and manly freedom"
of his ordinary tone—notes which he admired in the
writings of his maternal grand-father, Peter Folger
—rise in parts of his official correspondence to a
severity of decorum; for there is a trace of the
senatorial in the man, the dignity of antique Rome.
He is seldom too hurried, even in a private letter,
to gratify the ear by the turning and cadence of
sentence and phrase; and one feels that the harmony of his periods is the right and predestined
vesture of his essential blandness and suavity of
temper. His stylistic drapery, however, is never
so smoothed and adjusted as to obscure the sinewy

vigor of his thought. His manner is steadily in the service of his matter. He is adequate, not copious; for his moral "frugality and industry" prompt him to eschew surplusage and to make his texture firm. His regard for purity of diction is classical; he avoids vulgarity; he despises the jargon of scientific pedants; but like Montaigne he loves frank and masculine speech, and he likes to enrich the language of the well-bred by discreet drafts upon the burry, homely, sententious, proverbial language of the people. Like Lord Bacon and like many other grave men among his fellow countrymen, he found it difficult to avoid an opportunity for a jest even when the occasion was unpropitious; and he never sat below the Attic salt. When his fortune was made he put by the pewter spoon and earthenware bowl of his apprenticeship for silver and fine china. His biographer reminds us that he kept a well-stocked cellar at Passy and enjoyed the distinction of suffering from the gout. With affluence and years he acquired a "palate," and gave a little play to the long repressed tastes of an Epicurean whom early destiny had cast upon a rockbound coast. The literary expression of his autumnal festivity is to be found in the *bagatelles*. The tallow chandler's son, having entered on the cycle of his development by cultivating thrift like Defoe, completed it like Lord Chesterfield by cultivating "the graces." *The Ephemera* proves that this great eighteenth century rationalist had a fancy. It is no relative, indeed, of that romantic spirit which pipes to the whistling winds on the enchanted greens of Shakespeare. It is rather the classic sprite which summons the little rosy-winged Loves and Desires to sport among the courtiers and philosophers and the wasp-waited ladies in the delicate *fête champêtre* of Watteau.

IV

THE EMERSONIAN LIBERATION

Some books, like some persons, convey to us all that they will ever have to give at a single sitting. Others hold our attention profitably through two or three encounters. Of the wives we marry we ask more than that; and the books to frequent, the books to be shipwrecked with, the great books into which rich and substantial lives have been distilled and packed—the *Dialogues* of Plato, Montaigne's *Essays*, Boswell's *Johnson*, the *Essays* and *Journals* of Emerson—these are to be lived with and returned to and made the companions of hours and days and moods as various as those in which they were written. You cannot discover what Emerson has been to others or what he may be to you by any cursory turning of his pages. Still less can you "get him up" by studying any summary of his philosophical system. Philosophers tell us indeed that his philosophical system is hopelessly antiquated, and fancy that they have disposed of him. But Emerson himself remarked: "I need hardly say to anyone acquainted with my thoughts that I have no system." The value of his thoughts depends scarcely

63

more upon the metaphysical filaments among them than the value of a string of alternating beads of gold and pearl depends upon the string. The figure has a momentary illustrative force but is very inadequate. Emerson lives, still speaks pertinently of our current affairs, and to-morrow we shall still find him commenting with equal pertinency on to-morrow's affairs. To know him is not mere knowledge. It is an experience; for he is a dynamic personality, addressing the will, the emotions, the imagination, no less than the intellect. His value escapes the merely intellectual appraiser. Analysis cannot deal properly with his pungent wit—it must be savored; nor with the impetus that he gives to the will—it must be felt; nor with the purgation and serene rapture of the mind towards which his noble discipline tends—this rapture must be attained as a state of grace by imitation of those who have attained it, by lifelong intercourse with men whose tone and habit of life is noble.

I

Since we are to consider him primarily as an unspent force in our own times, what it most concerns us to enquire about him is what he can do for us. If we approach him with that question, we need not tarry long over biographical details, interesting and rewarding as they may be to the student of literary history. We pretty well sum up his ex-

ternal career when we say that he was a New Englander of Boston, where he was born in 1803, and
of Concord, where he died in 1882, after a studious
life of irreproachable purity, dignity, and simplicity
becoming the descendant of several generations of
New England gentlemen and scholars. His formal
education he received at the Boston Latin School
and at Harvard College, from which he was gradu-
ated in 1821, with a well-formed bias towards an
intellectual life. The son of a Unitarian minister,
he inherited an ethical impulse which directed him
to the Harvard Divinity School in 1825–6. In 1829
he was appointed pastor of the Second Unitarian
Church of Boston. He was married in the same
year to Ellen Tucker, who died two years later,
leaving him a sweet and unfading memory of her
fragile loveliness. After he had served his parish
acceptably for three years, he felt obliged to announce, in 1832, that he was no longer able to
administer the sacrament of communion in the general sense of his congregation, and resigned his
charge. In December of that year he visited Europe and made acquaintance with three or four men
whose residence in Europe constituted for him the
chief reason for going abroad: Landor in Italy,
Carlyle at Craigenputtock, and Coleridge and
Wordsworth in England. He returned to America
in October, 1833, and in the following year settled
permanently in Concord. In 1835 he married his
second wife, Lidian Jackson. For three or four

years he preached with some regularity in various pulpits, but he gradually abandoned the church for the lyceum, which invited him as far west as Wisconsin and Illinois. He made a second visit to England in 1848. For the most part, barring his winter lecturing tours and an occasional excursion to deliver a commencement address or a Phi Beta Kappa oration, he lived placidly in Concord, reading, meditating, writing, editing the short-lived transcendental *Dial,* looking amusedly askance upon the Brook Farm experiment, and walking and talking with his famous fellow-villagers, the Alcotts, the Hawthornes, Margaret Fuller, Ellery Channing, and Thoreau.

What ferment of radical thought went on beneath the decorous exterior of that quiet scholar's life we know with remarkable fulness and accuracy. From early boyhood Emerson kept a journal—a habit, in his case, denoting a mind disposed to make unusual exactions of the "hypocritic days." At first, he is much occupied with what he has read or proposes to read; but presently his note-book becomes a kind of storehouse for mellowing the fruits of his daily meditations, and an experimental garden for planting the seeds of new thoughts gathered on his intellectual adventures. The *Journals,* now published in twelve volumes, give us an invaluable commentary upon the long-familiar essays, and they enrich greatly our sense of the personality behind them. Especially they illuminate the turning point in Emerson's life, when he abandoned the pulpit and became a wholly free thinker and speaker. With their help, one perceives that for years before the open break, the inner emancipation had been proceeding. One observes the young thinker expanding steadily beyond the formulas of his parish, reaching out towards the life of his nation, feeling his way into the higher spirit of his times, daily becoming more eager to exchange messages and compare visions with the leaders of his generation.

It is a vulgar error of our day to think of Emerson and his friends as living in a rude and mentally poverty-stricken era. In his formative period, say from 1820 to 1832, society around the Golden Gate and at the southern end of Lake Michigan was indeed in a somewhat more primitive state than at present. But in compensation, such civilized society as the country possessed was concentrated in a much smaller geographical area. To reside in Boston or New York was not then, as now, to live on the rim but at the centre of population, within reach of the molding pressure of all the great Americans of one's time. The "moment," furthermore, was peculiarly rich in the presence of eminent men who had been shaped by the Revolution, and in the presence of men who were to become eminent in the movement which led to the Civil War. To a young man of Emerson's quality, the period of the Adamses, Jefferson, Randolph, and Jackson, the period of Webster, Clay, Calhoun, Everett, and Garrison, was not a dull period, not a dead interval, but a most stirring and exciting time between two epoch-making crises, with the thunder of a political Niagara at one's back, and the roar of wild rapids ahead. The air was full of promise and of peril and of conflicting measures for avoiding the one and fulfilling the other.

Politically-minded men—the Jacksons, the Clays, the Calhouns—brought to the problems of the hour political solutions. But the more sensitive spirits among the younger generation in New England had already experienced a certain reaction against the political faith and enthusiasms of their fathers. Already they heard the ominous creaking of democratic machinery under the manipulation of unskilful and unscrupulous hands. To them it began to appear that the next great improvement in the condition of society must depend less upon the alteration of laws and institutions than upon the intellectual and moral regeneration of men. The new movement was genuinely Puritan by its inwardness, by its earnest passion for cleansing the inside of the cup, and by its protest against external powers which thwarted or retarded the efforts of the individual soul to move forward and upward by light from within. Looking back in 1844 over the multifarious projects for "the salvation of the world" unfolded by reformers in his part of the country, Emerson remarks: "There was in all the practical activities of New England, for the last quarter of a century, a gradual withdrawal of tender consciences from the social organization. There is observable throughout, the contest between mechanical and spiritual methods, but with a steady tendency of the thoughtful and virtuous to a deeper belief and reliance on spiritual facts."

Those who place their reliance on spiritual facts have always been thought a little queer and rather dangerous by those who do not. Nor can it be denied that the radical protestantism of the Puritans, which Emerson inherited, has contained from the time of Wycliff an anarchical germ, a latent suspicion of church and state, a tendency towards "coming out," till one shall stand alone in utter freedom and count for one and nothing more. It is hardly possible to exaggerate the individualism which characterized the movement in New England. For Emerson above all, the very rapture of the time rose from its challenge to a perfectly independent, a perfectly fearless, scrutiny and testing of received values in every field—art, politics, morals, religion.

Emerson was preserved from the fanaticism of a secession from "the social organization" partly by his culture. A moral reformation which undertakes to investigate the bases of morals will develop and transform itself into an intellectual renascence as soon as those who are conducting it perceive that everything in heaven and earth has a bearing on their questions. Emerson discovered early that the first step towards thinking greatly and freely on moral matters is to consult the world's accumulated wisdom. Hasty writers speak of his "jaunty" attitude towards the past. If he is jaunty about the past, it is because he is very familiar with it. What impresses the thoughtful student of his journals is his steady effort to hold himself and his contemporaries under the searching cross-lights of human experience. He reads Plato, Cicero, Hafiz, Confucius, Buddha, Mahomet, Dante, Montaigne, Milton, Voltaire, Kant, Goethe, Napoleon, Coleridge, Carlyle, because that, he finds, is the effective way to set his own intelligence free, and because freedom, he finds, means ability to move at ease and as an equal among such minds as these.

But Emerson was also preserved from excessive individualism by a passion which, properly elevated and directed, may be a young man's guardian angel, the passion of ambition. "All young persons," he observes, "thirst for a real existence for a real object,—for something great and good which they shall do with their heart. Meanwhile they all pack gloves, or keep books, or travel, or draw indentures, or cajole old women." By habitual imaginative association with great men, he had assimilated their thoughts and virtues, and had accustomed himself to look forward with an almost Miltonic assurance to playing a part above the ordinary in the life of his country. At the age of twenty-one he is sketching a series of papers on the improvement of the nation. He thinks the demand for a moral education the best sign of the times, and deems the exploration of the field a task fit for a new Columbus. He queries whether it were not an "heroic adventure" for him to "insist on being a popular speaker." And with perceptible elation at the prospect he concludes: "To address a great nation risen from the dust and sitting in absolute judgment on the merits of men, ready to hear if any one offers good counsel, may rouse the ambition and exercise the judgment of a man."

II

There is some disposition at present to look upon Emerson's ambition as extravagant and to regard his work as a closed chapter in the intellectual life of America. It is even asserted that he never much affected the thinking of his countrymen. Says a recent writer, "What one notices about him chiefly is his lack of influence upon the main stream of American thought, such as it is. He had admirers and even worshippers, but no apprentices." But this judgment will not stand examination. Emerson was a naturalist with a fresh vision of the natural world: he had Thoreau for an apprentice, and between them they established relations with the natural world, which successive naturalists like John Burroughs and John Muir have maintained and broadened to the dimensions of a national tradition.

Emerson was a poet with a fresh vision of the poetic field in America: he had Whitman for a disciple, and a large part of what passes with us as poetry to-day, whatever is indigenous and racy of the soil and native character and ideals, is ultimately traceable to their inspiration. Emerson is our great original force in criticism; he left the imprint of his spirit upon Lowell, who said: "There is no man living to whom, as a writer, so many of us feel and thankfully acknowledge so great an indebtedness for ennobling impulses." Whatever is finely academic, high-bred, and distinguished in our critical literature to-day has felt the influence of Emerson and Lowell. "To him," according to Lowell, "more than to all other causes together did the young martyrs of our Civil War owe the sustaining strength of thoughtful heroism that is so touching in every record of their lives." By his aid innumerable preachers and teachers have found a way to translate the message of ancient scriptures into the language of modern men. Every American who pretends to know anything whatever of the American classics has at one time or other read the *Essays;* and the "idealism" which was once thought to be characteristic of the American people is most readily formulated in a half dozen of his "familiar quotations," which every one knows, whether he has read a line of Emerson or not. Directly and indirectly Emerson probably did as much as any other writer in our history to establish what we mean by "a good

American"; and that, in the long run, is the most important sort of influence that can be exerted by any writer in any country.

That his influence abroad has been considerable may be briefly suggested by the reminder that he touched deeply such various men as Carlyle, Matthew Arnold, Nietzsche, and M. Maeterlinck. When Arnold visited America in 1883, he lectured on Emerson, on whom thirty years earlier he had written a sonnet of ardent admiration and homage. The lecture, the fruit of his ripest critical reflection, was not altogether satisfactory to his American audience. It impressed them as quite inadequately appreciative of their chief literary luminary. For Arnold very firmly declared that Emerson is not to be ranked with the great poets, nor with the great writers of prose, nor with the great makers of philosophical systems. These limitations of Emerson's power are commonly quoted as if detraction were the main burden of Arnold's message. As a matter of fact they are preliminary to his deliberate and remarkable declaration that in his judgment Emerson's essays are the most important work done in prose in our language during the nineteenth century. This is high praise from an exacting critic who was little given to the use of superlatives in any case, least of all in the case of American authors.

For what merit does Emerson deserve this preeminent place? Because, says Arnold, in a phrase full of significance, because "he is the friend and aider of those who would live in the spirit." Let us unfold a little the implications of this phrase and make its application more precise. Important as Emerson may have been to young Englishmen in the first half of the last century, he was still more important to young Americans. Helpful as he may become to European minds, he will always remain peculiarly the friend and aider of those who would live in the spirit amid an environment which, as is generally thought, tends powerfully to confirm on the one hand the hard and merely practical genius of the Yankee, and, on the other hand, the narrow and inflexible righteousness of the merely traditional Puritan, the Puritan who feels no longer the urgency and progressive force of new moral life within him. To the posterity of Franklin and Edwards, Emerson is the destined and appropriate counsellor because he brings them undiminished the vital force of their great moral traditions while at the same time he emancipates them from the "dead hand," the cramping and lifeless part of their past. To children of the new world, Emerson is a particularly inspiring friend, because with deep indigenous voice he frees them from unmanly fear of their elders, lifts from their minds the overawing prestige of Europe, liberates the powers and faith of the individual man and makes him "at home" in his own time and place.

A great part of our lives, as we all recognize in what we call our educational period, is occupied with learning how to do and to be what others have been and have done before us. We come abreast of our predecessors by imitating them, and are grateful to the masters when they reveal to us their secrets, to the older men when they give us the benefit of their experience. But presently we discover that the world is changing around us, and that the secrets of the masters and the experience of our elders do not wholly suffice—much though they aid us—to establish us effectively in our younger world. We discover within us needs, aspirations, powers of which the generation that educated us seems unaware, or towards which it appears to be indifferent, unsympathetic, or even actively hostile. We perceive gradually or with successive shocks of surprise that many things which our fathers declared were true and satisfactory are not at all satisfactory, are by no means true, for us. Then it dawns upon us, perhaps as an exhilarating opportunity, perhaps as a grave and sobering necessity, that in a little while we ourselves shall be the elders, the responsible generation. Our salvation in the day when we take command will depend, we are constrained to believe, upon our disentanglement from the lumber of heirlooms and hereditary devices, and upon the discovery and free wise use of our own faculties. The vital part of education begins in the hour when consciousness of self-dependence breaks upon the mind. That is the hour for Emerson.

He appeals to unfolding minds because he is profoundly in sympathy with the modern spirit. By this phrase we mean primarily the disposition to accept nothing on authority, but to bring all reports to the test of experience. The modern spirit is first of all a free spirit open on all sides to the influx of truth. But freedom is not its only characteristic. The modern spirit is marked further by an active curiosity which grows by what it feeds upon, and goes ever enquiring for fresher and sounder information, not content till it has the best information to be had anywhere. But since it seeks the best, it is, by necessity, also a critical spirit, constantly sifting, discriminating, rejecting, and holding fast that which is good only till that which is better is within reach. This endless quest, when it becomes central in a life, requires labor, requires pain, requires a measure of courage; and so the modern spirit, with its other virtues, is an heroic spirit. As a reward for difficulties gallantly undertaken, the gods bestow on the modern spirit a kind of eternal youth with unfailing powers of recuperation and growth. This spirit—free, actively curious, upward-striving, critical, courageous, and self-renewing—Emerson richly possesses; and that is why he is so happily qualified to be a counsellor of youth in the period of intellectual emancipation.

There are many prophets abroad in the land today, offering themselves as emancipators, who have only very partially comprehended their task. By the incompleteness of their message they bring the modern spirit itself into disrepute. They understand and declare that the modern spirit is free and curious. They have failed to recognize that it is also critical and upward striving. When the well-born soul discards the "old clothes" of outworn custom and belief, it seeks instinctively for fresh raiment; but these Adamites would persuade it to rejoice in nakedness and seek no further. They know that man is an animal; but it escapes their notice that man is an animal constituted and destined by his nature to make pilgrimages in search for a shrine, and to worship, till he finds it, the Unknown God. Because they understand so ill the needs and cravings of man, they go about eagerly hurrying him from a predicament into a disaster. They conceive that they have properly performed the emancipative function when they have cut the young generation loose from the old moorings, and set it adrift at the mercy of wind and tide.

It is these partial liberators who produce in our young people that false and bewildering sense of illumination, so eloquently described by John Henry Newman. Says that penetrating analyst of modern libertinism: "When the mind throws off as so much prejudice what it has hitherto held, and, as if waking from a dream, begins to realize to its imagination that there is no such thing as law and the transgression of law, that sin is a phantom, and punishment a bugbear, that it is free to sin, free to enjoy the world and the flesh; and still further, when it does enjoy them, and reflects that it may think and hold just what it will, that 'the world is all before it where to choose,' and what system to build up as its own private persuasion; when this torrent of wilful thoughts rushes over and inundates it, who will deny that the fruit of the tree of knowledge, or what the mind takes for knowledge, has made it one of the gods, with a sense of expansion and elevation,—an intoxication in reality, still, so far as the subjective state of the mind goes, an illumination?"

The true emancipator, the man who has entered fully into the modern spirit, is always a reconstructionist. The enlargement of mind which he offers is always, to modify slightly the words of Newman, an enlargement not of tumult and intoxication but of clearer vision and fruitful peace. In our Civil War slaves set free by proclamation flung up their caps and shouted with a vague joy. But shortly afterwards, we are told, many of them returned to their old masters and sought reemployment at their former tasks. So little was their undirected freedom worth. The true liberator strikes off the old shackles but immediately he suggests new service, a fuller use of our powers. He cuts us loose from the old moorings; but then he comes aboard like a good pilot, and while we trim our sails, he takes the wheel and lays our course for a fresh voyage. His message when he leaves us is not, "Henceforth be masterless," but "Bear thou henceforth the sceptre of thine own control through life and the passion of life."

III

Religious emancipation as conducted by Emerson makes a man not less but more religious. It frees the restless modern soul from ancient sectarian fetters, from ceremonial that has become empty, and from the litter of meaningless creeds. But straightway it reestablishes the soul in a new doctrine of "continuous revelation" and in works and conduct proper to those who have been freshly inspired. There is an element that looks like mystical experience underlying this fundamental part of Emerson's religious teaching. But since mysticism constitutes a difficulty and an obstacle to the average modern mind, let us reduce the irrational or super-rational element as far as possible. Let us explain what we can.

Emerson's belief in continuous revelation is clearly ascribable in large measure to the breadth of his spiritual culture. Throughout his life he was a student of the religions of the world. With free and open mind he compared the teachings of Plato, Confucius, Jesus, Buddha, Mahomet, seeking the spirit beneath the letter transmitted by each. This comparison did not bring him to the hasty thinker's conclusion that the Bible of Christians is an uninspired book, but rather to the conclusion that all the bibles are inspired books. The farther he pressed his studies in religion, in philosophy, in poetry, the more obvious it became to him that elevated thought and noble emotion are not the exclusive endowment of any special period or person, but are common to the highest representatives of all great peoples in all the great ages.

How account for that undeniable and really very inspiriting fact? Emerson explained it by what might be called the law of the conservation of spiritual energy. The mortal forms, momentarily fixed in the shape of Plato or Confucius, decay and are dispersed, yet their elemental force, as modern science teaches us, is not destroyed, but resumed and conserved in the all-encompassing energy of the universe, and is recreated for ever and ever in new shapes of men and things. In like fashion, as it appeared to Emerson, the thought and feeling of men, since thought and feeling are also forms of energy, must be resumed and conserved indestructibly in the general reservoir of moral energy, the "over-soul," from which they flow again into individuals, generations, races, with such sustaining recurrence as the vernal sap observes.

The vividness of his belief in this inflowing power may be ascribed to certain personal experiences, emotional and exalting, for which the entire discipline of his life had prepared him. From his youth up he had conversed in his reading with strong-souled men, with the saints, heroes, and sages. He had meditated on their counsels not occasionally but daily, persistently, for hours together, till the bounds between their minds and his disappeared, and their thoughts actually became his thoughts and their temper his temper. It is a discipline which breaks down the walls of personality and merges the individual with the over-soul. By books, he writes in his journal in 1824 at the age of twenty-one, "my memory goes back to a past immortality, and I almost realize the perfection of a spiritual intercourse which gains all the good, and lacks all the inconvenience and disgust of close society of imperfect beings. We are then likest to the image of God, for in this grateful rapidity of thought a thousand years become one day."

A mind thus stored and sensitized will respond now and then to an apparently slight stimulus with an extraordinary excitement and something in the nature of "vision" and "illumination." The young man reads in quiet solitude one of the more poetical dialogues of Plato, or he walks in flowering fields communing with his thoughts, or he lifts his head from his sick-bed at sunrise and beholds "the spotless orange light of the morning streaming up from the dark hills into the wide universe." Suddenly, to him unaccountably, there is a profound stirring of his emotional depths. A sense of sublimity fills his consciousness. His will appears to him godlike, invincible. He is elate with benign resolution. In a delighted ecstasy he feels streaming through all his being eternal forces,—all the wisdom and all the virtues that have ever been in the world. However we may attempt to explain, or to explain away, his sensations, he himself is incontrovertibly convinced that he has been visited and breathed upon by a power-not-himself. He has been but a passive vessel filled to the brim by an inrush of energy from the Over-soul, from the circumfluent seas of moral power.

Such inspiration, Emerson holds, is natural to man. It is probably open to everyone who will subject himself to the requisite preliminary discipline—who will live steadily with such thoughts as Emerson entertained. Record of these visitations one may find here and there in the *Journals* in such statements as this: "I am surrounded by messengers of God who send me credentials day by day"— statements which an intelligent reader may accept as substantially true and essentially verifiable by the method just indicated. This personal and direct relationship which he cultivated with the Over-soul had a two-fold effect. On the one hand it quite indisposed him to render allegiance to intermediate powers. Thus he declares in a poem of 1833, "Self-Reliance":

> Henceforth, please God, forever I forego
> The yoke of men's opinions. I will be
> Light-hearted as a bird, and live with God.
> I find Him in the bottom of my heart,
> I hear continually His voice therein.

On the other hand, this direct relationship with the source of moral power made him joyfully obedient to the impulses of what he at various times designated as the heavenly vision, the divine necessity, or the overlord of his soul. A certain levity, almost a frivolity, which he exhibits now and then in the presence of creeds, churches, pious organizations, is actually the consequence of his entire reverence in the presence of every unmistakable manifestation of spiritual life. Like his friend Carlyle, he feels that the religious edifices of the day are become uninhabitable; the religious spirit is seeking a new house. "Religion," he remarks, "does not seem to me to tend now to a cultus as heretofore, but to a heroic life. We find difficulty in conceiving any church, any liturgy, any rite that would be genuine."

This sounds like a radical utterance. It is radical with the root and branch thoroughness of Emerson's inherited Puritanism, a vital Puritanism urgent with fresh power, impatient of a corrupted tradition and a conformity that withholds one from the living truth. The tendency of the traditional religious culture he criticizes, as indifferent to æsthetic development, narrowly and incompletely moral, and averse from the wide reaches of living truth which are open to the modern mind in the domains of science. He holds that the founder of the faith in which most of his countrymen were bred was indeed a pure beam of truth whose ethical utter-

ances cannot be overprized, yet that he exhibited a
"very exclusive and partial development of the
moral element. . . . A perfect man should exhibit
all the traits of humanity, *and should expressly
recognize intellectual nature.* [Italics mine.] Socrates I call a complete, universal man."

That Emerson's is the radicalism of a conservative bent upon holding fast that which is good is
indicated by many other references to the character
and teaching of Jesus, to whom he returns again
and again with perceptions quickened and sharpened by his secular culture. "How strange," he
exclaims, "that Jesus should stand at the head of
history, the first character of the world without
doubt, but the unlikeliest of all men, one would say,
to take such a rank in the world." Approaching
the subject from a quite different quarter, he says:
"I think the true poetry which mankind craves is
that Moral Poem of which Jesus chanted to the
ages, stanzas so celestial, yet only stanzas." And
finally from still another angle: "The heart of
Christianity is the heart of all philosophy."

IV

Much has been written of Emerson's philosophical indebtedness to Kant and his German followers,
and to Coleridge and Carlyle and Madame de Staël,
who were intermediaries between the German and
the New England transcendentalists. It is not in

my power, happily it is not much to our purpose,
to enter into the details of this discussion. Briefly
speaking, it may be said that the German thinkers
and their interpreters by their combined influence
did undoubtedly strengthen Emerson's instinctive
reaction against the dry and incomplete rationalism
of the eighteenth century and against the Utili-
tarians of the nineteenth century, who to his nostrils
brought a peculiarly repugnant odor of "profit and
loss." But Emerson was no systematic student of
metaphysics, and most of such general impulses as
he was capable of receiving from the German
system-makers, he had perhaps encountered in Plato
and Berkeley and the seventeenth century divines
before he had much cultivated his German. He ultimately made his way through Goethe, but he never
became intimately attached to him or even quite
reconciled to him, finding him and his æsthetic
friends deficient in "moral life."

What is still more to the point, the vital features
of Emerson's philosophy are due less immediately
to his reading than to that religious illumination of
which we have already spoken. He arrived at the
centre of his beliefs by intuition. From the mechanical conception of the universe which reduced
Carlyle almost to despair, Emerson emancipated
himself, or rather he perfected his emancipation,
by a critical examination of his own experience.
This scrutiny disclosed a real world, the world of
things, moved by physical energies in accordance

with the laws of things.   But it disclosed also an
equally real world, the world of ideas, moved by
moral energies in accordance with the laws, perhaps
less clearly understood, of ideas.   One world is
associated with the other as the eye is associated
with seeing; yet seeing, not the instrument of sight,
is the sovereign matter.   An important continua-
tion of the Emersonian influence in our times, Professor Irving Babbitt, takes as the point of departure for his own developments these lines from
Emerson's Ode to W. H. Channing:

> There are two laws discrete,
> Not reconciled,—
> Law for man, and law for thing;
> The last builds town and fleet,
> But it runs wild, and doth the man unking.

As philosopher, Emerson conceives it his chief
business to explore the "law for man," to formulate
it, and to obtain recognition of it as the supreme
authority in human relationships.   His entire effort
aims at establishing human independence and a
human mastership.   Man liberates himself and exchanges servitude for mastery in proportion as he
obeys the "law for man" and learns to make the
"law for things" serve him.   In thus firmly insisting
upon a radical distinction between the two parallel
planes of experience, Emerson is in accord with the
wisdom of the ages and at variance with the folly
of the times, which tends to obliterate distinctions

and, surrendering to a physical fatalism, to accept
the law for things as also the law for man. Those
who still contend for the identity of the two laws
like to speak of their view as "realistic." It is a
word to conjure with. Emerson's view will prevail
against theirs only when it is finally established as
more realistic than theirs, as more accurately and
adequately descriptive of the facts of nature, the
experience of men.

It is important to note that what Emerson con-
tends for as the realistic view is the "twoness" of
the universe. He does not oppose a physical monism with a spiritual monism, but with a fairly clean-
cut dualism. It is a man asserting the equal realness
but radical dissimilarity of things and ideas who
remarks in his *Journal*, "Realist seems the true
name for the movement party among our Scholars
here. I at least endeavor to make the exchange
evermore of a reality for a name." When the
"solid men" of his day complain that his way of
thinking neglects the fundamental facts, he replies
that their way of thinking neglects the hypaethral
facts, but that his way of thinking takes due cogni-
zance of both: "Turnpike is one thing and blue sky
another." "The poet complains that the solid men ·
leave out the sky." This is the sunny mockery of
one who was both a poet and a solid man. Emerson
wove a net for casting in fathomless seas and
brought home his catches by ways unknown to the
fishermen; but this did not prevent his raising good

apples in his Concord orchard and taking the customary road to market.

His philosophical emphasis is, however, of course upon the order of facts most likely to be ignored by the "solid men," and because of his emphasis upon this order of facts we speak of him as an idealist and as a great fountain of American idealism. What idealism meant to him is expressed in his *Journal* in words which Molière's cook might have understood: "We are idealists whenever we prefer an idea to a sensation. . . . The physical sciences are only well studied when they are explored for ideas. . . . The book is always dear which has made us for moments idealists. That which can dissipate this block of earth into shining ether is genius. I have no hatred to the round earth and its grey mountains. I see well enough the sandhill opposite my window. Their phenomenal being I no more dispute than I do my own. . . . Religion makes us idealists. Any strong passion does. The best, the happiest moments of life, are these delicious awakenings of the higher powers and the reverential withdrawing of nature before its God. . . . We are all aiming to be idealists, and covet the society of those who make us so, as the sweet singer, the orator, the ideal painter."

V

It is commonly said that Emerson's interest in morals is his inheritance from the Puritans. In this connection it is interesting to find him in the *Journal* associating himself consciously with the loftiest Puritan of the seventeenth century, John Milton, of whom he writes: "Milton describes himself to Diodati as enamored of moral perfection. He did not love it more than I." Here indeed is a visible link in what we have grown accustomed to call the Puritan tradition. But, as a matter of fact, were Emerson and Milton more in love with moral perfection than Spenser, or was Spenser more in love with it than Dante, or Dante than Augustine, or Augustine than the Emperor Marcus Aurelius, or the Emperor than Socrates? There is a great community of minds enamored of moral perfection. It is no novel passion originating in New England or among the English Puritans. How explain the antiquity of the tradition? Dante, following Aristotle, explains it by declaring that "all things, by an intuition of their own nature, seek perfection." Emerson, then, rediscovered what Aristotle had observed: that the impulse to self-perfection is a tendency in the constitution of man.

In America, the most important predecessor of Emerson in this rediscovery was a free-thinking man of the world, entirely out of sympathy with strait-laced and stiff-necked performers of barren rites and observances. I refer to the greatest liberalizing force in eighteenth century America, Benjamin Franklin. Was he a Puritan? No one thinks of him as such; yet in truth he represents the normal reaction of a radical protestantism, of a living Puritanism, to an "Age of Enlightenment." By the courage of his moral realism he prepares the way for Emerson. He, too, begins his independent studies after a revolt against ecclesiastical authority, as narrow and unrealistic. The course of his emancipation is set forth in the *Autobiography,* where he relates his disgust at a sermon on the great text in Philippians: "Finally, brethren, whatsoever things are true, honest, just, pure, lovely, or of good report, if there be any virtue, or any praise, think on these things." In expounding this text the clergyman confined himself to enjoining scrupulous Sabbath observances, respect to ministers, etc., etc. "These might," says Franklin, "be all good things; but, as they were not the kind of good things that I expected from that text, I despaired of ever meeting with them from any other, was disgusted, and attended his preaching no more."

Franklin attended that preaching no more. But note what follows, apparently as the consequence of his break with the church: "It was about this time that I conceived the bold and arduous project of arriving at *moral* perfection. I wished to live without committing any fault at any time, and to conquer all that either natural inclination, custom or company might lead me into." Everyone will recall how Franklin drew up his table of thirteen moral virtues, and how he studied the means for putting them into effect. But for us the most significant feature of this enterprise and of his proposed Art of Virtue was the realistic spirit in which they were conceived, the bold attempt to ground the virtues upon experience rather than upon authority, the assertion of the doctrine "that vicious actions are not hurtful because they are forbidden, but forbidden because they are hurtful, *the nature of man alone considered.*"

Emerson as moralist takes up the work which Franklin's political duties prevented him from carrying out. He repeats Franklin's revolt in the name of sincerity, truth, actuality. "Whoso would be a man," he declares in "Self-Reliance," "must be a nonconformist. He who would gather immortal palms must not be hindered by the *name* of goodness, but must explore if it be goodness." He does not take up the virtues so methodically and exhaustively as Franklin does. That is mainly because he conceives morality to lie in a right condition and attitude of the whole self, from which particular acts will result with a kind of instinctive and inevitable rightness. "The less a man thinks or knows about his virtues," he says in "Spiritual Laws," "the better we like him." He concerns himself less with particular acts than many less exacting moralists, because he demands as the evidence of goodness that one's entire life shall be "an alms, a battle, a conquest, a medicine." The grand business of the moral explorer, as he understands it, is to push past conduct to the springs of conduct, to blaze a path behind the virtues to that general moral power which is the source of all the virtues.

There is a familiar saying of Emerson's which would epitomize, if it were understood, most of what is important and dynamic in all the Emersonian messages. Taken from its context in the essay on "Civilization," it has perhaps been more widely quoted than anything else that he uttered. Unfortunately one never hears it quoted with any sense of what it means in the thought of Emerson, where its position is absolutely central. The saying is this: "Hitch your wagon to a star." If one asks a man from whose lips it has glibly slipped what "Hitch your wagon to a star" means, he replies, "Aim high," a useful enough maxim of archery, but as a moral precept dreadfully trite and unproductive. What Emerson really means is: Put yourself in connection with irresistible power. In the physical world, let water turn your mill, let steam pull your cars, let the atmospheric electricity carry your words around the world. "That is the way we are strong, by borrowing the might of the elements." Likewise in the moral world, go where the gods are going, take the direction of all good men and let them bear you along, strike into the current of the great human traditions, discover the law of your higher nature and act with it. Presently you will notice that you are no longer fuming at obstacles and fretting at your personal impotence, but are borne forward like one destined.

At just this point many stern critics have cried out against Emerson as a moral teacher, and have charged him with counselling an optimistic passivity. Emerson bids us go with the current. The stern critic snatches at a figure and comes away with an error. Have not all the orthodox doctors taught that the good man goes *against* the current? Such misapprehension is the penalty for being a poet—for not sticking faithfully to the technical jargon. Without resorting to that medium, however, it should be possible to clear Emerson of the charge of counselling a foolish optimism, an indiscreet or base passivity. It should, at any rate, be possible to clear him in the eyes of any one whose morals have, like his, a religious basis—for example, in the eyes of the sad and strenuous author of that great line: *"In la sua volontade è nostra pace*—In his will is our peace." The point is, that Emerson does not urge us to confide in all currents, to yield to all tendencies. It is only after we have arrived by high thinking at a proud definition of man that we are to take for our motto: "I dare do all that may become a man." It is only after we have discovered by severe inquisition the law of our higher self that we are to trust our instincts and follow our nature. We are to be confident and passive. Yes: when we are doing the will of God.

What made Emerson's teaching take hold of his contemporaries, what should commend it to us to-day, is just its unfailingly positive character, the way it supplements by the restoration of classical virtues our Christian gospel of long-suffering. There is a welcome in it for life, even before the quality is disclosed: "Virtue is uneducated power." There is a place in it for manly resistance: "Be as beneficent as the sun or the sea, but if your rights as a rational being are trenched on, die on the first inch of your territory." There is the strong man's relish for difficulty and hostility: "We must have antagonisms in the tough world for all the variety of our spiritual faculties or they will not be born." There is precept for use of the spur: "He that rides his hobby gently must always give way to him that rides his hobby hard." There is warrant for choosing one's path: It is a man's "essential virtue to carry out into action his own dearest ends, to dare to do what he believes and loves. If he thinks a sonnet the flower and result of the world, let him sacrifice all to the sonnet." Even in his definition of friendship, Emerson drives at action: "He is my friend who makes me do what I can." It is obvious that he restores ambition, an aspect of magnanimity, to its proper place in the formation of the manly character, ambition to bring one's life to its fullest fruit.

This accounts for his extraordinary emphasis upon the virtue of courage: "It may be safely trusted—God will not have His work made manifest by cowards." Read from that cue, and presently you fancy that all forms of virtue appeared to him as aspects and phases of courage. He has praise for the courage of nonconformity, the courage of inconsistency, the courage of veracity, the courage to mix with men, the courage to be alone, the courage to treat all men as equals—but at this thought he remembers his proud conception of man, his imagination kindles, and he cries: "Shall I not treat all men as gods?" and, elsewhere, "God defend me from ever looking at a man as an animal." It sounds like extravagance. It may turn out to be a maxim of the higher prudence. Treating men like worms has been tried—without particularly gratifying results. Why not explore the consequences of assuming that men have a nobler destiny? If you are educating a prince, all the classical manuals enjoin it upon you to treat him like a prince. Why should not this hold of uncrowned sovereigns in general? Courage to do these extraordinary things Emerson learned of his Aunt Mary Moody Emerson, who taught him in his boyhood to face whatever he feared. Such courage he praised in his last word on Carlyle, "He never feared the face of man."

Moralists present to us in general three distinguishable sanctions for the virtuous life, or as Emerson would have preferred to call it, the heroic life. They may commend conduct as conducive to happiness in the future world—the theological sanction. They may commend it as conducive to pleasure or happiness or convenience on earth—the utilitarian sanction. Or finally they may commend it as in accordance with the proper nature of man—the humanistic sanction. This is the position taken by Marcus Aurelius in a passage extolled by Matthew Arnold. Which of these is Emerson's sanction? In the essay on "Compensation," which he thought one of his prime contributions, he argues that divine justice executes itself in this world in accordance with inevitable laws. It is essentially the argument of Franklin; one is still concerned with reward and punishment. But the general tenor of Emerson's life and teaching rises above this level. Habitually he speaks in the spirit of the Roman Emperor, so deeply appealing to the well-born soul: "A third in a manner does not even know what he has done, but he is like a vine which has produced grapes, and seeks for nothing more after it has once produced its proper fruit. As a horse when he has run, a dog when he has caught the game, a bee when it has made its honey, so a man when he has done a good act, does not call out for others to come and see, but he goes on to another act, as a vine goes on to produce again the grapes in season."

VI

Though Emerson had thought much about the relation of the individual to society and to the state, he was not in any practical diurnal sense of the word

a politically-minded man. Politics is the art and
science of governing masses. The art and science
which appealed to his ambition is that which enables
the individual to govern himself. So far as he
was concerned, he felt little need of external government. Indeed, like many of the saints and sages,
conscious that he himself was actuated by the purest
internal motives, he looked with wary and somewhat
jealous eye upon the existence of an external controlling power in the state which might be actuated
by motives far less pure and in the exercise of its
constituted activity, warp him from the bias of his
soul. In this respect, he was distinctly a child of
the time-spirit which followed the Revolution and
preceded the Civil War, that period when the first
dire need of a powerful union had passed and the
second dire need of it had not yet been fully manifested. He could sympathize with his friend
Thoreau, who withdrew from the social organization to the extent of refusing to pay his taxes. But
his Yankee common sense preserved him from imitating this fanaticism. He perceived, as every intelligent lover of freedom does, that a decent conformity is the very secret of freedom.

He loved freedom too much to coquet with
anarchy. The imaginative masters of his political
speculations, Plato, More, Milton, Burke, Montesquieu, had confirmed him, furthermore, in the conviction that "politics rest on necessary foundations,
and cannot be treated with levity." The foundation

of government, he recognized, is in the constitution
of man: "Every human society wants to be officered
by the best class, who shall be masters instructed
in all the great arts of life; shall be wise, temperate,
brave, public men, adorned with dignity and accom-
plishments." He perceived that it is no true
function of the philosopher to bring into contempt
even imperfect instruments of order and liberty till
better instruments are at hand.

Like most Americans, however, he had pretty
much lost respect for government by an hereditary
aristocracy. He acknowledges the virtues of the
hereditary principle but with a touch of disdain:
it has "secured permanence of families, firmness of
customs, a certain external culture and good taste;
gratified the ear with historic names." Its defect
was its failure to make the laws of nature serve it.
Nature did not cooperate with the system: "the
heroic father did not surely have heroic sons, and
still less heroic grandsons; wealth and ease corrupted the race."

He goes a long way towards accepting the principles of the French Revolution. His respect for
efficient power makes him betray, in *Representative Men,* a great admiration for Napoleon Bona-
parte, qualified by grave reservations. He desires,
with Carlyle, to bring forward a natural aristocracy,
an aristocracy of talent. He would like to believe
that democracy is the means for recruiting that
talent, for organizing the superior class by which

society needs to be officered. But his study of the tyrannies of an "efficient state" administered by Napoleonic officers to whose talents a career was opened, has awakened in him as it never did in Carlyle, a deep suspicion of the "natural method," has put him on a criticism of democracy, which is the most valuable element in his political writing.

Might with right, Emerson never confused as Carlyle confused them—hopelessly; as democracies may at any time, under bad leadership, confuse them. "Our institutions," he declares in his "Politics," "though in coincidence with the spirit of the age, have not any exemption from the practical defects which have discredited other forms. Every actual State is corrupt. *Good men must not obey the laws too well.*" His patriotism was free, emancipated. In the year when he became of age, 1824, he wrote in his Journal: "I confess I am a little cynical on some topics, and when a whole nation is roaring Patriotism at the top of its voice, I am fain to explore the cleanness of its hands and the purity of its heart." In his Journal of 1833-5 he wrote "the life of this world has a limited worth in my eyes, and really is not worth such a price as the toleration of slavery." He cried out at the land-grabbing of the Mexican War. He spoke repeatedly between 1837 and 1861 in behalf of free speech, in behalf of emancipating the slaves, and in favor of violating the Fugitive Slave Law. Against the howling of mobs, as Mr. Woodberry shows in an admirable summary of his participation in the Anti-slavery movement, "his civic courage was flawless." He interrupted his lecture on Heroism in 1838 to praise the brave Lovejoy "who gave his breast to the bullets of a mob, for the rights of free speech and opinion, and died when it was better not to live." He received John Brown in Concord, and when two years later the law doomed him to die, he declared publicly in Boston that the new saint would "make the gallows glorious like the cross."

Efficient nature, the source of political power, herself requires to be checked. Where is the check to be found? "The wise man is to settle it immovably in his mind, that he only is fit to decide on his best action; he only is fit to praise it; his verdict is praise enough, and as to society, 'their hiss is thine applause'" (*Journals,* 1833-5). The contention of parties cannot be trusted to guard the interests of truth. Emerson has no naive respect for numbers. He has looked with disillusioned eye upon the wisdom of majorities. He confides to his Journal, for example, that if Jackson is elected, "we shall all feel dirty." He says that if he were unduly in love with life, he would attend a Jackson caucus, and "I doubt not the unmixed malignity, the withering selfishness, the impudent vulgarity, that mark those meetings would speedily cure me of my appetite for longevity." Yet despite this bitterness, the Jackson party was, as he himself recognized, that towards which his own principles and sympathies—in theory, broadly popular —should have inclined him. Speaking for publication, in his essay on "Politics," he reveals, with less asperity, the fact that he is not captivated by either party. The paragraph that follows might have been written by a disappointed independent of 1920:

"The vice of our leading parties in this country . . . is that they do not plant themselves on the deep and necessary grounds to which they are respectively entitled. . . . Of the two great parties which, at this hour, almost share the nation between them, I should say that the one has the best cause, and the other contains the best men. The philosopher, the poet, or the religious man will, of course, wish to cast his vote with the democrat, for free-trade, for wide suffrage, for the abolition of legal cruelties in the penal code, *and for facilitating in every manner the access of the young and the poor to the sources of wealth and power.* [My italics]. But he can rarely accept the persons whom the so-called popular party proposes to him as representatives of these liberalities. They have not at heart the ends which give to the name of democracy what hope and virtue are in it."

Possibly Emerson's concern for the "unwashed masses" forged a bit ahead of his sympathies as a man of flesh and blood. Theoretically, he was not afraid of dirt. Before Whitman bade us shun "delicatesse," Emerson had perceived that the effective democrat must not be a "high priest of the kid-glove persuasion." Writing in his Journal at the age of thirty-two, he says: "I would not have a man dainty in his conduct. Let him not be afraid of being besmirched by being advertised in the newspapers, or by going into Athenaeums or town-meetings or by making speeches in public. Let his chapel of private thoughts be so holy that it shall perfume and separate him unto the Lord, though he lay in a kennel."

It ought to be possible to feel "inwardly perfumed and separated unto the Lord" without either showing or feeling that Brahminical spirit of exclusiveness which men like Holmes and Lowell exhibited, and of which they were obviously proud. Emerson was quite earnestly opposed to the celebrated Brahminism of Boston and Cambridge. As Mr. Brownell has finely said: "A constituent of his refinement was an instinctive antipathy to ideas of dominance, dictation, patronage, caste, and material superiority whose essential grossness repelled him and whose ultimate origin in contemptuousness— probably the one moral state except cravenness that chiefly he deemed contemptible—was plain enough to his penetration." Henry Adams suggests, indeed with a touch of characteristic humor, that Emerson, from the spiritual altitude of Concord, probably looked down on the Brahmins themselves, looked down, for instance, on the Adamses, as worldlings.

Now there is interesting evidence in the *Journals*

that Emerson might have looked down on Henry Adams but from a point of view remote from that indicated by Adams:

"I do not forgive in any man this forlorn pride, as if he were an *Ultimus Romanorum*. I am more American in my feelings. This country is full of people whose fathers were judges, generals, and bank presidents, and if all their boys should give themselves airs thereon and rest henceforth on the oars of their fathers' merit, we should be a sad hungry generation. Moreover, I esteem it my best birthright that our people are not crippled by family and official pride, that the best broadcloth coat in the country is put off to put on a blue frock, that the best man in town may steer his plough-tail or may drive a milk-cart. There is a great deal of work in our men, and a false pride has not yet made them idle or ashamed. Moreover, I am more philosophical than to love this retrospect. I believe in the being God, not in the God that has been. I work; my fathers may have wrought or rested. What have I to do with them, or with the Fellatahs, or the great Khan! I know a worthy man who walks the streets with silent indignation as a last of his race, quite contemptuously eyeing the passing multitude."

Emerson goes farther than that in welcoming the "new man," the power without known antecedents. In a notable passage of his Journal for 1845, one sees him, as it were, shaking off the dust of the house of his fathers, breaking out of the old New England, in order to enter America, to participate in that national spirit which we know today must learn to enfold and assimilate men of all races:

"I hate the narrowness of the Native American Party. It is the dog in the manger. It is precisely opposite to all the dictates of love and magnanimity; and therefore, of course, opposite to true wisdom. . . Man is the most composite of all creatures . . . Well, as in the old burning of the Temple at Corinth, by the melting and intermixture of silver and gold and other metals a new compound more precious than any, called Corinthian brass, was formed; so in this continent—asylum of all nations—the energy of Irish, Germans, Swedes, Poles, and Cossacks, and all the European tribes—of the Africans, and of the Polynesians—will construct a new race, a new religion, a new state, a new literature, which will be as vigorous as the new Europe which came out of the smelting-pot of the Dark Ages, or that which earlier emerged from the Pelasgic and Etruscan barbarism. *La Nature aime les croisements.*"

No man who honestly and earnestly contemplates the making of a nation out of such heterogeneous elements as Emerson here enumerates, no man who truly cherishes the potentialities of human power, wherever they lie, is disposed to assign to political agencies an undue part in shaping the product of

the melting pot. Emerson did not. If we were
to sum up his attitude towards the state in a single
sentence, it would take some such form as this: The
State exists for the benefit of all the individuals in
it: and its stability and its welfare depend primarily
on the effort of each individual in it. All concrete
advance towards social regeneration, he believed,
is accomplished by minorities—by minorities of
one! In a country with a strong inclination towards
beginning all efforts for moral reformation by the
election of a president and a secretary, he proposes this modest method: "Count from yourself
in order the persons that have near relation to you
up to ten or fifteen, and see if you can consider
your whole relation to each without squirming.
That will be something." Commenting, in "Life
and Letters in New England," on a socialistic
scheme for imposing economic salvation on the
world from No. 200 Broadway, he surmises that
it would be better to say: "Let us be lovers and ser-
vants of that which is just, and straighway every
man becomes a center of a holy and beneficent republic, which he sees to include all men in its law,
like that of Plato and Christ." Let the great state
arch above us, but let it beware of pressing too near,
lest it crush more natural and vital powers—the
power of the individual over himself; the power of
the family, the neighborhood, the town-meeting, the
local enterprise; the "atmospheric" power of culture, the gradual and beneficent pressure of a

natural society steadily growing stronger by the diffusion of science and humane learning.

The Emersonian doctrine of democratic individualism has its defects. In these days it appears rather homely and old-fashioned. Yet it has merits towards which one occasionally turns with nostalgic yearnings, merits which may yet restore it to some of its former favor. After many a popular election, is it not still the chief available consolation to go quietly home and close the door and reflect that the wise man "occupies all the space between God and the mob?" And in spite of all the allurement of centralized power, with its promise of prompt and "nation-wide" progress in the sense of the men at Washington, shall we not find in the years to come that the preservation of individuality in the private citizen and of pride and initiative in the "parish," the province, and the separate states, is as vital to the health of the far-flung nation as the use of hands and feet?

VII

It has ordinarily been assumed and asserted that Emerson was very little developed on the aesthetic side. This assumption is intimately associated with two other popular errors, which, in the light of our examination, we may now dismiss. We may first dismiss the popular error which holds that the center of his being was ethical; for we have seen that the center of his being was religious. We may dismiss, also, the popular error of regarding him as a representative of Puritan decadence; for we have seen that he represents rather a renascence and fresh flowering of the ancient passion for self-perfection. We think rightly of Emerson when we think of him as a humanist bent upon liberating and developing not some but all of the properly human powers. He builds his many-chambered house of life around a private oratory, because like every successfully exploring humanist, he finds a private oratory at the center of his heart. But this innermost shrine of religious inspiration is emphatically not a Calvinistic chapel, hostile to the arts. It is a retreat friendly to all the Muses that ever haunted Siloa's brook or Heliconian springs.

Emerson believed, indeed, like his great predecessor of the seventeenth century, that the pulsing spirit which "voluntary moves harmonious numbers" prefers before all temples "the upright heart and pure." But no one who has approached that inner shrine will ever picture him as summoning the Sacred Nine about him in order to give them a lesson in conduct. No one understands Emerson who fails to perceive that he trusts his inspiration, like a Pythian prophet, like a celebrant of Dionysian mysteries. "If I am the devil's child," he defiantly retorted in his youth to one who had urged him to beware of his instincts, "I will live from the devil."

Well assured that he was not the devil's child, he opened communication with his sources of power, resolute to receive and utter whatever they sent, though it might sound like blasphemy, though it might whiff received ethics down the wind. Through a great part of his prose and verse, there is the peculiar beat and throb which marks work conceived in creative heat, under the sway of the "divine madness." Some of the friends who came closest to him testified to receiving from him not counsel but a sheer access of vital energy exhilarating to the verge of intoxication. It is above all a generative and fecundating impulse that he seeks for himself. It is this above all that he desires to impart to others.

We all tend to slip at times into colorless and meaningless routine, into lives of grey commonplace and insignificance. Emerson seems to have apprehended this as a peril to which our democratic society is peculiarly exposed. He cultivates the means of combating it. He cultivates, for example, the color of Oriental poetry. He follows Hafiz, this Unitarian in revolt against the tedium and dead level of the cold New England virtue, and cries: "Let us be crowned with roses, let us drink wine, and break up the tiresome old roof of heaven into new forms." He writes an essay on "Inspiration," which is a study under ten headings of the technique of exaltation, of ecstasy. He chants an ode to Bacchus, calling for

Wine of wine,
Blood of the world,
Form of forms, and mould of statures,
That I intoxicated
And by the draught assimilated,
May float at pleasure through all natures.

Under the heading "Morals" in his discourse on
"Poetry and Imagination," he comes to the conclusion, entirely characteristic of him, that "Power,
new power, is the good which the soul seeks."   On
this theme Emerson writes occasionally with a recklessness not often associated with the "Victorian"
period in America.   For power, he intimates in
"Mithridates," a poet may perhaps well pay with
his soul:

Too long shut in strait and few,
Thinly dieted on dew,
I will use the world, and sift it,
To a thousand humors shift it,
As you spin a cherry.
O doleful ghosts, and goblins merry!
O all you virtues, methods, mights,
Means, appliances, delights,
Reputed wrongs and braggart rights,
Smug routine, and things allowed,
Minorities, things under cloud!
Hither! take me, use me, fill me,
Vein and artery, though ye kill me!

As a priest of the "being God, not the God that
has been," Emerson finds that even the greatest of
the old poets do not wholly content him.   As a

believer in the doctrine of continuous revelation, he demands a new revelation. "In a cotillon," he declares in "Poetry and Imagination," "some persons dance and others await their turn when the music and the figure come to them. In the dance of God there is not one of the chorus but can and will begin to spin, monumental as he now looks, whenever the music and figure reach his place and duty. O celestial Bacchus! drive them mad—this multitude of vagabonds, hungry for eloquence, hungry for poetry, starving for symbols, perishing for want of electricity to vitalize this too much pasture, and in the long delay indemnifying themselves with the false wine of alcohol, of politics, or of money."

Emerson knew pretty well what he wanted in the way of a new poet. He was not in the least interested in the production of more "parlor or piano verse." He wanted such utterance as could come only from a great and noble soul immersed in the realities and filled with the spirit of the modern world. His poet must be radical, revolutionary, formative: "Bring us the bards who shall sing all our old ideas out of our heads, and new ones in; men-making poets . . . poetry which finds its rhymes and cadences in the rhymes and iterations of nature, and is the gift to men of new images and symbols, each the ensign and oracle of an age; that shall assimilate men to it, mould itself into religions and mythologies, and impart its quality to centuries." In his essay on "The Poet," he regrets that

"we have yet had no genius in America, with tyran-
nous eye, which knew the value of our incomparable
materials, and saw, in the barbarism and material-
ism of the times, another carnival of the same gods
whose picture it so much admires in Homer; then
in the middle age; then in Calvinism . . . Our
log-rolling, our stumps and their politics, our fish-
eries, our Negroes, and Indians, our boats, and our
repudiations, the wrath of rogues, and the pusil-
lanimity of honest men, the northern trade, the
southern planting, the western clearing, Oregon and
Texas, are yet unsung. Yet America is a poem
in our eyes; its ample geography dazzles the imagination, and it will not wait long for metres."
Clearly, Emerson was calling for a singer in many
important respects resembling Whitman; and Whitman answered.

It is not yet adequately recognized to what extent
Emerson anticipated not only Whitman but also the
poets of the present hour. He anticipates their desire to strike up for the new world a new tune. He
thinks that we leaned too much in the past upon
England. Our literature has become lifelessly traditional through uninspired imitation. We require
some sort of break and shock to liberate our own
native talents. In an extremely interesting passage
of the third volume of the *Journals,* he records the
surmise that salvation may come from that very
element which, in politics, he thought of as consti-
tuting the party of unkempt pioneers, barbarians,

slave-holders, and corruptionists: "I suppose the evil may be cured by this rank rabble party, the Jacksonism of the country, heedless of English and of all literature—a stone cut out of the ground without hands—they may root out the hollow dilettantism of our cultivation in the coarsest way, and the new born may begin again to frame their own world with greater advantage."

As literary critic, Emerson has, with only an occasional trace of reluctance, the courage of his free religion, his philosophy, his politics. His thought in these matters underlies and supports his Poetics and his Rhetoric. Mystic, symbolist, and democrat, he is constrained to declare that there is no vulgar life save that of which the poetry has not yet been written. He urges us bravely to paint the prospect from our doors, wherever they open. He asserts the possibility of all subjects: "A dog drawn by a master, or a litter of pigs, satisfies, and is a reality not less than the frescoes of Angelo." He detests a bookish and fossilized phrase and diction: "He only is a good writer who keeps one eye on his page, and with the other sweeps over things, so that every sentence brings in a new contribution of observation." He has meditated deeply on image, rhyme, and rhythm; and has discovered the literary value of colloquial cadence, the picturesque language of children, the scoff and violence of the "yeoman," the pungency of natural persons expressing their mother-wit. His essays contain more great "free verse" than any one has written since. Poems, such as "Hamatreya," "Woodnotes," "Monadnoc," and "Musketaquid," prove his possession of senses tinglingly responsive to the touches of native color, scent, and sound; show a poetical nature that has struck root and has been richly nourished "in haunts which others scorned." As for his general theory of art, in his more sanguine and exalted moments he goes beyond our most radical leaders in his passion for reconciling art with nature and restoring it to "all the people," so that the ultimate phase of artistic development would be an habitual happy improvisation.

That aspiration, as Emerson would have been the first to admit, was ideal, was Utopian. It could be realized only in a profoundly regenerated and enriched society. In this world as it is at present, he recognized that great poetry, for example, must be the result of special culture and austere discipline. It must therefore be submitted for judgment to the cultivated and the disciplined. He has no immediate intention of accepting the standards of the mob. Our radical anti-critical friends would indeed dispose of him as "academic." For he comforts himself, in the absence of a national Academy, with this reflection, in the second volume of the *Journals:* "Consider the permanence of the best opinion: the certainty with which a good book acquires fame, though a bad book succeeds better at first. Consider the natural academy which the best heads of the time constitute, and which 'tis pleasant to see, act almost as harmoniously and efficiently, as if they were organized and acted by vote."

For a writer who is often classified nowadays as a "mere moralist," Emerson liberated an extraordinary number of ideas about both the major and the minor problems of the literary art. You may say, if you like, that his literary scrupulousness is but an aspect of his moral rectitude; but any other writer of his exacting artistic conscience would be saluted by all the anti-Puritans as a "lover of beauty," a "martyr of style." In 1831, long before Flaubert or Pater had announced it, he committed to his Journal the doctrine of the "unique word:" "No man can write well who thinks there is any choice of words for him. The laws of composition are as strict as those of sculpture and architecture. There is always one line that ought to be drawn, or one proportion that should be kept, and every other line or proportion is wrong, and so far wrong as it deviates from this. So in writing, there is always a right word, and every other than that is wrong. There is no beauty in words except in their collocation. The effect of a fanciful word misplaced, is like that of a horn of exquisite polish growing on a human head."

Economy, Emerson regards as the poet's chastity: "Let the poet, of all men, stop with his inspiration. The inexorable rule in the muses' court, *either inspiration or silence,* compels the bard to report only

his supreme moments. It teaches the enormous
force of a few words and in proportion to the inspiration checks loquacity." Despite his desire for
fresh beginnings in America, he finds it necessary
to turn back to the old English writers, "not because
they are old, but simply because they wrote well.
If we write as well, we may deviate from them and
our deviations shall be classical." Every one, it is
to be hoped, remembers the little poem called "The
Test," in which Emerson challenges his reader to
find the "five lines" in his verses which outlasted
five hundred. It is a virtue in him, which our present loquacity should some day make esteemed, that
he so often anticipates the winnowing of time, as
in the firm Landorian carving of the Concord Hymn
with its cumulative solemnity, reaching its climax
in the breathless pause of the flawless final stanza,
before the ultimate foot:

> Spirit, that made those heroes dare
> To die, and leave their children free,
> Bid Time and Nature gently spare
> . The shaft we raise to them and thee.

The popular taste in poetry, as is proved by many
of the great reputations, is a little waterish. Emerson served "wine of wine." He has been underrated
as a poet because he did not understand, or would
not practice, dilution. One suspects that he might
be reinstated if some student of Japanese verse
would display in a wide-margined volume some fifty

or a hundred of his "images," selected here and there from his baskets of cut gems, for example:

> I am a willow of the wilderness
> Loving the wind that bent me.

Or possibly the reviver of Emerson should remind the Chicago School of these lines:

Bulkeley, Hunt, Willard, Hosmer, Meriam, Flint, Possessed the land which rendered to their toil Hay, corn, roots, hemp, flax, apples, wool and wood.

Critics have sufficiently harped upon certain defects in the prose style of Emerson: the apparent lack of firm design and evolution in the larger divisions of his discourse; the difficult transitions, the imperfect coherence, within the paragraphs. It is perhaps worth observing that some of these faults are closely connected with his characteristic virtues, and are truly due to the excess of these virtues. Emerson is characteristically rich and economical. He is so rich that he can put into a sentence as much as another would put into a paragraph, and as much into a paragraph as another would put into his entire discourse. He is so economical of space, so bent on filling every inch with solid matter, that he deliberately prunes away what is merely explanatory and transitional. If one compares passages in the *Journals* with parallel passages in the essays, one remarks at first with surprise that the superiority on the side of fluency and texture is frequently with the *Journals*. The superiority of the essays is in condensation and intensity.

It should be observed, furthermore, that in the prose which Emerson himself published the degree of fluency and stylistic coherence varies greatly with the subject. The moral essays, such as "Self-Reliance" and "Compensation," are written more or less in the manner of the Book of Proverbs or the Essays of Bacon. They are built of distinct injunctions, maxims, and fragments of wisdom, twenty or thirty of them to a paragraph. "Solid bags of duckshot," Carlyle called these paragraphs, and urged Emerson to fuse them into a solid luminous bar. They are close packed enough, in all conscience, without fusion. There is stuff enough for a morning's meditation in any half-dozen of the hundreds of maxims which make up the essay on Self-Reliance. But no ordinary mind can read easily page after page of epitomized moral experience: "Be it how it will, do right now. Always scorn appearances, and you always may. The force of character is cumulative. All the foregone days of virtue work their health into this." Before such matter can be made to flow, it must be diluted. Read in youth and for the first time, a page of such writing seems pebbly and difficult. But at each re-reading one discovers more pebbles that are interestingly translucent, opalescent, with a fire at the heart of them. Returning later in life, after perhaps the twentieth reading, one may discover that the pattern in the page comes out, that the gaps are bridged by one's own experience, that each sentence is illustrated by one's own verification of it, and that somehow this swift "saltation" from epitome to epitome of moral wisdom makes all other moral writing seem thin and flat.

But Emerson has many other prose manners, to which the stock criticisms and the traditional jests are not at all applicable. Turn, for example, to his "Thoreau," a biographical portrait executed in the firm objective manner of Suetonious yet with the gusto of Plutarch—a superbly vital piece of characterization, unsurpassed if not unequalled by anything of like scope in American literature. Or consider the flow of his reminiscences of Brook Farm and his bland comment on Fourierism in *Life and Letters in New England;* it is beautiful writing, urbane, luminous, exquisitely ironical. Or for still another vein, turn to the pages in *English Traits* where he describes meeting Thomas Carlyle, with something of the Scotch master's graphic force:

On my return, I came from Glasgow to Dumfries, and being intent on delivering a letter which I had brought from Rome, inquired for Craigenputtock. It was a farm in Nithdale, in the parish of Dumscore, sixteen miles distant. No public coach passed near it, so I took a private carriage from the inn. I found the house amid heathery hills, where the lonely scholar nourished his mighty heart. Car-

lyle was a man from his youth, an author who did
not need to hide from his readers, and as absolute a
man of the world, unknown and exiled on that hill-
farm as if holding on his own terms what is best in
London. He was tall and gaunt, with a cliff-like
brow, self possessed and holding his extraordinary
powers of conversation in easy command; clinging
to his northern accent with evident relish; full of
lively anecdote, and with a streaming humor, which
floated everything he looked upon.

If Emerson writes comparatively little in the
descriptive and narrative veins, it is neither from
impotence nor by chance but on consideration. "Do
you see," he asks himself, "what we preserve of history? a few anecdotes of a moral quality of some
momentary act or word." The word of Canute on
the sea-shore, he observes, is all the world remembers of the Danish conquest. Under the influence of
this thought, he seems, for a time, to have meditated
composing "a modern Plutarch," British and American—in which his "Thoreau" would well have
taken the place of Cato, and his "Lincoln" a place
of its own. His *Representative Men* was a partial fulfilment of the design. But quite early in life
Emerson was much occupied by a rival thought, thus
recorded in the fourth volume of the *Journals:* "I
said to Bryant and to these young people, that the
high poetry of the world from the beginning has
been ethical, and it is the tendency of the ripe modern mind to produce it. . . . As, I think, no
man could be better occupied than in making up his

own bible by hearkening to all those sentences which now here, now there, now in nursery rhymes, now in Hebrew, now in English bards, thrill him like the sound of a trumpet." In fulfilment of that design Emerson wrote his great essays.

To many a lonely student, obscure and friendless, meditating in the long cold spring and adolescence of his talent on his untried powers, Emerson has come as with the sound of a magical trumpet, shattering the dungeons of fear, sending the young knight on his quest inwardly fortified and resolute to give soul and body to that undertaking, whatever it may be, for which he was sent into the world. Such is the primary function of the religious and democratic ethos with which he sought to impregnate American letters. He, too, had been lonely, obscure, uncertain of his way, feeble, and prone to husband his strength and gifts. But when he found which way the planets are going and the well where the gods drink, he faltered no longer. "What a discovery I made one day, that the more I spent the more I grew, that it was as easy to occupy a large place and do much work as an obscure place to do little; and that in the winter in which I communicated all my results to classes, I was full of new thoughts." To this, let us add that other thought, so precious to him that it appears repeatedly in various forms in the *Journals* and in the essays: "If a man knows the law, he may settle himself in a shanty in a pine forest, and men will and must find their way to him as readily as if he lived in the City Hall." We shall keep near the main stream of Emersonian virtue, if we close with a variation and enlargement of the same theme: "Penetrate to the bottom of the fact that draws you, although no newspaper, no poet, no man, has ever yet found life and beauty in that region, and presently when men are whispered by the gods to go and hunt in that direction, they shall find that they cannot get to the point which they would reach without passing over that highway which you have built. Your hermit's lodge shall be the Holy City and the Fair of the whole world."

V

HAWTHORNE: A PURITAN CRITIC OF PURITANISM

Of that group of eminent New Englanders who made American literature in the middle of the last century it has become the fashion among our youth to speak with a certain condescension as of country cousins or old friends outgrown. Since Emerson and Lowell and Holmes and the other worthies of the age laid the author of *The Scarlet Letter* to rest in Sleepy Hollow, new generations have arisen, who have looked for a less austere leadership than New England followed, and for interpreters of appetites and passions in human nature which the "spiritual patricians" of an elder time deliberately suppressed and disdainfully ignored. Our literary historians tell us that the "national period" has arrived, and that in the widened domain of our letters the voices of the "Puritan aristocracy" must inevitably sound somewhat thin and provincial. Under the influence of European example our authors, particularly our novelists, are learning to overcome the Anglo-Saxon, or rather the Victorian, diffidence. In the choice and treatment of their themes they enjoy a liberty which neither public opinion nor private conscience granted to the novelist of 1850; and with the new freedom and the tolerant national public, they are supposed to have become more secular, more sensuous, more erudite, and, above all, more vital and realistic.

To whatever disadvantages New England birth and breeding exposes the artist, Hawthorne was exposed. Born in Salem, Massachusetts, in 1804, he had in his veins the blood of Puritans, counted a witch-hanging judge among his ancestors, and was probably the first of his line who did not regard the writing and reading of romances as idleness and vanity. After nearly all his important literary work was done he saw something of England and Italy, but his experience till late in life was provincial, not to say parochial, and he himself avowed that New England was as large a lump of earth as his sympathies could embrace. The society of his native town he found so unremunerative or so formidable that he lived there for twelve years, following his graduation from Bowdoin, in virtual solitude, writing in obscurity and publishing anonymously the stories later collected as *Twice Told Tales*. In personal relations he ordinarily exhibited a taciturnity and reserve no doubt fostered by his hermit years but alleged to be characteristic of those who live too steadily by the "rockbound coast." In his art he maintained a reticence about many things which are now cried from the housetops. He lacked the stimulus of fellow-workers in his own kind, and he labored in a romantic vein which even in his own day was on the point of appearing old-fashioned. Associated with an intellectual movement animated by an hereditary passion for righteousness, he was interested in the moral significance of his narratives; and his moral sympathies are said to have been at least deeply tinged with what the impatient young people of our day impatiently, not to say wrathfully, designate as Puritanism.

It should follow that his treatment of forbidden love has been quite overshadowed by the masterpieces of successors working with so many superiorities of circumstance and method. But as a matter of fact *The Scarlet Letter* appears to be as safe from competitors as *Pilgrim's Progress* or *Robinson Crusoe*. It is recognized as the classical treatment of its particular theme. Its symbols and scenes of guilt and penitence—the red letter on the breast of Hester Prynne, Arthur Dimmesdale on the scaffold—have fixed themselves in the memory of men like the figure of Crusoe bending over the footprint in the sand, and have become a part of the common stock of images like Christian facing the lions in the way. When a book has achieved this sort of celebrity, it needs ask for nothing more; it has entered into immortal life, and passes through all changes of fashion unscathed. But Hawthorne and this book have won the critical as well as the popular tribute. Nearly thirty years after the publica-

tion of *The Scarlet Letter,* Henry James, the most
fastidious and the most sophisticated of critics, declared him to be "the most valuable example of
the American genius," and *The Scarlet Letter* the
finest specimen of his art. And in 1909, Mr. W. C.
Brownell, an exacting critic, as free from suspicion
of indulgence to the New England school as Henry
James and more severe than James in his attitude
towards Hawthorne's general reputation, finds this
scarlet leaf among his withered laurels undamaged
by the ruinous touch of time or rival splendors.

With the most restricted permanent glory Hawthorne himself would certainly have been better con-
tented than with the widest transitory blaze. If he
has left one book that cannot die, it is rather idle
to make a pathetic story of his straitened circumstances and the narrow field in which his beautiful
talent was perfected. Had he lived in a great
literary center, kept his mind brisk by frequent intercourse with men of letters, and enriched his
stores by travel and observation of various societies
in the "grand style," his production might have been
more abundant; it would probably have had more
of the realistic virtue so highly valued at present;
but it is doubtful whether it would have included
The Scarlet Letter or the other works in which we
recognize his special and unique quality. For the
charm, with difficulty definable, which pervades his
best writing is due to the felt presence of a subtle
and exquisite spirit that has dwelt apart from the

throng in still and shadowed places, preserving with a kind of virginal jealousy its own internal vision of beauty, its own internal scale of values. If we value him in proportion as he approaches the interests and methods of contemporary realism, we miss what is most precious in him, namely, his power of reducing the insolent pretensions of circumstance to insignificance, and of giving to the moral and ideal world reality, importance, and supreme interest.

Hawthorne was at times a close and shrewd observer of external fact, but he did not dwell habitually in the world of external fact, and other men have far surpassed him in their notation of manners and the visible aspects of nature. External nature he tended to regard as hieroglyphic and symbolical. It engaged his attention chiefly for the correspondences which he could discern between it and the forms and relations of his ideas. His notebooks are full of brief jottings of apparently trivial scenes and incidents intended to serve as starting points for his interpretive imagination: "A cloud in the shape of an old woman kneeling, with arms extended towards the moon." "An old looking-glass. Somebody finds out the secret of making all the images that have been reflected in it pass back again across its surface." "A person to catch fireflies, and try to kindle his household fire with them. It would be symbolical of something." Underlying this search for ulterior meanings and spiritual significances there was doubtless in Hawthorne a certain disdain for primary meanings, for the immediate gross reports of the senses. His imagination he sets continually at work contriving an avenue of escape from the vulgar and the humdrum. On a fine day in February he notes as follows the aspiration of the poor wingless biped man to raise himself a little above the earth: "How much mud and mire, how many pools of unclean water, how many slippery foot-steps, and perchance heavy tumbles, might be avoided, if one could tread but six inches above the crust of this world. Physically we cannot do this; our bodies cannot; but it seems to me that our hearts and minds may keep themselves above moral mudpuddles and other discomforts of the soul's pathway."

To the development of his peculiar imaginative faculty it would not be difficult to show that his circumstances, far from being inauspicious, were highly favorable—as favorable, perhaps, as exile in Ireland was to his favorite poet, the author of *The Faerie Queene*. Solitude drives the hungry man to intensive cultivation of the inner life, and a plain domicile reminds him of the necessity of building for his soul a more stately mansion. After his engagement to Sophia Peabody, looking back in 1840 upon the long lonely years when he was learning his art in the locked room in Salem, he feels the pathos of his earnest and externally cheerless prime, and yet he testifies, in a passage deeply moving and beautiful, that those were the richest and

happiest years of his life till love transformed it;
and in the quiet exultation of the new emotion he
blesses them still because they made and kept him
fit for the transformation:

. . . Here I sit in my old accustomed chamber, where I used to sit in days gone by. . . .
Here I have written many tales—many that have
been burned to ashes, many that doubtless deserved
the same fate. This claims to be called a haunted
chamber, for thousands upon thousands of visions
have appeared to me in it; and some few of them
have become visible to the world. If ever I should
have a biographer, he ought to make great mention
of this chamber in my memoirs, because so much of
my lonely youth was wasted here, and here my mind
and character were formed; and here I have been
glad and hopeful, and here I have been despondent.
And here I sat a long, long time, waiting patiently
for the world to know me, and sometimes wondering
why it did not know me sooner, or whether it would
ever know me at all—at least, till I were in my
grave. And sometimes it seemed as if I were already in the grave, with only life enough to be
chilled and benumbed. But oftener I was happy—
at least as happy as I then knew how to be, or was
aware of the possibility of being. By and by, the
world found me out in my lonely chamber, and
called me forth—not, indeed, with a loud roar of
acclamation, but rather with a still, small voice—
and forth I went, but found nothing in the world
that I thought preferable to my old solitude till
now. . . . And now I begin to understand why I
was imprisoned so many years in this lonely chamber, and why I could never break through the view-

less bolts and bars; for if I had sooner made escape into the world, I should have grown hard and rough, and been covered with earthly dust, and my heart might have become callous by rude encounters with the multitude, . . . but living in solitude till the fulness of time was come, I still kept the dew of my youth and the freshness of my heart. . . . I used to think I could imagine all passions, all feelings, and states of the heart and mind; but how little did I know! . . . Indeed, we are but shadows; we are not endowed with real life, and all that seems most real about us is but the thinnest substance of a dream—till the heart be touched. That touch creates us—then we begin to be—thereby we are beings of reality and inheritors of eternity. . . . .[1]

By the time he was appointed weigher and gauger at the Boston Custom House, in 1839, Hawthorne had learned to live, somewhat according to the Emersonian injunction, in business, if not in society, with his hands and in solitude with his head and heart. One who reads in the *American Note-Books* his memoranda of that period cannot fail to be impressed with the fact that his thraldom and drudgery and the sordidness of his daily occupation intensified his delight in his inner freedom and perfected it. All day long he measures coal in a black little British schooner, in a dismal dock at the north end of the city. He thinks that his profession is somewhat akin to that of a chimney-sweeper. He grieves

---

[1] *American Note-Books*, October 4, 1840.

occasionally at the havoc it makes with his wits and at the waste of blessed hours; yet he thanks it for teaching him to "know a politician," and to acquit himself like a man in a world of men. Then this strange coal-gauger walks home under the cloud-rack of a scattered storm—"so glorious indeed, and so lovely, that I had a fantasy of heaven's being broken into fleecy fragments and dispersed through space, with its blest inhabitants dwelling blissfully upon those scattered islands." He enters his room and lies down to read his Spenser, or records in his journal some such half-mystical experience as this: "Besides the bleak, unkindly air, I have been plagued by *two* sets of coal-shovellers at the same time, and have been obliged to keep two separate tallies simultaneously. But I was conscious this was merely a vision and a fantasy, and that, in reality, I was not half frozen by the bitter blast, nor tormented by those grimy coal-heavers, but that I was basking quietly in the sunshine of eternity. . . . Any sort of bodily and earthly torment may serve to make us sensible that we have a soul that is not within the jurisdiction of such shadowy demons,—it separates the immortal within us from the mortal." [2]

It was doubtless in the hope of bringing the inner and the outer worlds into harmony that Hawthorne in the spring of 1841 joined the socialistic commu-

---

[2] *American Note-Books*, April 7, 1840.

nity at Brook Farm, an adventure commemorated
in his *Blithedale Romance.* His sojourn among
these interesting Utopians seems to have dispelled
the hope and to have confirmed his instinctive deep-
seated individualism. It is significant that Clover-
dale even at Brook Farm retreats from his socialistic brethren to a hermitage in a circumjacent wood
—"It symbolized my individuality, and aided me
in keeping it inviolate." "The real Me," Hawthorne declared later, "was never an associate of
the community; there has been a spectral Appearance there, sounding the horn at daybreak, and
milking the cows, and hoeing potatoes, and raking
hay, toiling in the sun, and doing me the honor to
assume my name. But this spectre was not myself." [3]   The effort to externalize felicity and to
make of it common property impressed him on the
whole as a failure, renewing in him the old passion
for seclusion in which "to think, to feel, to dream."
His cutting private judgment of Margaret Fuller,
the Zenobia of *The Blithedale Romance,* represents
his mature conviction that beauty and perfectness
of character result from the gradual unfolding of
some innermost germ of divine grace, and are un-
attainable by mechanical means and local applica-
tions. As this passage illustrates forcibly an aspect
of Hawthorne ordinarily little emphasized, his occasionally severe and penetrating critical faculty, it

---

[3] Moncure Conway's *Hawthorne,* p. 89,

may be quoted here to offset our emphasis upon his tendency to revery and fantasy:

She was a person anxious to try all things, and fill up her experience in all directions; she had a strong and coarse nature, which she had done her utmost to refine, with infinite pains; but of course it could only be superficially changed. The solution of the riddle lies in this direction; nor does one's conscience revolt at the idea of thus solving it; for (at least, this is my own experience) Margaret has not left in the hearts and minds of those who knew her any deep witness of her integrity and purity. She was a great humbug,—of course with much talent and much moral reality, or else she could never have been so great a humbug. But she had stuck herself full of borrowed qualities, which she chose to provide herself with, but which had no root in her. . . . It was such an awful joke, that she should have resolved—in all sincerity, no doubt—to make herself the greatest, wisest, best woman of the age. And to that end she set to work on her strong, heavy, unpliable, and, in many respects, defective and evil nature, and adorned it with a mosaic of admirable qualities, such as she chose to possess; putting in here a splendid talent and there a moral excellence, and polishing each separate piece, and the whole together, till it seemed to shine afar and dazzle all who saw it. She took credit to herself for having been her own Redeemer, if not her own Creator; and, indeed, she was far more a work of art than any of Mozier's statues. But she was not working on an inanimate substance, like marble or clay; there was something within her that she could not possibly come at, to re-create or refine it; and, by and by, this rude old potency bestirred itself, and undid all her labor in the twinkling of an eye. On the whole, I do not know, but I like her the better for it; because she proved herself a very woman after all, and fell as the weakest of her sisters might.[4]

After his departure from Brook Farm, Hawthorne married that fine intelligent Emersonian woman Sophia Peabody, July 9, 1842, and lived for the next four years at the Old Manse in Concord. There in former days, as he remembers in the quietly rapturous introduction to *Mosses from an Old Manse,* Emerson had written *Nature;* "for he was then an inhabitant of the Manse, and used to watch the Assyrian dawn and Paphian sunset and moonrise from the summit of our eastern hill." For Hawthorne it was a return from an uncomfortable hot-bed of culture to Eden, and he was accustomed indeed to speak of himself and his wife at that period as Adam and Eve. In a serene felicity of mutual understanding and perfect sympathy they dwelt in their *solitude à deux,* each sufficient for the other, though occasionally he would hunt Indian arrowheads or water lilies with Thoreau and Ellery Channing, or they would meet Emerson "in the woodpaths, or sometimes in our avenue, with that pure, intellectual gleam diffused about his presence like the garment of a shining one; and he, so quiet,

---

[4] Extract from *Roman Journal* quoted in *Nathaniel Hawthorne and His Wife,* by Julian Hawthorne, 1889, vol. I, pp. 260 *ff.*

so simple, so without pretension, encountering each man alive as if expecting to receive more than he could impart." At another period, he says, "I, too, might have asked of this prophet the master word that would solve me the riddle of the universe, but now, being happy, I felt as if there were no question to be put, and therefore admired Emerson as a poet of deep beauty and austere tenderness, but sought nothing from him as a philosopher."

This deep happiness of the Hawthornes, as nearly perfect as any recorded in literature, this happiness that asked little of friends or fortune or metaphysical philosophy, was in truth for both of them the fruit of solitude, the reward of a prolonged silent discipline in living, as the Transcendentalists would say, "in the Ideal," a discipline that determined the level of their meeting and enabled them, when they were united, to maintain without effort their ideal relations. To her in 1839, in the days of their engagement, he had written: "I never, till now, had a friend who could give me repose; all have disturbed me, and, whether for pleasure or pain, it was still disturbance. But peace overflows from your heart into mine. Then I feel that there is a Now, and that Now must be always calm and happy, and that sorrow and evil are but phantoms that seem to flit across it." [5] Of him, in October, 1842, she writes to her mother: "His will is

---

[5] *Nathaniel Hawthorne and His Wife*, vol. I, p. 203.

strong, but not to govern others. He is so simple,
so just, so tender, so magnanimous, that my highest
instinct could only correspond with his will. I never
knew such delicacy of nature. His panoply of reserve is a providential shield and breastplate. . . .
He is completely pure from earthliness. He is
under the dominion of his intellect and sentiments.
Was ever such a union of power and gentleness,
softness and spirit, passion and reason?" [6] As this
was written but two or three months after marriage, it may be subject to interpretation as the
sweet effusion of an uncritical young bride. But
living with one's husband eight years on a few hundred dollars a year ordinarily makes an adequate
critic of the most emotional bride. Hear this same
witness eight years later:

He is as severe as a stoic about all personal
comforts, and never in his life allowed himself a
luxury. It is exactly upon him, therefore, that I
would like to shower luxuries, because he has such
a spiritual taste for beauty. It is both wonderful
and admirable to see how his taste for splendor and
perfection is not the slightest temptation to him;
how wholly independent he is of what he would
like, all things being equal. Beauty and the love
of it, in him, are the true culmination of the good
and true, and there is no beauty to him without
these bases. He has perfect dominion over himself
in every respect, so that to do the highest, wisest,
loveliest thing is not the least effort to him, any

---

[6] *Ibid.*, pp. 271–2.

more than it is to a baby to be innocent. . . . I never knew such loftiness, so simply borne. I have never known him to stoop from it in the most trivial household matter, any more than in a larger or more public one. If the Hours make out to reach him in his high sphere, their wings are very strong. But I have never thought of him as in time, and so the Hours have nothing to do with him. Happy, happiest is the wife who can bear such and so sincere testimony to her husband after eight years' intimate union.[7]

Is this the portrait of a Puritan? If Puritanism means, as many of our over-heated young people would have it mean, fear of ecclesiastical and social censure, slavish obedience to a rigorous moral code, a self-torturing conscience, harsh judgments of the frailties of one's fellows, morbid asceticism, insensibility and hostility to the beauties of nature and art, Hawthorne was as little of a Puritan as any man that ever lived. But if Puritanism in America means to-day what the lineal and spiritual descendants of the Puritans exemplified at their best in Emerson's New England—emancipation from ecclesiastical and social oppression, escape from the extortion of the senses and the tyranny of things, a consciousness at least partly liberated from the impositions of space and time, freedom for self-dominion, a hopeful and exultant effort to enter into right, and noble, and harmonious relations with the highest impulses of one's fellows, and a vision, a love, a

_____
[7] _Ibid.,_ pp. 372–3.

pursuit of the beauty which has its basis in "the good and true"—if Puritanism means these things, then Hawthorne was a Puritan. If, however, our young people will not permit us to use the term in this high derivative sense, if they persist in employing it as a term of dire derogation, then let us call Hawthorne a Transcendentalist, let us call him a subtle critic and satirist of Puritanism from the Transcendental point of view. But let us make this concession to our over-heated young people with a strict understanding that in return they shall abjure their ill custom of applying to a fanatic or to a starched hypocrite the same term that they apply to Emerson. If Puritanism is to mean what they would have it, they must cease and refrain entirely from referring to the leaders of the Renaissance in New England as Puritans. The essence of that movement of which Hawthorne is an admirable representative is a deliverance from the letter of the law and a recovery of happiness through the right uses of the imagination.

The close relationship between Hawthorne's Transcendental point of view and the character of his fiction has hardly received the attention that it deserves. Henry James, who can with difficulty forgive him for not being a realist, declares that "he was not a man with a literary theory," and goes on to complain that "he has been almost culpably indifferent to his opportunities for commemorating the variations of colloquial English that may

be observed in the New World." But there is
abundant evidence that Hawthorne was conscious
of the realistic method and that he deliberately rejected it. What should a man whose wife "never
thought of him as in time" care for the variations
of colloquial English in the New World? It is very
clear that he sought to winnow out of his fiction
everything that can be brought or carried away by
the Hours. His literary theory becomes explicit
enough in his exquisite chapter on "Lichfield and
Uttoxeter" in *Our Old Home*. He had made a
pilgrimage "to indulge a solemn and high emotion"
to the scene of Samuel Johnson's penance in the
market place of Uttoxeter. Arrived at the spot
where his pious errand should have been consum-
mated, he confesses that his first act was to step
into a hostelry and order a dinner of bacon and
greens, mutton-chops, gooseberry pudding, and ale
—"a sufficient meal for six yeomen." On enquiry
he finds the Doctor's fellow-townsmen generally un-
acquainted with the story which had consecrated
the place "in the heart of a stranger from three
thousand miles over the sea." And his own emotions remain unstirred till he has left the visible
Uttoxeter behind him and returned to the Uttoxeter of his inner vision. His comment on this incident may serve us as a commentary on his literary
method:

A sensible man had better not let himself be
betrayed into these attempts to realize the things

which he has dreamed about, and which, when they cease to be purely ideal in his mind, will have lost the truest of their truth, the loftiest and profoundest part of their power over his sympathies. Facts, as we really find them, whatever poetry they may involve, are covered with a stony excrescence of prose, resembling the crust on a beautiful sea-shell, and they never show their most delicate and divinest colors until we shall have dissolved away their grosser actualities by steeping them long in a powerful menstruum of thought. And seeking to actualize them again, we do but renew the crust. If this were otherwise—if the moral sublimity of a great fact depended in any degree on its garb of external circumstances, things which change and decay—it could not itself be immortal and ubiquitous, and only a brief point of time and a little neighborhood would be spiritually nourished by its grandeur and beauty."

When Hawthorne was settled in the Old Manse, an abode so happily adapted to his still contemplative habit, he had pondered, he intimates, various grave literary projects, and had "resolved at least to achieve a novel that should evolve some deep lesson and should possess physical substance enough to stand alone." He wrote there some of his finest short stories, "The Birthmark," "Young Goodman Brown," "Rappaccini's Daughter," "Roger Malvin's Burial," "The Artist of the Beautiful"; but the production of his novel was to take place in another scene and under a rather singular stimulus. By 1846 the prospect of being able to make both

ends meet in Concord was so unpromising that to
relieve himself of the anxiety occasioned by his
small debts and his keen sense of obligation he obtained appointment as surveyor of customs at Salem.
How he meditated Hester Prynne's story as he
passed "with a hundred-fold repetition, the long
extent from the front-door of the Custom-House to
the side entrance, and back again," he has told in
his fascinating introductory chapter. And there he
admits that despite his long practice in creative
revery he found himself not wholly independent of
circumstances and "atmospheric" conditions. His
imagination was dimmed, and the shadowy creatures of his dream turned upon him and said:
"What have you to do with us? The little power
you might once have possessed over the tribe of
unrealities is gone! You have bartered it for a pit-
tance of the public gold. Go, then, and earn your
wages." After three years of service, which we
understand was efficiently performed, the politicians
turned him out of office. Him the dismissal appears
to have filled temporarily with chagrin and a measure of bitterness; but Mrs. Hawthorne, in her admirable superiority to the loss of their visible means
of support, showed herself at this crisis a guardian
angel—or at least a more finished Transcendentalist
than her husband. Let us have this beautiful incident as reported by George Parsons Lathrop:

On finding himself superseded, he walked away
from the Custom-House, returned home, and enter-

ing sat down in the nearest chair, without uttering a word. Mrs. Hawthorne asked him if he was well.

"Well enough," was the answer.

"What is the matter, then?" said she. "Are you 'decapitated'?"

He replied with gloom that he was, and that the occurrence was no joke.

"Oh," said his wife, gayly, "now you can write your Romance!" For he had told her several times that he had a romance "growling" in him.

"Write my Romance!" he exclaimed. "But what are we to do for bread and rice, next week?"

"I will take care of that," she answered. "And I will tell Ann to put a fire in your study, now." [8]

Hawthorne's introductory account of the origin of the romance in papers and relics discovered in the Custom-House is a part of the fiction. The original germ of it had probably begun to strike root in his imagination years before when he had come upon an historical record of a punishment like Hester's. In "Endicott and the Red Cross" (included in the second installment of *Twice Told Tales*), he had introduced for a moment among a group of culprits suffering various ingenious penalties, "a young woman, with no mean share of beauty, whose doom it was to wear the letter A on the breast of her gown, in the eyes of all the world and her own children. And even her own children knew what that initial signified. Sporting

---

[8] "A Biographical Sketch of Nathaniel Hawthorne," in *Tales, Sketches, and Other Papers by N. H.* Houghton Mifflin, n. d., p.496.

with her infamy, the lost and desperate creature had embroidered the fatal token in scarlet cloth, with golden thread and the nicest art of needle-work; so that the capital A might have been thought to mean Admirable, or anything rather than Adulteress." There, for him, was the typical nucleus of an imaginative tale.

We have not much information about the course of its development into *The Scarlet Letter* beyond what James T. Fields, the publisher, has related in his *Yesterdays With Authors*. In the winter of 1849 Fields went to Salem to call on Hawthorne and to urge him to publish something. His author, whom he seems to have found in low spirits, replied that he had nothing to publish, and sent him away empty-handed. But before he had reached the street, Hawthorne overtook him and thrust into his hands a manuscript which he read on the way back to Boston. It was a sketch or first draft of *The Scarlet Letter*. "Before I slept that night," says Fields, "I wrote him a note all aglow with admiration of the marvellous story he had put into my hands, and told him I would come again to Salem the next day and arrange for its publication. I went on in such an amazing state of excitement, when we met again in the little house, that he would not believe that I was really in earnest. He seemed to think I was beside myself, and laughed sadly at my enthusiasm." In the *English Note-Books,* Hawthorne instances as a case of remarkable phlegm the fact that Thackeray read the touching last number of *The Newcomes* to James Russell Lowell and William Story in a cider-cellar. In this connection he remarks: "I cannot but wonder at his coolness in respect to his own pathos, and compare it with my emotions, when I read the last scene of *The Scarlet Letter* to my wife, just after writing it— tried to read it rather, for my voice swelled and heaved, as if I were tossed up and down on an ocean as it subsides after a storm. But I was in a very nervous state then, having gone through a great diversity of emotion, while writing it, for many months. I think I have never overcome my own adamant in any other instance." [a]

The success of the book on its publication in 1856 was immediate and, considering the restrictions put upon novel reading in the days of our fathers and grandfathers, extensive. In a striking passage of a most charming piece of criticism, Henry James records the reverberation of its fame registered in his own then youthful breast, an instrument more than ordinarily sensitive to such impressions, yet reacting in a sufficiently representative fashion to serve as a general indicator:

. . . . The writer of these lines, who was a child at the time, remembers dimly the sensation the book produced, and the little shudder with which people

---

[a] *English Note-Books*, September 14, 1855, quoted by James.

alluded to it, as if a peculiar horror were mixed
with its attractions. He was too young to read it
himself; but its title, upon which he fixed his eyes
as the book lay upon the table, had a mysterious
charm. He had a vague belief, indeed, that the
"letter" in question was one of the documents that
come by the post, and it was a source of perpetual
wonderment to him that it should be of such an un-
accustomed hue. Of course it was difficult to explain
to a child the significance of poor Hester Prynne's
blood-coloured A. But the mystery was at last
partly dispelled by his being taken to see a collection of pictures (the annual exhibition of the National Academy), where he encountered a representation of a pale, handsome woman, in a quaint black
dress and a white coif, holding between her knees
an elfish-looking little girl, fantastically dressed,
and crowned with flowers. Embroidered on the
woman's breast was a great crimson A, over which
the child's fingers, as she glanced strangely out of
the picture, were maliciously playing. I was told
that this was Hester Prynne and little Pearl, and
that when I grew older I might read their interesting history. But the picture remained vividly im-
printed on my mind; I had been vaguely frightened
and made uneasy by it; and when, years afterwards,
I first read the novel, I seemed to myself to have
read it before, and to be familiar with its two
strange heroines. I mention this incident simply
as an indication of the degree to which the success
of *The Scarlet Letter* had made the book what is
called an actuality. . . . The book was the finest
piece of imaginative writing yet put forth in the
country. There was a consciousness of this in the
welcome that was given it—a satisfaction in the

idea of America having produced a novel that belonged to literature, and to the forefront of it.
Something might at last be sent to Europe as exquisite in quality as anything that had been received,
and the best of it was that the thing was absolutely
American; it belonged to the soil, to the air; it came
out of the very heart of New England.[10]

No commentator can fail to remark that the
story of Arthur Dimmesdale and Hester Prynne
begins where a seductive love-story hastens to end,
with the bitterness of stolen waters and the unpala-
tableness of bread eaten in secret. Without one
glance backward over the secret path that led to
the jail door, we are invited to fix our attention
upon the sombre drama of punishment, atonement,
remorse. "To Hawthorne's imagination," says
Henry James, "the fact that these two persons had
loved each other too well was of an interest comparatively vulgar; what appealed to him was the
idea of their moral situation in the long years that
follow." This is probably to represent the case as
more exclusively a matter of artistic interest than
it was to Hawthorne, though not more so than it
might have been to James. When, in the *Inferno*,
Dante confronts a pair of lovers at a similar point
in their progress, the first question he raises is how
they fell into that predicament. Hawthorne would
hardly have regarded either the answer or the curi-

---

[10] *Hawthorne* (in The English Men of Letters series), 1879,
pp. 107–8.

osity which evoked it as vulgar. But by refraining in *The Scarlet Letter* from lifting the veil that hides the antecedent history of this passionate experience he evades what would have been for him, or for any novelist, the extremely difficult problem of representing Arthur Dimmesdale in love. By this abridgment he obtains, furthermore, an intense concentration of interest upon that portion of the history which a writer wishing to "evolve some deep lesson" would desire to emphasize. Finally, it is obvious that he has striven sedulously to avoid all occasion for exhibiting an aberrant passion in its possible aspects of alluring and romantic glamour, so that one desperate embrace of the lovers and Hester's entreaty for forgiveness under the deep shadow of foreboding (in the seventeenth chapter) remain almost the only vivid evidence and certification of their continuing tenderness and attraction for each other.

Arthur Dimmesdale is ordinarily considered the figure of primary importance, and, so far as the external evolution of the story is concerned, unquestionably he is. His, apparently, is the main tragic problem, and his is the solution of it. Undoubtedly, also, we are admitted from first to last very much more fully into his consciousness than into Hester's. While she remains for the most part in isolation with her enigmatic child, he is defined by his relations to the elder clergyman and the officials of the colony in that superbly ironical scene in which Governor Bellingham says: "Good Master Dimmesdale, the responsibility of this woman's soul lies greatly with you. It behooves you, therefore, to exhort her to repentance, and to confession, as a proof and consequence thereof." He is defined by his peculiarly excruciating relations with Roger Chillingworth, a creature of somewhat uncertain significance even to his creator, who sometimes invites us to think of him as the devil incarnate, sometimes as an avenging fury, sometimes as the Puritan conscience, but never as merely a wronged husband. He is defined by his relations to a series of his parishioners in the great temptation scene of the twentieth chapter, where the baser elements of his nature are exhibited in riot and all but victorious. He is defined by the passionate exaltation of his Election Sermon and by his last words on the scaffold. His is the character that is most adequately realized and presented and that affects us as most unquestionably human. And yet when all is said and done, he does not become an individual; he remains a type. The forms of his temptation, sin, suffering, struggle, and aspiration are all strictly determined for him by the pressure of Puritan society and his clerical profession. Our special interest in him is due not to any noteworthy differentiation of his character but to the tremendous irony of his situation.

In Hester, on the other hand, it is manifest that Hawthorne intended to present an individual. She is differentiated by her rich dark beauty, her voluptuous Oriental taste for the gorgeously beautiful, and by her aspect, when she is flushed with momentary joy, of a heroine of romance. But her most interesting distinction is her moral independence and originality. It is to be noted that though her punishment causes her shame and suffering, it does not appear to bring her to any clear state of contrition or repentance. She feels that society by making her an outcast has severed her obligation to it. For it, she exists only as a terrible example. For herself, she is a free spirit liberated in a moral wilderness with her own way to make and take. In these circumstances her thinking has little reference to the doctrines expounded in the meeting-house. She thinks as her heart prompts; and her heart tells her that Arthur Dimmesdale is still her supreme good, and devotion to him her highest duty. The world's frown she had endured and the frown of heaven; "but the frown of this pale, weak, sinful, and sorrow-stricken man was what Hester could not bear and live!" To save him she had borne in silence the burden of her knowledge of Roger Chillingworth's presence. To redeem him from misery she is ready to flee with him to other lands. Though in the years of her exile she had quietly conformed to the external regulations of society, "the world's law," says her historian, "was no law for her mind." Her readiness to leave the colony with the minister, Hawthorne desires us to understand, was no mere impulse of unreflecting emotion. It was due to her vision of the possibility of reconstructing their shattered lives, and this vision in turn was the consequence of her internal emancipation from the power of the Puritan system of ideas: "She assumed a freedom of speculation, then common enough on the other side of the Atlantic, but which our forefathers, had they known it, would have held to be a deadlier crime than that stigmatized by the scarlet letter. In her lonesome cottage, by the seashore, thoughts visited her, such as dared to enter no other dwelling in New England; shadowy guests, that would have been as perilous as demons to their entertainer, could they have been seen so much as knocking at her door." This free speculative impulse in Hester, her reaching out for "spiritual laws" not generally recognized by the society of her time, makes her a Transcendentalist before the appointed hour.

In the forest scene Hawthorne represents Nature as in mysterious and joyous sympathy with the bliss of the lovers in their vision of a new life together. That he does not accept Nature as moral oracle, however, he indicates by an emphatic parenthesis—"that wild, heathen Nature of the forest, never subjugated by human law, nor illumined by higher truth." On the other hand, his giving the solution of the problem to Arthur Dimmesdale does not prove by any means that his sympathies were wholly on the side of the Puritans. His comment upon the two possibilities of escape from the predicament in which he has placed his hero and heroine is more subtle than is ordinarily noticed. What he has made clear is, that for the minister, who at the end is as thoroughly dominated by Puritan forms of thought as at the beginning, confession was fated and inevitable. For him Hester's solution would have involved the repetition of a deadly sin. His temporary decision to flee with her is therefore consistently represented as filling his mind with perverse suggestions of evil. Arthur Dimmesdale, we may be sure, was happier dying on the scaffold than he would have been sailing to Europe.

It is to be observed, however, that the devilish persecution which afflicts him does not touch Hester. Nor is she exhibited as participating in the ecstasy of his confession. To his question, "Is not this better than what we dreamed of in the forest?" she only murmurs, "I know not! I know not!" And her last words express her quite heretical hope of union with the minister in another world. She believes that in her seven years of suffering she has made amends to heaven for her wrongdoing. With the lapse of time even her rigorous fellow-townsmen relent, take her again into their affections, and even turn to her for counsel "in the continually recurring trials of wounded, wasted, wronged, misplaced, or erring and sinful passion." Hawthorne, while remarking that she often thinks amiss, obviously admires the natural desire of her rich warm nature to regain a place of usefulness and happiness in society. In the conclusion, furthermore, he intimates pointedly enough that the Puritans of the seventeenth century had not received the final word on the regulation of human relationships; that, when the world is ripe for it, there will be a "higher law" declared, a new revelation, "showing how sacred love should make us happy, by the truest test of a life successful to such an end!"

In his preface to *The House of the Seven Gables* Hawthorne deprecates attempts to "impale the story with its moral, as with an iron rod." "A high truth," he declares, "fairly, finely, and skilfully wrought out, brightening at every step, and crowning the final development of a work of fiction, may add an artistic glory, but is never truer, and seldom more evident, at the last page than at the first." In the face of this caution it would be imprudent to speak directly of the moral intentions wrought into the fabric of *The Scarlet Letter*. It may be permissible, however, to call attention to the singular union of judgment with compassion which characterizes Hawthorne's treatment of his principal personages, and which he also solicits for them from the reader. He solicits compassion in this romance, as in the little tale of "The Minister with the Black Veil," by perpetually suggesting to the reader that search in his own heart would discover at least the seeds and latent possibilities of kindred tragic guilt. He solicits judgment on the ground which the most gentle-spirited Transcendentalist may take, and so save himself from dissolution in sympathy, namely, that we should abide firmly by the law we have till the higher law is ready. The method of Hawthorne's moral appeal is the method of tragic poetry: the image of anguish that never fades, the cadenced cry that, like the despairing wail of Lady Macbeth, lingers in the memory—"Is there not shade enough in all this boundless forest to hide thy heart from the gaze of Roger Chillingworth?"

WALT WHITMAN

Whitman interests and disquiets us beyond all other American poets by that personality of his, so original, so indolent yet intense, so fearlessly flaunted yet so enigmatically reserved, so palpably carnal yet so illuminated with mystical ardor that at the first bewildering contact one questions whether his urgent touch is of lewdness or divinity. There is something daimonic in the effluence of the man, which visitors remark and remember months and years afterwards as an impulse unaccountably affecting the temper of their lives. It is a sign by which one recognizes native power of one sort or another quite above talent. Hawthorne and other observers were conscious of such an effluence from Whitman's master, Emerson—"a pure, intellectual gleam diffused about his presence like the garment of a shining one." But the aura of the disciple, who roved so far from the decorous circle of the Concord Platonist, was, I fancy, spiked with yellow flame, like the gold-colored nimbus that he sought to paint above the heads of his fellow countrymen—"I paint

153

many heads: but I paint no head without its nimbus of gold-colored light." "Something a little more than human," commented Thoreau, that cool-blooded New Englander, after an hour's conversation with the bard. Edward Carpenter, an English pilgrim who visited him in 1877, says that in the first ten minutes he became conscious "of an impression which subsequently grew even more marked —the impression, namely, of immense vista or background in his personality." As to the final quality of Whitman's personal effluence the testimony of John Burroughs, recorded in 1878, should be decisive: "After the test of time nothing goes home like the test of actual intimacy, and to tell me that Whitman is not a large, fine, fresh magnetic personality, making you love him, and want always to be with him, were to tell me that my whole past life is a deception, and all the perception of my impressions a fraud." His appeal to the imagination was not diminished by his offering to the eye. The mere physical image of him standing against the sky, so nonchalant and imperturbable in his workman's shirt and trousers, as in his first edition of 1855, is, or was, of a novel and compelling effrontery in the smooth gallery of our national statuary. Like the image of Franklin at Paris in his coonskin cap, the image of Lincoln as the rail-splitter, or of Mark Twain as the Mississippi pilot, or of Roosevelt as Rough Rider, so the image of

Walt Whitman as the carpenter or printer turned bard in Manhattan pleases one's taste for the autocthonous, the home-grown. More than that, it touches the heart by symbolizing the national sense that, after all our civilizing efforts, we live still in an unfinished world. He acquired blandness with the years; yet even in his mild old age he looked out from under his wide-brimmed hat and from the cloudy covert of beard and hair with no academic mien—rather with the untamed and heroic aspect of

Tiresias and Phineus, prophets old.

On the centenaries of most of the American poets who flourished at the time when the *Leaves of Grass* was first put forth, we enquire rather coldly and incuriously what is left of them. They have sadly dwindled—most of them—they have lost their warmth for us, they have become irrelevant to our occasions. Whitman still with astonishing completeness lives. He lives because he marvelously well identified that daimonic personality with his book, so that whoever touches it, as he himself declared, touches a man, and a man of singularly intense perceptiveness. One can hardly exaggerate the potency of Whitman's imaginative process—a process easier to illustrate than to define. Let us take, for example, these lines on the fugitive slave and consider the almost intolerable immediacy of the presentment:

The hounded slave that flags in the race, leans by
    the fence, blowing, cover'd with sweat,
The twinges that sting like needles his legs and neck,
    the murderous buckshot and the bullets—
All these I feel or am.
I am the hounded slave, I wince at the bite of the
    dogs;
Hell and despair are upon me, crack and again
    crack the marksman;
I clutch the rails of the fence, my gore dribs, thinn'd
    with the ooze of my skin;
I fall on the weeds and stones.
The riders spur their unwilling horses, haul close,
Taunt my dizzy ears and beat me violently over the
    head with whip stocks.
Agonies are one of my changes of garments.
I do not ask the wounded person how he feels; I
    myself become the wounded person;
My hurts turn livid upon me as I lean on a cane
    and observe.

This is the method of Whitman: imaginative
contemplation of the object, which identifies him
with the object. It does not suggest comparison
with the method of Longfellow or of Tennyson. It
reminds one rather of the imaginative contemplation practised by mediæval saints, which brought
out in hands and brow the marks of the Crucifixion.
The vitality and validity of Whitman's report is not
that of an experience observed but rather that of
an experience repeated.

But Whitman lives for another reason which is
worth dwelling upon for the sake of young poets

eager for immortality. He lives because of the richness of his vital reference, the fulness of the relations which he established between his book and the living world. There is a sect of poets to-day, with attendant critics, who expect to outlast their age by shunning contact with its hopes and fears, by avoiding commitments and allegiances, and by confining themselves to decorating the interior of an ivory tower in the style of Kubla Khan. Whitman made his bid for perpetuity on another basis. He identified himself and his chants with innumerable things that are precious and deathless—with his wide-extended land and the unending miracles of the seasons, with the independence and union and destiny of "These States," with common people and heroes, their proud memories, their limitless aspiration, and with the sunlight and starlight of the over-arching heaven. Committing himself to democratic America, he surrendered with "immitigable adoration" to a spirit that preserved and magnified him with its own unfolding greatness. And so as the seasons return, he returns with the spring and the musical winds and tides that play about his beloved Mannahatta, with the subtle odor of lilacs in the dooryard, with valor and suffering and victory, with the thoughts and words that perennially consecrate the old battlefield at Gettysburg, with the young men returning from the latest "great war," with civil labor resumed and civil comradeship, with furled flags and May-time and hopes recurrent. He returns; and if we wish to salute him, he will give us the tune:

Again old heart so gay, again to you, your sense,
    the full flush spring returning;
Again the freshness and the odors, again Virginia's
    summer sky, pellucid blue and silver;
Again the forenoon purple of the hills;
Again the deathless grass, so noiseless, soft and
    green,
Again the blood-red roses blooming.

But why is this interesting and vital personality important to us? Open the *Leaves of Grass,* and you will find this piquantly intimate answer: "I considered long and seriously of you before you were born." Other poets have given little thought to us, and we, in compensation, give little thought to them; for we modern men and women of realistic temper go not to literature to escape from life, but to intensify our sense of it and to find a spirit that will animate us in the thick of it. Whitman, proclaimer of egotism, foresaw our intentness upon our own enterprises, and prepared for the day when we should demand of him: "What have you said, Poet, that concerns us?" Though he is saturated with historical and contemporary references, nothing in him is merely contemporary, merely historical. He gathers up ages, literatures, philosophies, and consumes them as the food of passion and prophecy. He strides with the energy and momentum of the national past into the national future, towering above a poetical movement which he has fathered, scattering social and political and religious gospels, with troops of disciples and unbelievers in this and other lands, crying still proudly as of old: "All that I have said concerns you." He is important, because he recognized that, though there are many ways by which a man can attract attention and get a temporary hearing, there is only one way by which he can permanently interest and attach the affections of the American people and so hold a place among the great Americans: that is by helping them unfold the meanings, fulfil the promises, and justify the faith of democratic society.

By making himself important to the American people as the poetic interpreter of their political and social ideals, Whitman, as things are turning out, finds himself now mid-stream in the democratic movement which encompasses the earth. At the present time it is manifest that, in spite of obstacles and cross-currents, the central current of the world is making towards democracy. Whatever else it involves, democracy involves at least one grand salutary elementary admission, namely, that the world exists for the benefit and for the improvement of all the decent individuals in it. Till recently this admission in many quarters had never been made, had been savagely opposed. It is covertly, secretly, indirectly opposed in many quarters of our own country even to-day. Now the indications are that those who opposite it are going to

be outnumbered and overwhelmed. The movement
is on, and it will not be stopped. Wise men, ambitious men, far-sighted men will not attempt to block
it. They will adapt themselves to it, they will cooperate with it, they will direct and further it as
the only way in which they may hope to be of any
cheerful significance in the era opening before them.
The "ruling class," the statesmen, in all nations
will find their mission and their honor progressively
dependent upon their capacity for bringing the entire body of humanity into one harmonious and
satisfactory life.

Now the supreme power of Whitman consists in
this: that his spirit works inwardly, like religion,
upon other spirits, quickening and preparing them
for this general human fellowship, this world society, which to him, as to many of his great predecessors, appeared to be the legitimate far-off consequence of the principles declared by the American
fathers. "Cosmopolitanism" has of late suffered
many indignities as a word and as a conception;
and those who speak of an international society are
readily charged with treasonable and anarchical in-
novation. In the spiritual sense of the word no
aspiration is, as a matter of fact, more thoroughly
American and traditional than cosmopolitanism.
"God grant," exclaimed Franklin, "that not only
the love of liberty but a thorough knowledge of the
rights of man may pervade all the nations of the
earth, so that a philosopher may set his foot any-

where on its surface and say, 'This is my country.' "
By statesmen like Washington, Jefferson, John
Quincy Adams, or Lincoln this utterance would have
been accepted as suggesting the ultimate fruition of
the highest statecraft. The diffusion of a spirit
among men which will support and make possible
such statecraft appeared to writers like Emerson
and Whitman as perhaps the central function of the
serious man of letters.

"I hate literature," said Whitman, conversing in
Camden with colloquial over-emphasis. What he
meant was that he rejected the famous "play-
theory" of art and looked with disdain upon *belles-
lettres* in their merely recreative and decorative
aspects. "Literature is big," he explained on another occasion, "only in one way—when used as an
aid in the growth of the humanities—a furthering
of the cause of the masses—a means whereby men
may be revealed to each other as brothers." Recognizing that "the real work of democracy is done
underneath its politics," Whitman conceived of his
mission from first to last as moral and spiritual;
and nothing could be sillier than the current criticism which derides a sense of mission in the poet
and at the same time proudly salutes Whitman as
the chief American poet. It is as if one should
say, "I am very fond of walnuts, but I don't like
the meats." Not a part but the whole of his life-
work is permeated with religious and moral intention. What gives to the *Leaves of Grass* its cumu-

lative effect is its many-sided development of a single theme, of which I shall give one more of his conversational descriptions: "I am for getting all the walls down—all of them. . . . While I seem to love America, and wish to see America prosperous, I do not seem able to bring myself to love America, to desire American prosperity, at the expense of some other nation." "But must we not take care of home first of all?" asked Dudley. "Perhaps," replied Whitman, "but what is home—to the humanitarian what is home?"

It is easy and natural to disparage this diffusive humanitarian sentiment as it is to ignore that difficult central precept of Christianity which prescribes one's feeling towards one's neighbor. Every one knows, for example, Roosevelt's scornful comparison of the man who loves his own country no better than another to the man who loves his own wife no better than another. Roosevelt, who had a great talent for bringing forward and glorifying the simple elementary passions, has had his share of applause. When the applause dies away and reflection begins, it occurs to some of us that the simple elementary passions pretty well look after themselves. No very rare talent is required to commend to the average man the simple elementary passions. He takes to them by a primitive urge of his being as the bull moose takes to fighting and mating. Nature has given them a vigor and hardiness which provides against their extinction. Meanwhile our societies, national and international, do not run as smoothly and efficiently as men who hate waste and confusion desire. They seem to clamor from their discordant and jarring gear for some motive and regulative power other than the simple elementary passions. What nature has overlooked and neglected or inadequately attended to is the development of those feelings which fit men to live harmoniously in complex civil societies. So that the special task for those who would ameliorate our modern world is to bring forward and glorify an order of emotions quite unknown to the Cave Man —a mutual understanding and imaginative sympathy which begin to develop and operate only when the elementary urges of our nature have been checked and subdued by a reflective culture. Over most of the once-called great statesmen of Whitman's period and of our own generation—the Bismarcks, the Disraelis, the Roosevelts—there falls the shadow of great tasks from which they shrank and the darker and still present shadow of a great calamity which their fostering of the elementary passions helped to bring upon us. In the present posture of the world I think we should not scorn so resolute a patriot as Whitman, who had lived through two or three wars, for confessing the growth in himself and for promoting the growth in others of a sense like this:

This moment yearning and thoughtful sitting alone,
It seems to me there are other men in other lands
    yearning and thoughtful;
It seems to me I can look over and behold them in
    Germany, Italy, France, Spain,
Or far, far away in China, or in Russia or Japan,
    talking other dialects.
And it seems to me if I could know these men I
    should become attached to them as I do to men
    in my own lands.
O I know we should be brethren and lovers;
I know I should be happy with them.

There is at least an appearance of inconsistency
between this limitless humanitarian sympathy of
Whitman's and his enthusiastic nationalism. There
is at least an appearance of inconsistency between
his enthusiastic nationalism and his resolute individualism. But let us not forget the appearance
of fundamental conflict between the multitude of
the heavenly host crying peace on earth and the
words of him they heralded saying, "I came not
to bring peace but a sword." The exploration of
the ground between these opposites, the reconciliation of jarring antinomies, is a task from which
statesmen shrink. It is precisely the master task
of the poetic and religious imagination. Whitman,
as the opening lines of his book declare, recognized
it as the very heart of his theme:

One's-Self I sing—a simple, separate Person;
Yet utter the word Democratic, the word *En-masse.*

There is the mystery which enchanted him and

which perplexes us still—the mystery of the coexistence of personal freedom with social authority. He believed in both, just as for centuries men have believed in the coexistence of free-will with foreknowledge absolute. No one has a right to call his reconciliation of the individual with society inadequate who has not taken the trouble to hear the whole of his song and its commentaries in "Democratic Vistas" and "Specimen Days"; for part supports part, and the whole is greater than the sum of them. No other poet exhibits himself so inadequately in extracts. One gets nearly all of Gray in the "Elegy"; but one can no more get all of Whitman in "O Captain! My Captain" than one can get all of a modern symphony in the sound of the flutes or oboes. Whitman is not primarily a melodist. His strength is in the rich interweaving of intricate and difficult harmonies.

In the life-long evolution of his work, he was seeking a concord of soul and body, individual and society, state and nation, nation and the family of nations, some grand chord to unite the dominant notes of all. In his quest for this harmony he clothes himself in his country as in a garment; he becomes America feeling out her relations with the world. I seem to distinguish in his poems three great successive movements or impulses corresponding roughly to the three periods of the national life in which he had his being. The first is a movement of individualistic expansion corresponding to the period before the Civil War. The second is a movement of concentration corresponding to the period of the war. The third is a resumed movement of "individualistic" expansion following the war, and spiritualized by it."

It can hardly be too much emphasized that Whitman and America went through their adolescence together and that the arrogance of his advent in poetry matches the defiant attitude of the young republic. Born at West Hills, Long Island, May 31, 1819, Walt Whitman had a lively consciousness of his inheritance from the French and American revolutions. In his boyhood he had actually been touched by Lafayette. He knew an old friend of Tom Paine's. His own father, though an uneducated man, had caught the free-thinking habit of the eighteenth century. As he grew towards manhood, he felt stirring around him that intoxicating welter of radical enthusiasms and rosy idealisms which in the forties and fifties was loosely described as Transcendentalism, and which remains to this day the most variously fascinating and fragrant blossoming of mind that America has exhibited. It was a delighted movement of emancipation from the old world and her unholy alliances. It was still more a resolute affirmation of faith in the new world and her unexplored possibilities—faith in the resources of nature and the capacity of man to appropriate them. Inspiriting voices were in the air, and every voice cried in one fashion or another: "Trust thyself; every heart vibrates to that iron string. Acccept the place the divine Providence has found for you; the society of your contemporaries, the connexion of events. Great men have always done so and confided themselves childlike to the genius of their age, betraying their perception that the Eternal was stirring at their heart, working through their hands, predominating in all their being."

In his roving early days as teacher, printer, editor; reading his Dante and Shakespeare in a wood by the sea: visiting New Orleans and wandering home again by the Mississippi and the Great Lakes, Whitman heard these voices of his age pealing in his ear with an ever more imperative summons, "Trust thyself." And Whitman resolved to trust himself, soul and body, and to trust his time and place, and to commit himself for better or for worse to the society of his contemporaries and the spiritual current flowing beneath American events. There has been much discussion of Whitman's indebtedness at this point to the inspiration of Emerson. It seems clear on the one hand that Whitman sent a copy of his edition of 1855 to Emerson; that in his edition of 1856 he printed Emerson's letter of acknowledgment and spoke of him as "friend and master"; and that in the conversations of his later years with Traubel he repeatedly talked of Emerson with admiration and reverence. It is clear, on the other hand, that Emerson looked upon Whitman as a representative of the new America, for whom he had in some sense prepared the way, and that on July 21, 1855, he wrote to the then almost unknown poet the following memorable letter:

DEAR SIR: I am not blind to the worth of the wonderful gift of *Leaves of Grass*. I find it the most extraordinary piece of wit and wisdom that America has yet contributed. I am very happy in reading it, as great power makes us happy. It meets the demand I am always making of what seems the sterile and stingy Nature, as if too much handiwork or too much lymph in the temperament were making our Western wits fat and mean. I give you joy of your free and brave thought. I have great joy in it. I find incomparable things, said incomparably well, as they must be. I find the courage of treatment which so delights us, and which large perception only can inspire.

I, greet you at the beginning of a great career, which yet must have had a long foreground, for such a start. I rubbed my eyes a little to see if this sunbeam were no illusion; but the solid sense of the book is a sober certainty. It has the best merits, namely, of fortifying and encouraging.

I did not know, until I last night saw the book advertised in a newspaper, that I could trust the name as real and available for a post-office.

I wish to see my benefactor, and have felt much like striking my tasks, and visiting New York to pay you my respects.

R. W. EMERSON.

Now Whitman's "free and brave thought," his determination to trust himself, body and soul, impelled him in the first gush of his self-expression to glorify his earthy and instinctive impulses with a flamboyance which Emerson and many other critics were to condemn as distasteful, shocking, or even dangerous. The powerful virtue in the chants before the war, the virtue for the sake of which Emerson overlooked whatever in them he distasted, was their "fortifying and encouraging" individualism. It is an individualism of adolescent America, unchecked by political experience, modified and colored by emotional attachments to the American scene and the American actors. It is such a passion as made such an indigenous individual as Thoreau love Walden Pond and refuse to pay his taxes. It is an individualism further tempered, however, from the first by a profound sense of the general human brotherhood and a hatred of unearned special privilege. Heir of the Revolutionary Era, Whitman is an equalitarian of a sort. "By God," he exclaims, "I will accept nothing which all cannot have their counterpart of on the same terms." But for bringing in the reign of Equality he confides in men rather than in political mechanisms. "Produce," he asserts, "Produce great persons, the rest follows." He is the Declaration of Independence incarnate. He desires followers but only such as are moved by inner impulse; he will not have clubs studying him nor "schools" trooping after him. Markedly like Emerson and Thoreau in this respect, he is wary of organizations which prescribe the conduct of the individual and relieve him of his personal danger and responsibility. He will stand or fall in his own strength. He is wary of organized majorities. Almost in the spirit of Washington he warns against the savageness and wolfishness of parties, so combative, so intolerant of the idea of equal brotherhood and the interests of all. "It behooves you," he declared, "to convey yourself implicitly to no party, nor submit blindly to their dictators, but steadily hold yourself judge and master over all of them." "I am a radical of radicals," he repeats from youth to grey old age. Beside this utterance one should place his golden words to his biographer Traubel: "Be radical; be radical; be not too damned radical." Despite such cautionary modifications, however, one may say that Whitman's primary impulse is one of revolt against whatever deprives the simple separate person of his right to freedom and the pursuit of happiness.

But the second movement of Whitman's mind proves him a far more complex phenomenon than most of the critics have acknowledged. Mr. George Santayana represents him as a kind of placid animal wallowing unreflectively in the stream of his own sensations. This view of him may indeed be supported by reference to certain of his passages which express with unwise exuberance his delight in the reports of his senses. The unwisdom of his exuberance with reference to the sexual life, for example, is pretty nearly demonstrated by the number of critics whose critical faculty has been quite upset

by it; so that they can find nothing significant in this
prophet of the new world but his shamelessness.
"Hold off from sensuality," enjoined Cicero (who,
by the way, was not a Victorian) "for, if you have
given yourself up to it, you will find yourself unable
to think of anything else." This precept rests upon
physiological and psychological facts which Whitman's experiments in heliotherapy have not altered.
To put a serpent in a show-window does not blunt
its fangs. But to represent Whitman as exclusively
or finally preoccupied with the life of the senses is
not to represent him whole. It is to ignore a fact
which flames from the completed *Leaves of Grass,*
namely, that he is one of the "twice-born"—that
he had a new birth in the spirit of the Civil War
and a rebaptism in its blood. His book as it now
stands is built around that event, and the martyred
President is the palpitating heart of it. That Whitman emerged from the warm shallows of his individual sensibility, that he immersed himself in the
spiritual undercurrents of the national life,—this
significant alteration of his position is established
by his conduct and temper in the war.

Through the long agony of the struggle, Whitman went about the military hospitals, nursing the
sick and wounded from every state without excep-
tion; with malice toward none, with charity for all,
tenderly compassionate toward Northerner and
Southerner alike. In his "Notes of a Hospital
Nurse" he records his affectionate ministrations to

two brothers mortally wounded in the same battle but on opposite sides; and he remarks almost as if he himself were a neutral above the conflict. "Each died for his cause." The accent of his compassion recalls the perplexed sadness of that touching passage in the Second Inaugural where Lincoln reflects that "Both read the same Bible, and pray to the same God; and each invokes his aid against the other." Almost in the manner of an outraged pacifist, Whitman, after describing an attack on a hospital train, comments as follows: "Multiply the above by scores, aye hundreds—light it with every lurid passion, the wolf's, the lion's lapping thirst for blood—the passionate boiling volcanoes of human revenge for comrades, brothers slain—with the light of burning farms, and heaps of smutting, smouldering black embers—and in the human heart everywhere black, worse embers—and you have an inkling of this war." Yet despite his abhorrence of cruelty and despite his compassion for suffering, Whitman's sympathy does not blunt the edge of his judgment. He is no more a pacifist or a neutral than Lincoln himself. Though his eyes are fixed daily on the dreadful cost of his moral and political faith, he remains a passionate and unrelenting Unionist. Like the great captain whom he was to salute as "the sweetest, wisest soul of all my days and lands," he has sunk his personal sensibilities in the larger and more precious life of the nation. Till the war is over he cries with full heart: "Thunder on! stride on, Democracy! Strike with vengeful stroke." In his vision of the indispensable One encompassing the Many he salutes the sacrificial flag with an out-flaming national loyalty incomprehensible to the conscientious objector:

Angry cloth I saw there leaping!
I stand again in leaden rain your flapping folds
    saluting,
I sing you over all, flying beckoning through the
    fight—O the hard-contested fight!
The cannons ope their rosy-flashing muzzles—the
    hurtled balls scream,
The battle-front forms amid the smoke—the volleys
    pour incessant from the line,
Hark, the ringing word *Charge!* now the tussle and
    the furious maddening yells,
Now the corpses tumble curl'd upon the ground,
Cold, cold in death, for precious life of you,
Angry cloth I saw their leaping.

In the era of reconstruction after the war Whitman reconstructs his individualism in the light of his allegiance to the Union. Musing deeply of "these warlike days and of peace return'd, and the dead that return no more," he hears a phantom with stern visage bidding him chant the poem "that comes from the soul of America, chant me the carol of victory." Brooding once again upon the old mystery, why Lincoln wished to preserve the Union, what justified those rivers of fraternal blood, he bursts into this explanation of the ultimate purpose

of a modern democratic state, and offers it, as will
be noted at the end, to America militant:

I swear I begin to see the meaning of these things,
It is not the earth, it is not America who is great,
It is I who am great or to be great, it is You up
there, or any one,
It is to walk rapidly through civilizations, govern-
ments, theories,
Through poems, pageants, shows, to form indi-
viduals.
Underneath all, individuals,
I swear nothing is good to me now that ignores
individuals,
The American compact is altogether with individ-
uals,
The only government is that which makes minute of
individuals,
The whole theory of the universe is directed un-
erringly to one single individual—namely, to
You
(Mother! with subtle sense severe, with the naked
sword in your hand,
I saw you at last refuse to treat but directly with
individuals.)

There is a definition of purpose which cuts into
Treitschke's cold-blooded assertion that "the individual has no right to regard the State as a means
for attaining his own ambitions in life." And it cuts
with equal keenness into the conception of those
younger international, revolutionary statesmen who,
ignoring individuals, propose to deal with classes,
legislate for one class, and institute world-wide

class-war. But let us admit, also, that it strikes quite as deeply into the pretensions of any class whatsoever, which governing in its own interest, becomes the oppressor and parasite of the body politic. These stalwart American individuals whom Whitman demands in immense numbers as the counterpoise to the levelling State cut all classes to pieces. "The pride and centripetal isolation of a human being in himself," he says in one of his timely pregnant passages, is the check, "whereby Nature restrains the deadly original relentlessness of all her first-class laws."

There is no reconciliation of this haughty individualism with his haughty nationalism possible except through faith—faith to believe that the American type of democratic government is the form best adapted to the production of the largest possible number of great and happy individuals. Rise to that faith, and you find within reach a principle of reconciliation between your proud nationalism, and that profound and sacred instinct in you which impels you to join hands with men and women who live under other flags yet belong to the same great civil society. Keep your eyes fixed on the true goal of national life and you may keep your national loyalty even in a league of nations. You may say in all honesty and with the full ardor of patriotic exaltation: "O America, because you build for mankind, I build for you."

Whitman is not the altogether intoxicated believer in democracy that he is usually made out to be. We may as well embrace this faith, such is the entirely sober argument of "Democratic Vistas," because the experiment is going to be tried, whether we like it or not. The deep currents of the times set that way: "Whatever may be said in the way of abstract argument, for or against the theory of a wider democratizing of institutions in any civilized country, much trouble might well be saved to all European lands by recognizing this palpable fact (for a palpable fact it is), that some form of such democratizing is about the only resource now left. *That,* or chronic dissatisfaction continued, mutterings which grow annually louder and louder, till, in due course, and pretty swiftly in most cases, the inevitable crisis, crash, dynastic ruin. Anything worthy to be called statesmanship in the Old World, I should say, among the advanced students, adepts, or men of any brains, does not debate today whether to hold on, attempting to lean back and monarchize, or to look forward and democratize—but *how,* and in what degree and part, most prudently to democratize."

On the occasion of his centenary celebration there was much inconclusive discussion as to whether, had he lived in these days, he would have been a "Bolshevist."

If Whitman had lived at the right place in these years of the Proletarian Millennium, he would have been hanged as a reactionary member of the *bour-*

geoise. First, he distrusts schemes of doctrinaires instituting a new order in sudden and violent contravention of nature, as these lines witness:

Were you looking to be held together by lawyers?
Or argument on paper? or by arms?
Nay, nor the world, nor any living thing, will so
    cohere.

Secondly, he had a realistic scheme of his own for stabilizing democratic society by absorbing the upper and lower economic strata into a renovated and homogeneous middle: "The true gravitation hold of liberalism in the United States will be a more universal ownership of property, general homesteads, general comfort—a vast, intertwining reticulation of wealth. As the human frame, or indeed, any object in this manifold universe, is best kept together by the simple miracle of its own cohesion, and the necessity, exercise and profit thereof, so a great and varied nationality, occupying millions of square miles, were firmest held and knit by the principle of the safety and endurance of the aggregate of its middling property holders. So that, from another point of view, ungracious as it may sound, and a paradox after what we have been saying, democracy looks with suspicious, ill-satisfied eye upon the very poor, the ignorant, and on those out of business. She asks for men and women with occupations, well-off, owners of houses and acres, and with cash in the bank and with some cravings for litera, ture, too; and must have them." A passage by no means devoid of political sagacity.

Thirdly, Whitman is not in the least content as a final term of progress with the material civilization which he expects and demands as the stage following the founding of fundamental institutions and laws. "The fruition of democracy, on aught like a grand scale," he declares with emphasis, "resides altogether in the future." Like most imaginative writers who have striven to present a vast and complex vision, he has been grievously misunderstood. His great songs are songs of faith, winged with anticipative ecstasy, outflying the literal and the humdrum, soaring down that far vista at the end of which a "sublime and serious Religious Democracy" will sternly take command. He has been described as a noisy braggart about himself and his country; but he is complacent with hope, not fulfillment. What he is bragging about is God, that power not ourselves working through man and nature and mysteriously bringing vast designs to pass in spite of all that the almost infinite wickedness and ignorance of man can do to thwart him.

Finally, Whitman would have been hanged by a canny council of workmen because of the germs of a new aristocracy lurking in his "great persons," his powerful free individuals, and pervading, indeed, all that he says or sings. He is a reader of newspapers and passes for a shallow fellow with those who do not also observe that he is a de-

vourer of bibles and epics. He is called a blind
and silly optimist by those who overlook the fact
that he has made a clean breast of more evil in
himself and his countrymen than any other writer
had admitted as existing; and his optimism is said
to depend upon his championship of vulgarity and
mediocrity. It is true that he seems to rely a great
deal upon the "divine average." But, then, his
standards are not so low. He is not such a facile
leveler. His specimen of the average man, what
he means by the average man, is Ulysses Grant, is
Abraham Lincoln. Whitman adores America because she produces such men, and he clamors for
shoals of them—poets, orators, scholars—of the
same bulk and build and aplomb. He will not be
satisfied till he sees a hundred million of such superb
persons, such aristocrats, walking these States. He
is a democrat with an exorbitant thirst for distinction, of heroic mold, elate with a vision of
grandeurs and glories, of majesties and splendors
—like every good democrat with a spark of imagination.

I have set forth some of the main points in Whitman's system of ideas, but I recall his warning: "Do
not attempt to explain me; I cannot explain myself." And certainly his service to us is neither contained nor containable in an argument. He gives
us the sustaining emotion which prevents argument
from falling to pieces of its own dryness. He ful-
fills the promises and justifies the faith of demo-

cratic society in his own characteristic fashion, by being a great individual, by being a great poet. He chiefly serves our society as poets do: "We do not fathom you—we love you." He is a lover himself and the cause of love in others.

How do I know that he is a great poet? Not merely because such judges as Emerson, Tennyson and Swinburne have acknowledged his power. Not because he has achieved a wide international reputation and translations into French, Dutch, Danish, German, Italian, Russian and Spanish. The great court of glory has pronounced unmistakeably in his favor; and this award fortifies, to be sure, the individual judgment. But there is another very simple test, which for some reason or other, is seldom applied to our contemporary verse. What is the purpose and the effect of great poetry—of Homer, *The Psalms, Beowulf,* the *Song of Roland,* the *Divine Comedy, Richard III, Paradise Lost?* It is to raise man in the midst of his common life above the level of his ordinary emotion by filling him with a sentiment of his importance as a moral being and of the greatness of his destiny. Does Whitman's poetry accomplish that end? It does, and it will continue to do so with increases of power as the depth and sweep of his book, its responses to a wide range of need, become familiar in the sort of daily exploration through a number of years, in dull times and crucial, which such a book can repay.

It is ungracious to say that one can measure the magnitude of Whitman by comparing him with his successors in the free verse movement; yet a word of comparison is almost unavoidable. The way to get at the matter is to ask, for example, whether the *Spoon River Anthology* of Mr. Masters fills one with a sentiment of one's importance as a moral being and of the greatness of one's destiny. Does there not fall over most of the figures in our late poetic renaissance "the shadow of great events from which they have shrunk?" Whitman still towers above his American successors as Pike's Peak towers above its foothills; and not merely by the height of his great argument and the lift of his passion but also—though they surpass him in small subtleties and superficial finish—by the main mastery of his instrument, the marshalling of his phrases, the production of the poetic hypnosis, and the accent and winning freshness of his voice. I have spoken of his theme and the larger aspects of his emotion, and have not space to exhibit his surging cumulative effects:

"Here the doings of men correspond with the broadcast doings of the day and night,
Here is what moves in magnificent masses careless
of particulars.

But I should like to leave in a few lines a taste of the quality of his voice, responding first to simple rapture in the common loveliness of the natural world. Most of us ordinary people feel it when we are young and happy, but in Whitman it is a perennial incitement to benediction. No other American poet communicates so abundantly the sheer joy of living:

Beginning my studies the first step pleas'd me so
    much,
The mere fact consciousness, these forms, the power
    of motion,
The least insect or animal, the senses, eyesight, love,
The first step I say awed me and pleas'd me so much,
I have hardly gone and hardly wish'd to go any
    farther,
But stop and loiter all the time to sing it in ecstatic
    songs.

Add this impression of a prairie sunset:

Pure luminous color fighting the silent shadows to
    the last.

And that exquisite line:

I am he that walks with the tender and growing
    night.

Then for his note in compassion, read "Reconciliation," remembering that here is no feigned emotion, but the very spirit of the man bending above some Rebel soldier in the old Washington days—the bearded angel of spiritual Reconstruction:

Word over all, beautiful as the sky,
Beautiful that war and all its deeds of carnage must
in time be utterly lost,
That the hands of the sisters Death and Night in-
cessantly softly wash again and ever again,
this soil'd world;
For my enemy is dead, a man divine as myself is
dead,
I look where he lies white-faced and still in the
coffin—I draw near,
Bend down and touch lightly with my lips the white
face in the coffin.

Or read "A Sight in Camp in the Daybreak Gray
and Dim," another picture of the dead soldier, ending with a swift mystical vision of his transfiguration
by the love which passes understanding:

I think this face is the face of the Christ himself,
Dead and divine and brother of all, and here again
he lies.

There is more of the high pity and terror of war,
more of the valor and tenderness that come straight
from the magnanimous heart, in Whitman's battle
chants and dirges than in all our other war poetry
put together.

"In Homer and Shakespere," says Whitman truly,
one will find a "certain heroic ecstasy, which, or the
suggestion of which, is never absent in the works of
the masters." That heroic ecstacy is present in
Whitman himself. There is not a page of him in

which he does not impart it. The continuous miracle is that he manages to impart it with only a line here and there in the familiar grand style of the masters, and these remain, one suspects, by his inadvertence as in his salutation to a tawny headed warrior:

Now ending well in death the splendid fever of
        thy deeds,
        .   .   .   .

Leaving behind thee a memory sweet to soldiers,
Thou yieldest up thyself.

These are lines that the old masters would recognize as in their style; but the heroic ecstasy lives too in the new style of his own:

Fall behind me States!
A man before all—myself, typical, before all,
Give me the pay I have served for,
Give me to sing of the great Idea, take all the rest.

Or consider his salute: "To Him That Was Crucified":

My spirit to yours dear brother,
Do not mind because many sounding your name
        do not understand you,
I do not sound your name, but I understand you.

In nothing does a man measure himself more decisively than in his judgment of other men. Whitman has an instinct and talent for recognizing the heroic in literature, in history, among his own contemporaries. He recognizes it in Christ, in Lincoln, in the nameless crumpled corpse amid the debris of battle; and he responds to it with the adoration of a kindred spirit. This is a decisive test of his quality. This instinct keeps him near the central stream of our national life, an unperturbed and reassuring pilot in misty weather. In recognition of this virtue in him I choose for my last word this line of his:

The years straying toward infidelity he withholds by his steady faith.

VII

JOAQUIN MILLER: POETICAL CONQUISTADOR OF THE WEST

Joaquin Miller was a picturesque figure on the American scene for more than forty years. The romantic life which he had conceived and which he had, in considerable measure, enacted, he recorded in both verse and prose, with due regard for the attention of posterity. Though much of his work is a genuine conquest, he wrote too easily and he wrote too much. In the summer of 1921, only eight years after his death, though occasional curious pilgrims visited his home, The Hights, above San Francisco Bay, and carried off a stone from his monument to Moses, the Law-Giver, booksellers of a dozen shops in the cities that fringe the bay looked up with surprise when one inquired for a copy of his works, and replied that they had none. It is not strange that popular interest refuses to float a six-volume edition of Miller. But our literature is not so rich in distinctive national types that we can afford to let this poetical pioneer fade, as he is now in danger of fading, into a colorless shadow like the once famous scouts that accompanied Fremont into the West.

He is, to be sure, difficult to fix for an adequate portrait, because in his time he played several parts; and he himself was never quite sure in which of his various costumes and poses he would most adorn the national gallery. An emigrant from the Middle Border, a gold-hunter of the Far West, an Indian fighter, a frontier judge, he first rose above the horizon, in 1871, with assistance and cheers from England, as the long-haired, top-booted "poet of the Sierras." Even at the outset of his career, he was not quite satisfied with that rôle. His own early aspiration was rather to be known as "the American Byron;" and, in keeping with that high calling, he shook off the dust of his native land, wandered for a time in "exile," and bore through Italy and the Aegean Isles the pageant of his bleeding heart. Following his personal contact with the Pre-Raphaelites in London, this impressionable mountaineer of the new world discipled himself for a brief period in the early 'seventies to Swinburne and the Rossettis, was intensely "æsthetic," and contemplated devoting himself to the Orient. Returning to America about 1875, he made through his middle years numerous ventures in prose fiction and drama, ranging all the way from the Forty-Niners and the Indians of the Pacific slope to fast life in New York and to the more or less autobiographical affairs of the artist Alphonso Murietta in Italy (*The One Fair Woman*). In what we may call his final period, after his return to California in the middle 'eighties, there grew strong in him a sense that he was the leader of a native poetical movement, a spiritual seer with Messianic or at least prophetic mission, and in the flowing hair and beard of his last years, stalking majestically under the trees which he had planted by his monuments on The Hights, and gazing dreamily out over the Pacific, he looked the part.

Now, whatever one may think of Miller's actual contribution to poetry or to prose fiction, this evolution of an Indian fighter into the Moses of the Golden Gate is an extraordinary phenomenon. Considered merely as a detached individual, he is abundantly interesting to the biographer. But he repays sympathetic curiosity most generously perhaps when one regards and studies him as a register of the power exerted upon the individual by the American environment and the national culture, even at their thinnest and crudest. To study him in this fashion, the first requisite is a more coherent account of his career than has hitherto been available. Joaquin Miller was his own principal hero, but by a singular fatality his adventures have never been adequately written. Certain scenes and events he himself sketched repeatedly; but concerning many passages of his history he was extremely reticent. What is more serious, he had no steady narrative power.

Lifelong an adventurous rover, in love with action, he finds it next to impossible to stick to the thread of his story. As soon as he grasps the pen, he overflows with sentiment and moralization, and he riots in description. Consequently his longer poems frequently produce the effect of panorama, and the feeling which they present remains obscure till the shifting pictures are connected and explained by the events of his own life.

To the student of American culture, the case of Joaquin Miller is the more valuable from the fact that he did not—like Bret Harte, for example—put on the frontier as a literary garment, after an eastern upbringing. By birth and ancestry he belonged in the great migration which settled the Middle Border and the Far West. He was born in 1841, in a covered wagon, "at or about the time it crossed the line dividing Indiana from Ohio." His mother, Margaret Witt, of Dutch stock from North Carolina, and his father, Hulings Miller, of Scotch stock from Kentucky, were married in Indiana; and after some oscillation between Indiana and Ohio, gravitated slowly westward for a decade through the Miami Reservation and up along the banks of the Wabash and the Tippecanoe rivers, before they heard a clear call to follow the overland trail to the coast. Meanwhile they made various cabin homes for their young family. The mother cooked and sewed and wove and spun. The father worked his little clearings, failed as storekeeper, served as magistrate, and kept school for the children of the wilderness. It was a rough life, but every reference of Miller to his childhood indicates that it was in many respects a good and happy life; and every reference to his parents is marked by a tenderness without condescension. These simple people were impecunious, restless, and not very shrewd—rather sentimental and visionary. But they were honest and pious, with the pacificism of the Quaker discipline and the abolitionism of Horace Greely; they were loyal to one another and gentle and affectionate in all the family relationships; they were kindly in their intercourse with the Indians of the Reservation; and they were hospitable with their meager shelter to wanderers less fortunately circumstanced. Most of the parents' traits ultimately reappeared in the son, from their hospitality to their turn for roving.

The migratory influences from his immediate family were re-enforced by the spirit of the age. The Millers were not alone in finding it difficult to "settle down" in the eighteen-forties. It was an expansive and exploratory epoch in both the physical and the intellectual senses. The East was in a philosophical and social ferment. Descendants of the Puritans, corporeally resident in Concord, were extending their mental frontiers to Greece and India, and in 1841 Emerson published the first series of his essays, "striking up" for a new world. It is not clear that these expansive utterances promptly reached the Indiana settlement. But between 1842 and 1844 Fremont started a movement which was the material complement of Transcendentalism by his series of bold expeditions to the Rocky Mountains, Oregon, and California. Fremont's account of these explorations Hulings Miller borrowed from an Indian agent and read in the evenings to his assembled family. "I was never so fascinated," says Joaquin, "I never grew so fast in my life. Every scene and circumstance in the narrative was painted in my mind to last, and to last forever." The hide of the "woolly white horse" celebrated in Fremont's presidential campaign is exhibited to this day in Miller's home in California; and it may be mentioned here that Fremont's guide, the hunter and Indian fighter Kit Carson, is the hero of one of Miller's most readable poems. In 1845 Texas was admitted to the Union, and Sam Houston, another of the poet's western heroes, was elected to the United States Senate. At about this time the Mormons, whom he was to commemorate in *The Danites,* were drifting westward through Illinois and Missouri; and in 1847 Brigham Young led the faithful into the valley of the Great Salt Lake. In 1849 the cry—"Gold is discovered in California!"—ran like prairie fire among our middle-borderers, and doubled the attraction of the full section of land offered to each settler in Oregon, in a bill introduced by Senator Linn of Missouri. By 1850, still another of Miller's heroes, the enigmatic William Walker, was in California, soon to be preparing his filibustering excursions into Mexico and Nicaragua. To add the last attraction, General Joe Lane, once a pupil of Hulings Miller in the sugar camps of Indiana, had been appointed Governor of Oregon.

The multiplied appeals of the Far West had become irresistible. As soon as they could equip themselves for the journey, three years after the discovery of gold, the Millers started for the promised land. With a presentiment on his father's part that it would some day be a pleasure to go over the record, Joaquin, then in his eleventh year, kept a journal of the great expedition. Though this unfortunately was lost, the poetic residuum of his impressions is preserved in "Exodus for Oregon" and "The Ship In The Desert." As he recalled their adventure many years later, they set out in wagons on the seventeenth of March, 1852; in May, they crossed the Missouri above St. Joe, where they found the banks for miles crowded with tents of the emigrants; followed the Platte River; threaded Fremont's South Pass over the Rockies; rested at Salt Lake City; skirmished with the Indians in the desert; descended to the head waters of the Snake River; crossed the Cascade Mountains at The Dalles; and, after seven months and five days, ended their march of three thousand miles in Oregon, near the middle of the Willamette Valley— "the most poetic, gorgeous and glorious valley in flowers and snow-covered mountains on the globe."

Miller's enthusiasm for the scenery of Oregon is only equalled by his enthusiasm for the new settlers. "The vast multitude," he declares, that fought their way across the plains in the face of cholera, hostile Indians, famine, and drouth, "was, as a rule, religious, and buried their dead with hymns and prayers, all along the dreary half year's journey on which no coward ever ventured, and where the weak fell by the wayside, leaving a natural selection of good and great people, both in soul and body."

It was about two years after the establishment of the Millers in Oregon that Joaquin's independent adventures began. They had cultivated a little land, bought a few cows and sheep and hens, and were running a tavern in a small way. The father and elder brother were now absent teaching school, and Joaquin and his younger brother Jimmy were left with their mother to look after the place. Stories brought up from the mining camps of California by pedlars and itinerant preachers had for some time been making him restless; and it had been conceded, he says, that he was ultimately to be allowed to seek his fortune in the wicked and dangerous territory to the southward. In his fourteenth year, anticipating the parental consent, he ran away, and joining a party of miners who were opening a placer claim in a wooded gulch by the Klamath River, just below the border between Oregon and California, he offered his services as cook and dishwasher. Here began his more intimate acquaintance with the tougher and more miscellaneous element of the western population which was streaming through the Golden Gate—the Australians, the European adventurers, the Mexicans, the Chinese, and questionable wanderers from eastern cities. And here, if his memory is to be trusted, he wrote his first song, in celebration of an adjutant cook's marriage to a woman from Australia.

Joaquin was at this time small for his age, slender, pale, frail-looking, with hair of the color of "hammered gold," reaching to his shoulders. The camp diet of bacon and beans did not agree with him and his first mining experience was terminated by a serious attack of scurvy. He was nursed back to health in Yreka by Dr. Ream and a "kind little Chinaman;" and then was taken by a mysterious stranger to another camp for the winter by the forks of several little streams which flow into the Klamath River from the north of Mt. Shasta. Here, at a later period, he laid the scene of *The Danites*—"my famous play but have always been sorry I printed it, as it is unfair to the Mormons and the Chinese." The tall stranger with whom he spent the winter is another of his heroes whom at this time he seems to have regarded with unqualified adoration. He figures so largely and mysteriously in his work that he requires identification. In the introduction to the collected poems he is described merely as "the Prince," and is said to have gone "south," in the spring of 1855. But in the *Life Among the Modocs,* 1873, he is represented as a very handsome and romantic professional gambler of great courage and chivalrous nature who was generally understood to be a prince, but who, after fighting with Walker in Nicaragua, acknowledged himself to be only plain James Thompson, an American. In 1876, Miller dedicated his *First Fam'lies Of The Sierras* as follows: "To my old companion in arms, Prince Jamie Tomas, of Leon, Nicaragua." But that this "Prince Jamie Tomas" was the James Thompson of *"Life Among The Modocs* and the mysterious stranger of the autobiographical sketch is made clear at last by a footnote to the poem called "Thomas of Tigre," in the fourth volume of the *Bear* Edition.

After the departure of "the Prince," the most influential friend of the strange boyhood days on Mt. Shasta was another mysterious figure, Joseph De Bloney, whom Miller met in the spring of 1855. In an apparently serious sketch of him, included in *Memorie and Rime,* De Bloney is described as "a Californian John Brown in a small way." According to this account, he was of an old noble Swiss family, and had probably crossed the plains with Fremont under an impulse similar to that which animated Brigham Young in Utah and Walker in Nicaragua—an impulse to found a new state. "His ambition was to unite the Indians about the base of Mt. Shasta and establish a sort of Indian republic, the prime and principal object of which was to set these Indians entirely apart from the approach of the white man, draw an impassable line, in fact, behind which the Indian would be secure in his lands, his simple life, his integrity, and his purity. . . . It was a hard undertaking at best, perilous, almost as much as a man's life was worth to befriend an Indian in those stormy days on the border, when every gold-hunter . . . counted it his privilege, if not his duty to shoot an Indian on sight. An Indian sympathizer was more hated in those days, is still, than ever was an abolitionist. . . . De Bloney gradually gathered about twenty-five men around him in the mountains, took up homes, situated his men around him, planted, dug gold, did what he could to civilize the people and subdue the savages. . . . But he had tough elements to deal with. The most savage men were the white men. The Indians, the friendly ones, were the tamest of his people. These white men would come and go; now they would marry the Indian women and now join a prospecting party and disappear for months, even years. At one time nearly all went off to join Walker in Nicaragua."

Under the influence of this odd character, young Joaquin seems for the time to have forgotten the Oregon homestead, and to have embraced the dream of a little Indian republic on Mt. Shasta. Between 1855 and 1859 he represents himself as living in the shadow of the mountains with De Bloney and the Indians and "Indian Joe," a scout and horsetrader of German birth, who had been with Fremont, and who furnished Miller some of the materials for his poems. He was also on intimate terms with the Indian Chief Blackbeard, who, he remarks in *Memorie and Rime,* had a very beautiful daughter, and gave him a "beautiful little valley," where he built a cabin, and "first began to write." According to *Life Among the Modocs,* a romance with an auto-biographical core, he married the chief's daughter and became eventually the leader in the movement to unite the tribes in an Indian republic. These stories of his Indian bride and of his fighting de-fiance of the white men seem rather more plausible when one forgets that he was but fourteen when he remarked the beauty of the girl and only seventeen when he assumed the responsibilities for which, ac-cording to *Memorie and Rime,* De Bloney's grow-ing inebriety disqualified him.

Viewed from within by a romantic poet, this colony of adventurers and Indians was a noble en-terprise for the preservation of an oppressed race; viewed from without it probably seemed more like a nest of horse-thieves. Its importance for Miller was partly in its development of his romantic sym-pathy with the outlaw. In a paper on "How I Came To Be A Writer Of Books," contributed to *Lippincott's* in 1886, he illustrates this point, and, at the same time, explains the origin of his pen-name "Joaquin." His parents had called him Cincin-natus Heine (or Hiner); but, during his sojourn on

Mt. Shasta, his friends had already begun to employ the more familiar name. According to this account, he had made several trips with Mexican horse and mule drivers down into Arizona and northern Mexico, and, on these expeditions, "these Mexicans were most kind to me." They, on the contrary, were treated by the Anglo-Saxon conquerors of California with a brutality which was "monstrous." "It was this," says Miller, "that had driven Joaquin Murietta, while yet a youth, to become the most terrible and bloody outlaw our land has ever known. A reward of many thousands had been offered for his head, he had been captured, killed, and his head was in spirits and on exhibition in San Francisco,[1] when I took up my pen for the first time and wrote a public letter in defence of the Mexicans." In consequence of this letter, he was banteringly identified by a Sacramento paper with the bandit. His friends continued the banter. The name was revived when he returned to Oregon, and was employed to twit him, when he became an editor. And so he finally accepted it and used it in the title of his first book.

In the chapter of his relations with the Indians, there are manifold obscurities and contradictions. He adhered pretty consistently throughout his life to the assertion that he was in three Indian battles

---

[1] In spite of this capital evidence, Miller elsewhere raises a doubt whether Joaquin Murietta had actually been killed, and plays with the notion that he himself may have been the original "Joaquin."

or campaigns, the Battle of Castle Rocks, the "Pit River War," and a later campaign in Oregon. But according to one set of stories he figures as a renegade fighting with the Indians against the whites; while according to the other set of stories he is fighting with the whites against the Indians. The chief sources of the renegade story are *Life Amongst the Modocs* and *Memorie and Rime;* but he still calls himself a renegade in the introduction to the *Bear* Edition. On the other hand, there is in existance among the papers preserved by the Miller family a petition to the government for damages, drawn up by Miller but never presented, in which he represents himself as the victim of Indian depredations; and in his annotations of the poem "Old Gib At Castle Rocks," he establishes by a sworn affidavit that this first battle was *against* the "Modocs and Other Renegades," and that his wound in the head was received while he was fighting at Judge Gibson's side. In *Memorie and Rime,* however, he declares that the Battle of Castle Rocks was fought under the leadership of De Bloney, to punish unfriendly Indians for burning his camp. But in the introduction to the *Bear* Edition, he says nothing of De Bloney; the leader of Miller's party is there represented as Mountain Joe, who in the battle unites forces with Judge Gibson, the *alcalde* of the district.

The disparities in his various accounts may be explained in three ways. First, Miller did in his poems and prose narratives deliberately adulterate his facts with imaginary elements in the interest of romance, and like his early model Lord Byron, he enjoyed and encouraged identification of himself with all his hard-riding, hard-fighting, and amorous heroes. Secondly, he tells us that as a result of his arrow wound in the head and neck at the Battle of Castle Rocks, "on the 15th day of June, 1855," he lost his memory for months, was "nearly a year" in recovering, and was somewhat feeble minded for some time after. Thirdly, if he ever actually became a renegade and participated in outlaw raids, when he returned to civilization, he indulged in wise "lapses of memory."

With a consciousness, then, that we are treading the uncertain border between fact and fiction, we pull the arrow from Joaquin's neck in the summer of 1855, and commit him to the care of an Indian woman, who treats him as her son. Late in the fall, restored at last to his senses and beginning to recover his strength, he teaches school in a mining camp near Shasta City at night and tries to mine by day—rather strenuous activities for a feeble-minded convalescent! But in the following spring, 1856, he again joins the red men on the mountain. "When the Modocs rose up one night and massacred eighteen men, every man in Pitt River Valley, I alone was spared"—thus runs the introduction to the *Bear* Edition—"and spared only because I was *Los bobo*, the fool. Then more battles and two more wounds. My mind was as the mind of a child and my memory is uncertain here." But according to *Memorie and Rime,* news of the Pitt River massacre came to Joaquin in the spring of 1857, when he was encamped on the spurs of Mt. Shasta, *"sixty miles distant;"* so that it must have been in a later stage of the "war" that he got his "bullet through the right arm." Had he complicity in the massacre? He raises the question. He says that he knew in advance that it had been planned, and he sympathized with its perpetrators years later. Following it, he made an expedition to Shasta City for ammunition to arm De Bloney's Indians "against the brutal and aggressive white men"; had a horse shot under him by the pursuing whites, stole another horse, was overtaken, threatened with hanging, lodged in Shasta City jail, "and my part in the wild attempt to found an Indian republic was rewarded with a prompt indictment for stealing horses." This, he says, was in 1859. After long confinement, he was delivered from jail by the Indians on the night of the 4th of July, thrown upon a horse, "and such a ride for freedom and fresh air was never seen before." (See *Memorie and Rime,* pp. 234–235; *Life Amongst the Modocs,* chap. xxx, and *The Tale of the Tall Alcalde.*)

Miller hints, in *Memorie and Rime,* at one more disastrous attempt to carry out De Bloney's plan for the republic, followed by separation from his leader, and flight to Washington Territory. But in the introduction to the *Bear* Edition, he interposes at this point in his career, though without dates and vaguely and briefly, his connection with the filibuster William Walker. "I, being a renegade," he says, "descended to San Francisco and set sail for Boston, but stopped at Nicaragua with Walker." In his poem "With Walker in Nicaragua," he represents himself as riding side by side with the filibuster in his campaigns and as treated by him like a son; and he always encouraged the common belief that his poem had a substantial autobiographical core. There is a good deal of evidence for concluding that it had none. Walker sailed from San Francisco in May and landed in Nicaragua on June 16, 1855. On the previous day, Miller was wounded at Castle Rocks, in northern California. In May, 1857, Walker left Nicaragua and was a paroled prisoner in the United States till August, 1860, when he landed in Honduras, where he was executed on the 12th of September in the same year. Miller later associated himself with his hero by publishing the last words of Walker, obtained from the priest who attended the execution; but Miller says in his notes on the poem in the *Bear* Edition: "I was not with him on this last expedition." Of course the intended implication is that he *was* with Walker on a previous expedition. Recruits from California sailed down to join the filibuster at frequent intervals, it is true, and Miller may conceivably have visited Nicaragua with one of these parties; but if any credit is to be given to his Indian stories, he was recovering from his Castle Rocks wound from June, 1855, till the spring of 1856, when he joined the red men on the mountains; he spends the winter on the spurs of Mt. Shasta, and in the spring of 1857 he becomes implicated in the Pitt River Valley War, in which he is again seriously wounded; and his connections with this affair are not terminated till 1859. He might then have set out in time to join Walker's fatal expedition in Honduras; but he tells us that he did not. Walker, in his account of *The War in Nicaragua*, published in 1860, nowhere mentions the boy whom he is alleged to have fathered. One's final impression is that the poem is fiction, colored by the tales and published narratives of the filibusters and perhaps by Miller's subsequent acquaintance with Central America. And this impression is strengthened by Miller's reply to one who asked him point blank whether he was ever with Walker in Nicaragua: "Was Milton ever in Hell?" [2]

The fiasco of De Bloney's and Joaquin's Mt. Shasta "republic" fell, according to the legend, in the year of John Brown's raid at Harper's Ferry, and two years after the ejection of Walker from Nicaragua. In Miller's mind these three curious attempts to escape from the jurisdiction of the United States became closely associated memories

---

[2] For this anecdote I am indebted to Mrs. Miller.

of forlorn hopes, with a singular appeal to his imagination. Writing at Harper's Ferry in 1883 (*Memorie and Rime*, 228 *ff.*), he gives this account of his movements and sentiments following his alleged connection with Walker and De Bloney: "I made my way to Washington Territory, sold my pistols, and settled down on the banks of the Columbia, near Lewis River, and taught school. And here it was that the story of John Brown, his raid, his fight, his capture, and his execution, all came to me. Do you wonder that my heart went out to him and remained with him? I, too, had been in jail. Death and disgrace were on my track, and might find me any day hiding there under the trees in the hearts of the happy children. And so, sympathizing, I told these children over and over again the story of old John Brown there."

From 1860 to 1870, Miller was chiefly an Oregonian, though he made many excursions from his base. We shall have to notice one more interesting inconsistency which casts a suspicion over his account of his life with the Indians. In the introduction to the *Bear* Edition, he says in his baffling summary fashion, without dates, that on his return from being "with Walker," he "went home, went to college some, taught school some, studied law at home some." Now, in a note to the *Bear* Edition (vol. ii, p. 185), he speaks of teaching school in 1858 below Fort Vancouver, "during vacation at Columbia College, the forerunner of the Oregon

University"; and, in another note (vol. i, p. 170),
he says that he wrote "the valedictory class poem"
for Columbia College in 1859. It thus appears that
his attendance at "Columbia College" falls in the
period when, according to his other stories, he was
engaged in his last desperate efforts to establish De
Bloney's "Mt. Shasta republic"; and that his valedictory poem was apparently delivered in the year
in which he fled from Californian justice to hide in
Washington Territory.

If one thinks of Miller as having taken a regular
college course ending in 1859, then one must be
prepared to dismiss most of the Mt. Shasta stories
as mythical; and doubtless there is a large element
of fiction in them. They are not, however, quite
so inconsistent with the "college" course as at first
sight they appear. Eugene City, in which the "college" was located, was not settled till 1854; and
the institution, with its "pleasant campus," in which
the poem was perhaps delivered five years later, was
nothing more than a small-town high school or
seminary. And Miller, returning from California
in 1858, or even as late as 1859, might, after a very
brief instruction, have appeared as class poet in
1859. It is, moreover, unfortunately necessary to
regard the statements about his own life made towards the close of his literary career with almost
as much skepticism as those which he made near its
outset—and for an interesting reason. In his last
period, as the seer on The Hights, Miller desired

to be regarded as an authoritative man of letters; consequently he minimized his frontier upbringing and magnified his education and general culture. Furthermore, he ultimately desired to be regarded as devoutly American and as intensely pacifistic; consequently he touched very lightly in later years the period when he was a secessionist, he skilfully hinted here and there that the stories of his outlawry were mythical, and he worked over his poems, making great excisions and adding new passages, with the purpose of harmonizing them with his declaration that he would rather starve than be celebrated as the poetic glorifier of war.[3]   This was obviously a difficult task in the case of the bloody and imperialistic career of Walker.

In the summer of 1861 Miller began other interesting adventures which are better attested.   At this time he was riding Mossman and Miller's pony express, carrying letters and gold dust between Walla

---

[3] " 'The Tale of the Alcalde,' he says in his note in the *Bear* edition, "has been a fat source of feeding for grimly humorous and sensational writers, who long ago claimed to have found in it the story of my early life; and, strangely enough, I was glad when they did so, and read their stories with wild delight.   I don't know why I always encouraged this idea of having been an outlaw, but I recall that when Trelawny told me that Byron was more ambitious to be thought the hero of his wildest poems than even to be King of Greece, I could not help saying to myself, as Napoleon said to the thunders preceding Waterloo, 'We are of accord.' The only serious trouble about the claim that I made the fight of life up the ugly steeps from a hole in an adobe prison wall to the foothills of Olympus, instead of over the pleasant campus of a college, is the fact that 'our friends the enemy' fixed the date at about the same time in which I am on record as reading my class poem in another land."

Walla, Washington, and the newly opened mines
at Millersburg, in Idaho. Attracted by certain contributions of "Minnie Myrtle" appearing in the
newspapers of his pack, he wrote to her and had
replies. His mining ventures yielded him enough to
enable him to build "a beautiful new home" for his
parents, and also to buy a newspaper. In 1863 he
began to edit *The Democratic Register* in Eugene,
Oregon, and he avowed southern sympathies which
aroused the community. Though he had been
brought up an ardent abolitionist and his elder
brother John had entered the Northern army, he
himself had imbibed, in his "college," which was
tainted with disloyalty, or from the friends of Walker, who was a pro-slavery man, or elsewhere—he
had imbibed principles and sentiments obnoxious to
the aroused Unionist spirit of Oregon. As he explained it in *Memorie and Rime,* "when the war
came, and the armies went down desolating the
South, then with that fatality that has always followed me for getting on the wrong side, siding with
the weak, I forgot my pity for the one in my larger
pity for the other."

His entrance into journalism brought him again
to the attention of his unknown correspondent,
"Minnie Myrtle," who was then living in a mining
and lumber camp at Port Orford by the sea, not far
from the southern boundary of Oregon. Twenty
years later, when this lady died in New York, in
May, 1883, Miller told in his own fashion the story

of his brief unhappy relations with her. Since they
made a turning point in his career and introduced
into his poetry additional "Byronic" notes, let us
have an abridgement of his own version of the affair
as set forth in *Memorie and Rime:*

When I came down from the mountains and em-
barked in journalism, she wrote to me, and her
letters grew ardent and full of affection. Then I
mounted my horse and rode hundreds of miles
through the valleys and over the mountains, till I
came to the sea, at Port Orford, then a flourishing
mining town, and there first saw "Minnie Myrtle."
Tall, dark, and striking in every respect, . . . this
first Saxon woman I had ever addressed had it all
her own way at once. She knew nothing at all of
my life, except that I was an expressman and country editor. I knew nothing at all of hers, but I
found her with kind, good parents, surrounded by
brothers and sisters, and the pet and spoiled child
of the mining and lumber camp. . . . The heart of
the bright and merry girl was brimming full of romance, hope, and happiness. I arrived on Thurs-
day. On Sunday next we were married! Oh, to
what else but ruin and regret could such romantic
folly lead?

"Procuring a horse for her"—for she, too, was
an excellent and daring rider—"we set out at once
to return to my post, far away over the mountains."
After a week's ride, the bridal couple reached their
intended home in Eugene, "but only to find that my
paper had been suppressed by the Government, and
we resolved to seek our fortunes in San Francisco.

But we found neither fortune nor friends in that great city." In 1863 Mrs. Fremont was there, and Charles Warren Stoddard, and Prentice Mulford, and Ina Coolbrith. Bret Harte was writing for *The Golden Era*. The nucleus was already formed of the literary group which Mark Twain joined in 1864, and which launched *The Californian* and *The Overland Monthly*. Whether at this time Miller made any attempt to break into the "western school" does not appear. If he did so, we can understand his failure. He was still a very immature writer, though Stoddard records that he did contribute to *The Golden Era*, "from the backwood depths of his youthful obscurity." But coming as he did in the midst of the Civil War to the outskirts of a group animated by Bret Harte, then engaged in writing strongly patriotic verse and prose, the editor of a paper which had just been suppressed for disloyalty could hardly have expected a very cordial reception.

One is tempted to conjecture that Miller's failure to establish a literary or journalistic connection in the city may perhaps have dashed a little the spirits of his bride. At any rate, he says that even while they were living in San Francisco, she had presentiments of "wreck and storm and separation for us." If thwarted aspiration for more literary and social life than she had enjoyed in the lumber camp had stimulated these presentiments, they must have been strengthened when Joaquin bought a band of cattle and journeyed with his wife and baby to a new mining camp at Canyon City, in eastern Oregon. As for him, it was the life to which he had always been accustomed, and he threw himself into the task of establishing himself with unwonted application of his restless energy. He practised law among the miners, he planted the first orchard in the land, he led in his third Indian campaign; he was rewarded in 1866 by election, for a four-year term, as judge of the Grant County court, and finally, he had begun to occupy himself seriously with poetry. In 1868 he published a pamphlet of *Specimens,* and in 1869, at Portland, Oregon, his first book: *"Joaquin, Et Al.,* by Cincinnatus H. Miller"—dedicated "To Maud." [4]

Ambition and a multitude of business, as he depicted the matter, made him not the most genial of companions:

Often I never left my office till the gray dawn, after a day of toil and a night of study. My health gave way and I was indeed old and thoughtful. Well, all this, you can see, did not suit the merry-hearted and spoiled child of the mines at all. . . . She became the spoiled child here that she had been at her father's, and naturally grew impatient at my persistent toil and study. But she was good all the time. . . . Let me say here, once for all, that no man or woman can put a finger on any stain in this

[4] The contents were: "Joaquin," "Is It Worth While?" "Zanara," "In Exile," "To the Bards of S. F. Bay," "Merinda," "Nepenthe," "Under the Oaks," "Dirge," "Vale," "Benoni," and "Ultime."

woman's whole record of life, so far as truth and purity go. But she was not happy here. Impatient of the dull monotony of the exhausted mining camp, . . . she took her two children and returned to her mother, while I sold the little home, . . . promising to follow her, yet full of ambition now to be elected to a place on the Supreme Bench of the State. . . . She had been absent from me quite a year, when . . . I went to Portland, seeking the nomination for the place I desired. But the poor impatient lady, impulsive as always, and angry that I had kept so long away, had forwarded papers from her home, hundreds of miles remote, to a lawyer here, praying for a divorce. This so put me to shame that I abandoned my plans and resolved to hide my head in Europe.

To "hide" his head was hardly the prime object of Miller's first trip abroad, nor, except by a wide poetic license, can the phrase be used to describe his activities there. His object was more candidly presented in a line of his Byronic "Ultime," the last poem of the little volume, *Joaquin, Et Al.*, published in Portland in 1869—a poem written as if in premonition of death:

It was my boy ambition to be read beyond the brine.

As soon as *Joaquin, Et Al.* was published, what Miller burned for was literary recognition impossible on the Oregon frontier. In March of 1869, he wrote from Portland to Charles Warren Stoddard to solicit his interest in getting the book ade-

quately noticed in *The Overland Monthly,* which
had been launched two months before. Stoddard
was absent in Hawaii; but in January, 1870, Bret
Harte gave *Joaquin* a humorous but not unfriendly
salute in the new magazine: "We find in *'Joaquin,
Et Al.'* the true poetic instinct, with a natural felicity of diction and a dramatic vigour that are good
in performance and yet better in promise. Of
course, Mr. Miller is not entirely easy in harness,
but is given to pawing and curvetting; and at such
times his neck is generally clothed with thunder and
the glory of his nostrils is terrible."

Following this recognition from the leading literary periodical of the Far West, Miller came
down from Oregon to embrace the bards of San
Francisco Bay—so romantically addressed by him
in *Joaquin, Et Al.*—came to embrace them and to
be embraced by them—"clad," says Stoddard, who
had now returned from Hawaii, "in a pair of
beaded moccasins, a linen 'duster' that fell nearly
to his heels, and a broad-brimmed *sombrero."*
Fresh, breezy, ingenuous, Miller exclaimed at once,
"Well, let us go and talk with the poets." Stoddard
took him around to call upon Bret Harte, and presented him also to the most lyrical third of their
trinity, the local Sappho, Ina Coolbrith, who was
at once impressive and sympathetic. But on the
whole, literary glory at the Golden Gate was paler
than his expectations—"he had been somewhat
chilled by his reception in the metropolis." Had

he really desired to hide his head, he might have accepted Stoddard's invitation to flee away with him to the South Seas. Instead of doing so, Miller accepted a wreath of laurel from Ina Coolbrith, to lay on the tomb of Byron, and, in midsummer of 1870, "started for England in search of fame and fortune."

One dwells upon this first return to the old world, because now one sees for the first time adequately manifested the literary sensibility and the imaginative yearning which for years had been secretly growing in the heart of the judge of Grant County, Oregon. Here is an astounding fact: jottings from a diary, preserved in *Memorie and Rime,* prove that this backwoodsman went abroad, not with the jaunty insolence of Mark Twain's jolly Philistines, but rather in the mood of Henry James's delicately nurtured "passionate pilgrims" of the decade following the Civil War, those sentimental and æsthetically half-starved young Americans who in the middle years of the last century flung themselves with tearful joy on England and Europe as the dear homeland of their dreams. There is a touch, sometimes more than a touch, of the theatrical in his gesture; but there is an unquestionable depth of sincere feeling animating the performance as a whole.

There is even a touch of pathos—the more affecting because he himself, for once, seems hardly aware of it—in the memoranda of his departure

from New York. He bought his ticket on August
10, 1870, "second class, ship *Europa,* Anchor Line,
to land at Glasgow; and off to-morrow." While
waiting for the sailing, he notes that he has tried
in vain to see Horace Greeley and Henry Ward
Beecher, but has got some leaves from a tree by the
door of Beecher's church "to send to mother."
There, in a sentence, was his unconscious epitome
of what the higher culture of the American metropolis had to offer in 1870 to a passionate pilgrim, to
a romantic poet: the editorials of a great journalist,
the sermons of a great preacher—a rebuff from the
office of the one, and a leaf from a tree of the other.
A note of the voyage, which he seems to have found
very dreary, reminds us that the Franco-Prussian
War was then in progress: "A lot of Germans going home to fight filled the ship; a hard, rough lot,
and they ate like hogs."

Arrived in Scotland, he turns his back on commercial Glasgow, and makes straight for the haunts
of Burns. On September 10, he writes: "God bless
these hale and honest Scotch down here at peaceful Ayr. . . . One man showed me more than a
hundred books, all by Ayrshire poets, and some of
them splendid! I have not dared to tell any one
yet that I too hope to publish a book of verse. . . .
I go every day from here to the 'Auld Brig' over the
Doon, Highland Mary's grave, and Alloway's auld
haunted kirk. . . . Poetry is in the air here. I
am working like a beaver. . . . September 18: In

the sunset to-day, as I walked out for the last time toward the tomb of Highland Mary, I met a whole line of splendid Scotch lassies with sheaves of wheat on their heads and sickles on their arms. Their feet were bare, their legs were bare to the knees. Their great strong arms were shapely as you can conceive; they were tall, and their lifted faces were radiant with health and happiness. I stepped aside in the narrow road to enjoy the scene and let them pass. They were going down the sloping road toward some thatched cottages by the sea, I towards the mountains. How beautiful! I uncovered my head as I stepped respectfully aside. But giving the road to women here seems to be unusual. . . ." Having paid his devotion to Burns, his "brother," he goes on into the Scott country, wades the Tweed, and spends a night in Dryburg Abbey.

Thence he proceeds, with ever more reverential mood, to Nottingham, where he lays his western laurel on the tomb of his "master," Byron, and bargains with the caretaker "to keep the wreath there as long as he lives (or I have sovereigns)." "O my poet!" he cries, "worshipped where the world is glorious with the fire and the blood of youth! Yet here in your own home—ah, well!" The parallelism between Byron's fate and his own, on which he broods in Nottingham, stimulates him to fresh poetical efforts. On September 28, the record runs:

Have written lots of stuff here. I have been happy here. I have worked and not thought of the past. But to-morrow I am going down to Hull, cross the Channel, and see the French and Germans fight. For I have stopped work and begun to look back. . . . I see the snow-peaks of Oregon all the time when I stop work. . . . And then the valley at the bottom of the peaks; the people there; the ashes on the hearth; the fire gone out. . . . The old story of Orpheus in hell has its awful lesson. I, then, shall go forward and never look back any more. Hell, I know, is behind me. There cannot be worse than hell before me. . . . Yet for all this philosophy and this setting the face forward, the heart turns back.

After a glimpse of the war, he began on November 2, 1870, his adventures in London—which he found delightfully different from New York—by walking straight to Westminster Abbey, guided only by the spirit in his feet. Later, he continued his passionate pilgrimage by looking up the haunts of Washington Irving and Bayard Taylor, and he lived for a while in Camberwell, because Browning had lived there. In February, 1871, he was lodged in a garret of the poet Cowley's house, "right back of the Abbey," looking out on Virginia creepers planted by Queen Elizabeth, and listening to the sound of the city's bells. Refreshed from his bath in the stream of poetic tradition and "atmospherically" inspired, Miller made a little book called *Pacific Poems,* containing "Arazonian" (sic) and his drama "Oregonia," and having printed, at his own expense, a hundred copies, scoured the city seeking a publisher. But the publishers would have none of it. Murray, "son of the great Murray, Byron's friend," received him, indeed, and showed him many pictures of Byron, but rejected the proffered opportunity to become Joaquin's publisher, saying, with definitive uplifted finger: "Aye, now, don't you know poetry won't do? Poetry won't do, don't you know?"

In other quarters he met with better fortune. Knocking at the door of *Punch*, as a nameless American, he was cordially received by "my first, firmest friend in London," a man in whose arms Artemus Ward had died,—Tom Hood, son of the famous humorist. By March, 1871, he got his *Pacific Poems* to the reviews and into a kind of private circulation without a publisher. Almost at once both book and author began to catch the fancy of the London literary tasters, who are always hospitably inclined to real curiosities from overseas, and welcome a degree of crudity in a transatlantic writer as evidence that he is genuinely American. By the end of the month, "Arazonian" was attributed by the *Saint James Gazette* to Robert Browning; and, notes the diary, "Walter Thornbury, Dickens' dear friend, and a better poet than I can hope to be, has hunted me up, and says big things of the 'Pacific Poems' in the London *Graphic*." There are, moreover, "two splendid enthusiasts

from Dublin University." And, finally, Tom Hood
has introduced him to the society poet of the city,
who, in turn, has given him letters "to almost everybody"; and so he is socially launched. With this
encouragement and backing, he attacks the publishers again, this time successfully. By April, 1871,
Longmans has brought out his *Songs of the Sierras,*
and Miller's "boy ambition" is accomplished.

At one stride he had stepped from backwoods
obscurity into the full noontide of glory; and it is
not strange that the remembrance of his English
reception dazzled him for the rest of his life. It
is hardly an exaggeration to say that this acclaim
was instantaneous, enthusiastic, and unanimous—
"over-generous," he called it, years later, when he
published in the *Bear* Edition some thirty pages of
appreciations from the English press, including *The
Spectator, The Athenæum, The Saturday Review,
The Pall Mall Gazette, The Illustrated London
News, The Academy, The Evening Standard, The
Westminster Review, The Dark Blue, The London
Sunday Times, Chamber's Journal, Frazer's Magazine, The Evening Post, The Globe, The Morning
Post,* and others. These are largely concerned with
his first volume, *Songs of the Sierras.* The reviewers, in general, touch lightly upon his obvious
inequalities, blemishes, slips in grammar, and faults
in metre; some of them apologize slightly for his
frontier culture; more recognize it boldly as the
source of his power, and proceed to speak in glow-

ing terms of his freshness of theme and treatment, of his tropical color, his myth-making power, his fluent, rapid, and melodious verse, and "the supreme independence, the spontaneity, the all-pervading passion, the unresting energy, and the prodigal wealth of imagery which stamp the poetry before us."

They did not hesitate, this chorus of reviewers, to tell him that his poetry was the most important that had ever come out of America. Nor did they stop with this equivocal praise. *The Athenæum* found him like Browning in his humor and in the novelty of his metaphors. *The Saturday Review* dwelt on his Byronic qualities, and remarked in him "a ring of genuineness which is absent from Byron." *The Westminster Review* thought that he reminded one of Whitman, with the coarseness left out. And *The Academy* gravely declared that "there is an impassable gap between the alien *couleur locale* of even so great a poet as Victor Hugo in such a work as *Les Orientales,* and the native recipiency of one like our California author, whose very blood and bones are related to the things he describes, and from whom a perception and a knowledge so extremely unlike our own are no more separable than his eye, and his brain."

In the wake of the journalistic ovation, social invitations came in upon the poet faster than he could accept or answer them. Among those which he had pushed aside were three letters signed

"Dublin." His Irish friends discovered these and explained that they were from the Archbishop (Trench). "At 'Dublin's' breakfast," says Miller, "I met Robert Browning, Dean Stanley, Lady Augusta, a lot more ladies, and a duke or two, and after breakfast 'Dublin' read to me—with his five beautiful daughters grouped about—from Browning, Arnold, Rossetti, and others, till the day was far spent." The other great feast of the season was an all-night dinner with Dante Gabriel Rossetti, at which "the literary brain" of London was present. As he recalled the event, with an intoxication of delight, later in the summer: "These giants of thought, champions of the beautiful earth, passed the secrets of all time and all lands before me like a mighty panorama. . . . If I could remember and write down truly and exactly what these men said, I would have the best and the greatest book that was ever written."

What he recorded of the conversation is not overpoweringly impressive; but from this rather bewildering contact with the pre-Raphaelite group Miller departed with a vivid conviction that he, too, was above all else a lover of the beautiful, and he carried away a strong impression, which markedly affected his next volume of poems, that beauty is resident in "alliteration and soft sounds." Perhaps, however, the most noteworthy utterance which he preserved was his own reply to a question of Rossetti's:

"Now, what do you call poetry?" and he turned his great Italian eyes tenderly to where I sat at his side.

"To me a poem must be a picture," I answered.

There was more than a drop of bitterness mingled in the joy of his English welcome. With the cup raised to his lips, he wrote in his diary, "I was not permitted to drink." In the midsummer of this most triumphal year, he received news that his sister had died. He returned to the United States, only in time to attend the death-bed of his elder brother in Pennsylvania. Re-visiting his parents in Oregon, he found his mother in broken health and failing mind. Furthermore, the American reception of his poems lacked the warmth of the English cordiality. The traditional superciliousness of the East towards the West and a resentful unwillingness to have this uncouth frontiersman accepted abroad as a leading or even a significant representative of American letters——these not altogether unfamiliar notes are strident in a review in the New York *Nation* in 1871: "It is the 'sombreros' and 'serapes' and 'gulches,' we suppose, and the other Californian and Arizonian properties, which have caused our English friends to find in Mr. Miller a truly American poet. He is Mr. William Rossetti's latest discovery. We trust, however, that we have no monopoly of ignorance and presumption and taste for Byronism. In other climes, also, there have been Firmilians, and men need not be born in California to have the will in excess of the understanding and the understanding ill-informed. There are people of all nationalities whom a pinch more brains and a trifle more of diffidence would not hurt."

The chilliness of American literary criticism was not all, nor perhaps the worst, that Miller had to face on his return to the United States. During his absence in Europe, he had been accused at home, and not without a basis in fact, of deserting his wife. His celebrity as author of *Songs of the Sierras* gave newspaper value to the story. And in the fall of 1871, "Minnie Myrtle" made the entire subject a topic for editorial comment, both at home and abroad, by corroborating the story and then proceeding, in the spirit of magnanimity or of irony or of publicity, to justify the poet. Early in 1872, *The Saturday Review* summarized Mrs. Miller's communication to the American press, and discussed it at length, with elaborate comparison of the classical case of Lord Byron. From this discussion the following extract will suffice for our purposes:

The public, she holds [by her own act belying the contention] has nothing to do with Mr. Miller except as a poet, and has no right to sit in judgment on his conduct as a husband or father; and in the next place, poets are different from other people, and their lives must be judged, if at all, by a different standard. Mr. Miller, we are informed, "felt that he was gifted, and his mind being of a fine, poetic structure, and his brain very delicately organized, the coarse and practical duties of providing for a family, and the annoyance of children, conflicted with his dreams and literary whims." It had been for years his ambition to go to Europe and become famous. Time and money were of course necessary to his project, and when he wrote his wife that he should be absent for five or six years, and that she must not expect to hear from him often, she thought it would be better to release him at once from domestic obligations. . . . Mrs. Miller assures us that she fully sympathized with her husband's projects, and that she believes them to be justified by their practical results. "Mr. Miller," she says, "felt that he had gifts of the mind, and if his system of economy was rigid and hard to endure, it was at least a success; and if he needed all his money to carry out his plans, I am satisfied that he thus used it. . . . As we are both mortals, it would be affectation in me were I to profess to take upon myself all the blame, but I ask to bear my full share. . . . Good sometimes comes of evil. . . . Our separation and sorrows produced the poems of 'Myrrh' and 'Even So.'"

It was at about this point in his career that Miller proved the adage about a prophet in his own country.

And now perhaps he did seriously consider hiding his head for a time in Europe—hiding it in the Byronic fashion. From early in 1872 till 1875 "Childe" Miller wandered extensively, returning to Europe with a wide detour by way of South America and the Near East. From scattered references one gathers that he made acquaintance with the

Emperor of Brazil, that he went down the Danube
and up the Nile, saw Athens and Constantinople,
visited Palestine, and was "in and about the tomb
of buried empires and forgotten kings." These
wanderings, impossible to trace in detail, were interrupted and punctuated by considerable periods
of steady literary work, by visits to England, by a
sojourn in Italy, and by publications—all of which
can be dated with tolerable accuracy.

Beside the new edition of *Songs of the Sierras,*
he published in 1873 the first reflection of these
travels in *Songs of the Sun-Lands.* Of this, a reviewer in the *Athenæum* said: "Mr. Miller's muse
in this, its second flight, has taken the same direction as in its first essay, but, upon the whole, we
think, with a stronger wing." In the prelude to
the first long poem in the book, Miller cries with
fine bravado that "the passionate sun and the resolute sea" have been his masters, "and only these."
So far as the prosodical qualities of this collection
are concerned, this announcement is amusing, because nowhere else in his work does he show himself
so obviously the "sedulous ape" of his English contemporaries. The volume is dedicated to the Rossettis; in "Isles of the Amazons" he is affected by
the stanza of "In Memoriam" and he also echoes
Mrs. Browning; in "Sleep That Was Not Sleep" [5]
he attempts the Browningesque dramatic mono-

---

[5] A revision of "Zanoni" in *Joaquin, Et Al.*

logue; remembering the Rossetti dinner of 1871, he
works on the theory that "a poem must be a picture," and he is everywhere studious of "alliteration
and soft sounds"; finally in the Palestinian sequence
called "Olive Leaves." the influence of Swinburne
has quite transformed and disguised the sound of
his voice:

> With incense and myrrh and sweet spices,
>   Frankincense and sacredest oil
> In ivory, chased with devices
>   Cut quaint and in serpentine coil;
> Heads bared, and held down to the bosom;
>   Brows massive with wisdom and bronzed;
> Beards white as the white may in blossom,
>   And borne to the breast and beyond,—
> Came the Wise of the East, bending lowly
>   On staffs, with their garments girt round
> With girdles of hair, to the Holy
>   Child Christ, in their sandals.

Despite all this mimicry in the manner, the stuff
in the *Songs of the Sun-Lands* is, in great measure,
Miller's own. In "Isles of the Amazons" he conceives himself as a scout of the imagination, a Kit
Carson of poetry, who has carried his banner from
Oregon and the Sierras to plant it in South American islands by a mighty unsung river. His hero,
a singing warrior fleeing from strife to seek a Utopian peace and felicity, is once more a kind of
self-projection. "From Sea to Sea" is a poetical
reminiscence of a transcontinental journey by the
new Pacific Railway. *By the Sundown Seas,* which

he later cut up into its constituent pictures, sings the glories of Oregon and the emigrants. In "Olive Leaves," his garland from Palestine, he begins a peculiarly American reappropriation of Christianity and an assimilation of it to his growing humanitarian sentiment. And "Fallen Leaves" are for the most part memories of the West. So that if he does not exhibit any very daring unconventionalities in form, he does employ his forms with a good deal of flexibility in imaginatively molding the raw stuff of American experience.

In 1873, also, Miller published in France and England the most original and the most poetical of all his books in prose, and, on the whole, perhaps the most interesting book that he ever produced, *Life Among the Modocs*, which circulated in translations, later editions, and abridgments, pirated or otherwise, under various titles—as *Unwritten History*, *Scènes de la Vie des Mineurs et des Indiens de California*, *Paquita*, *My Own Story*, and *My Life Among the Indians*. In 1872 and 1873 the Modoc Indians were attracting the attention of the public by their stubborn resistance to the government's attempt to move them from their old lands to a new reservation. In the course of this resistance their killing of two peace commissioners naturally excited popular indignation. But in Miller, instinctively sympathetic with the under dog, the last hopeless stand of this warlike tribe, which he had known in his boyhood, appealed strongly to the humanitarian sentiment, stirred up old memories, and aroused the imagination. He had, as we have seen, in at least one of his "campaigns," fought against them; but now, as a poet and Utopian, he is all on their side, he embraces their cause, he speaks from their point of view, he makes himself one of them.

In the introduction to the *Bear* Edition, he gives this brief account of the origin of the book: "Having met the Prince, on a visit from Nicaragua at the time, he helped me to recall our life among the Modocs, adding such romance of his own as he chose." Elsewhere he acknowledges the collaboration of Prentice Mulford. How much is due to the influence of these collaborators one cannot say, but there is a continuity of narrative and dramatic and idyllic interest in the tale unequalled in Miller's other prose fiction. The authors enter with genuine enthusiasm into the exhibition of the white man's inhumanity, the virtues of the "noble savage," the chivalry of the Prince, the heroic fidelity of Paquita, the yellow-haired poetic renegade and his dusky bride, and the romantic and melancholy charm of life on the forested slopes of Mt. Shasta. There is a wavering thread of autobiographical fact running through the romance, but the romance is here far more significant than the thread of fact; all that Miller, as a poetic dreamer, longed to have been, all that he could not be, inextricably fused with what he was, is here projected, beautifully, by his

imagination. He so long encouraged the acceptance
of the book as "history" that perhaps in his later
years he actually lost the ability, never notable in
him, to distinguish what he had done from what
he had dreamed. In 1874 this book, with the title
Unwritten History: Life Amongst the Modocs, was
brought out in a subscription edition by the American Publishing Company, and in the advertising
pages of this edition is third in a list beginning with
Mark Twain's *The Gilded Age* and Josh Billings's
Everybody's Friend. This will suggest to those who
remember the American Publishing Company the
sort and size of the audience that Miller was addressing in the middle 'seventies.

In *Memorie and Rime,* Miller says that he returned to London in November, 1874, from his long
wanderings in Europe. Apparently, however, he
had returned to England in the preceding year, perhaps partly to enjoy the réclame of his two new
books. In 1873, at any rate, he made his acquaintance with that poet and patron of the arts and
great organizer of literary breakfasts, Lord Houghton. In Reid's *Life of Lord Houghton* little record
remains of this friendship, except a letter of August
5, 1873, addressed to Gladstone, in which Miller is
commended as "most interesting as poet and man;
I have known and asked nothing as to his private
life." Augustus Hare (*The Story of My Life,* vol.
iv) makes a supercilious reference to the poet's
appearance at one of these breakfasts: "Joaquin

Miller would have been thought insufferably vulgar if he had not been a notoriety: as it was, everyone paid court to him." But various letters and references in Traubel's *With Walt Whitman in Camden* show that Miller returned Lord Houghton's courtesies in America, in 1875, and attempted to bring about a meeting between his English friend and Whitman. Furthermore, Miller speaks of traveling with Lord Houghton in Greece; and in a note of the *Bear* Edition he gives interesting hints at the sort of figure that he himself made in English country life:

Born to the saddle and bred by a chain of events to ride with the wind until I met the stolid riders of England, I can now see how it was that Anthony Trollope, Lord Houghton and others of the saddle and "meet" gave me ready place in their midst. . . . In all our hard riding I never had a scratch. One morning Trollope hinted that my immunity was due to my big Spanish saddle, which I had brought from Mexico City. I threw my saddle on the grass and rode without so much as a blanket. And I rode neck to neck; and then left them all behind and nearly every one unhorsed. Prince Napoleon was of the party that morning; and as the gentlemen pulled themselves together on the return he kept by my side, and finally proposed a tour through Notts and Sherwood Forest on horseback. And so it fell out that we rode together much.

With so much cordiality manifesting itself abroad and so little at home, it is not strange that Miller, after this second visit to England, should have entertained for a time the notion of fixing his residence in a foreign land. It behooved him, furthermore, as a faithful follower of Lord Byron, to dwell in Italy. He says, with customary indefiniteness as to dates, that, in the footsteps of his hero, he "lived long enough at Genoa to find that his life there, along with the Shelleys, was simple, sincere, and clean. From Genoa I went to Florence, as the guest of our Consul General, Lorimer Graham. I wanted to live with Mr. Graham because he and his most amiable lady lived in the house occupied by Byron and the Shelleys, when they made their home in Florence. At Venice, under the guidance of Browning, who had left Florence to live in this latter place, after the death of his gifted wife, I found only the same story of industry, sobriety and devotion to art." Charles Warren Stoddard gives a glimpse of Miller's secretive life in Rome, picturing him driving out with the "Pink Countess," and declares that Miller's Italian novel, *The One Fair Woman*, 1876, with its epigraphs from Byron, Browning, Swinburne, and Hay, "embodies" much of Miller's Roman life, and is "one of the truest tales he ever told." Additional light on this period is thrown by *Songs of Italy*, 1878, a collection manifestly produced under the influence of Browning. *The Ship in the Desert*, published in book form in 1875, is preceded by an eloquent prose inscription to his parents, dated August, 1874, at Lake Como. At about this time, Miller bought some land near Naples and, in company with an English poet, meditated settling there; but malarial fever attacked them both, his friend died, and the Italian chapter of his life was ended.

In November, 1875, Miller dated at Chicago an introductory allegorical poem, prefixed to Mary Murdock Mason's little Italian novel, *Mae Madden,* published in 1876. In the course of the next decade he roved widely, as was his wont, but this is, in general, the period of his experiments at living in eastern cities, including Boston, New York, and Washington, where he built himself a log cabin, and, in his frontier costume, became the picturesque publicity man for the "Western school." Bret Harte and Mark Twain, now at the height of their production, were creating a lively demand for the tales of the pioneers; and Miller perhaps perceived that if he was to have his due profit of the popular interest he must renounce his Italian and Oriental inclinations and return to his native fields. In 1876, at any rate, he published *First Fam'lies of the Sierras,* a prose tale of the Forty-Niners, marked by that chivalric sentiment for women and by that idealization of the noble men in red shirts, which are distinctive "notes" of this literary movement. In *The Baroness of New York,* 1877, a long romantic medley in verse, he dismally failed in his attempt to extend the adventures of his western heroine into the society of the metropolis. A presentation copy of this book, now in the possession of the University of Chicago, bears the author's own veracious comment that it "isn't worth a damn." Though he salvaged a portion of it in "The Sea of Fire," the original title disappeared from his collective edition. Soon after his return to America, he began to be visited by dramatic aspirations; and in 1881 he achieved considerable success with *The Danites in the Sierras*. The three other plays which he preserved—*Forty-Nine, Tally-Ho*, and *An Oregon Idyl*—are like *The Danites* in presenting incidents in the story of the frontier. In 1881, he published also *The Shadows of Shasta*, a prose tale anticipating Helen Hunt Jackson's *Ramona* in indignation at our treatment of the Indians. In 1884 falls the interesting but very fragmentary autobiographical miscellany called *Memorie and Rime*. With *The Destruction of Gotham*, 1886, a sensational novel of class-conflict in New York City, Miller somewhat significantly terminated his search for fortune and glory in the Eastern states.

He had been a sentimental pilgrim in England, a poetic refugee in Italy, and a picturesque visitor—an ambassador from the Sierras—even in New York and Washington. Though he had enjoyed playing all these parts, perhaps by 1886 he felt that he and his public were beginning to lose their zest for one another. Furthermore he had now married again and at least entertained the thought of settling down. The loss of considerable money in Wall

Street speculations had shaken his faith in "capitalistic society" and had weakened the Babylonian attractions of metropolitan life. He remembered the mountains and the seas of the West. He remembered also Sir Walter Scott's castle and estate at Abbotsford as a general model of the fashion in which a great poet should live. Mingled with these memories, in the background of his mind there was a curious accumulation of Utopian and Arcadian dreams which from his boyhood he had vaguely desired to realize. And so at last the prophet returned to his own country, and, entering upon a tract of land upon the hills looking over Oakland to San Francisco Bay, he built there a little wooden house for his wife, which he called The Abbey (commemorating at once her name and Dryburgh and Newstead Abbeys), a second cottage for his old mother, a "bower" for his daughter, and a little guest-house for whatever visitor, white, black, or yellow, cared to occupy it. There, too, he planted thousands of trees in the shape of a gigantic cross, and beneath them on the crest of the hill he built for himself a funeral pyre of the rough cobble, and he erected three monuments of stone to three heroes: General Fremont, Robert Browning, and Moses.

Miller says that his choice of this retreat on the hills was determined by the relative cheapness of the land; but he was not a practical man, and he must soon have forgotten this practical consideration in the more characteristic reflection that The Hights was just the right setting for a man like him. His primary purpose there was not to follow any gainful occupation, but to live as all poetic Utopians have held that a man should live, toiling a couple of hours each day at honest labor of the hands and devoting the rest of life to love, friendship, art, and preaching the gospel of beauty. The literary expression of his dream appears in *The Building of the City Beautiful,* 1893, a Utopian romance obviously related to the writings of Ruskin and William Morris, but apparently inspired directly by Miller's conversations with a Jewish radical in Palestine. He had it in mind also to gather around him like-minded workers and friends, who should give to the world below them an illustration of the felicity in store for humanity when the base passions which now govern society are eradicated. Several young poets and artists came to him and tarried for a time in his guest-house, moved by curiosity or the hopes of youth—among them several Japanese, including Yone Noguchi. And students from the University in Berkeley and travellers from remoter places made little pilgrimages up into the hills to visit this romantically costumed poet and seer who had fought with Indians and now preached universal peace. To his disciples and lovers he lectured in a somewhat oracular tone on the laws of the new American poetry, on the conduct of life, and on the new religious spirit which is to embrace all mankind.

Miller's visitors did not always, however, find him preaching peace. His pacificism, like the popular American variety, was tempered by hatred of oppression and readiness to fight "on the side of the Lord." He accepted the "idealistic" interpretation of the Spanish-American War, and chanted lustily his encouragement of the struggle to free the Cubans from the tyranny of Spain. On the other hand, in his *Chants for the Boer*, 1900, he protested indignantly against the British imperial policy in South Africa; and his strong pro-English sympathies give a certain moral quality to his indignation. "Find here," he cries, "not one ill word for brave old England; my first, best friends were English. But for her policy, her politicians, her speculators, what man with a heart in him can but hate and abhor these? England's best friends to-day are those who deplore this assault on the farmer Boers, so like ourselves a century back."

There was an interesting element of inconsistency between the popular American humanitarianism which Miller had gradually adopted as his religion and his strongest poetical impulses, which were adventurous and imperialistic. In these later years the fire of his fighting youth slumbered in the veins of the white-bearded seer, but it was never extinguished, and, every now and then, it flashed out. In such seasons pilgrims to The Hights found that he was not at home.　He was a restless soul—like most Utopists, ill adapted to the permanency of a Paradise.　There was, moreover, a steadily disquieting feature in the prospect from his hills.　At his feet, the great ships rode at anchor.　But before his eyes daily they lifted anchor and spread their wings and sailed away, out through the shining Golden Gate into the Pacific, and disappeared on pathless ways over the rim of the world.　For him, even at the age of sixty, the attraction of unknown places was magical.　He followed "the gleam" to the islands of the South Seas, to Japan, to Alaska. In 1897–8 he was correspondent of the New York *Journal* in the Klondike.　Trying to pass from the Klondike to the Bering Sea by way of the Yukon, he finds the river closed at the edge of the Arctic Circle.　"It was nearly two thousand miles to the sea, all ice and snow, with not so much as a dog-track before me and only midnight round about me. There was nothing to do but to try to get back to my cabin on the Klondike.　In the line of my employment I kept a journal of the solitary seventy-two days and nights—mostly night—spent in the silent and terrible ascent of the savage sea of ice." The imaginative harvest of these later adventures was first gathered up in *As It Was in the Beginning,* 1903, a curious poetical fantasy, oddly brought forth in San Francisco in pamphlet form with a cover decorated by a figure of a stork bearing in his bill the infant Roosevelt in spectacles.　In 1907, worked over and shorn of its more grotesque features, the poem reappeared in dignified form as *Light*, with the interesting prefatory avowal: "My aspiration is and ever has been, in my dim and uncertain way, to be a sort of Columbus—or Cortez." (In the collective edition the title is changed once more to *A Song of Creation*.)

When Miller finally reviewed his own work and prepared his collective edition, he saw that much of his verse had been hastily written, journalistic, prolix, lacking in form and concentration; and he manfully discarded many long passages of it. At the same time, he felt as never before the importance of his own position in American poetry. He had not really achieved a distinctive poetical style. He had not been a thinker. He had been a pathfinder of the imagination; like Whitman, he had blazed a way into new territories. He had brought something of undiscovered beauty and splendor into American literature. He exulted in the wide lands and seas which he first had annexed to the provinces of song. He had sung the exodus across the plains. He had pictured the great American desert. He had celebrated the forested heights of the Sierras, the giant trees of the Mariposa Grove, and the falls of the Yosemite. He had been a myth-maker and had sown with poetic legends all his western land from the snowy peaks of Mt. Rainier and Mt. Shasta through the golden poppy fields of the central valleys to San Diego Bay, Nicaragua, and the

Amazon River. He had made captive for romance the outlaws of old Spanish California, the priests and bandits of Mexico, the scouts of Fremont, dusky Indian heroines, and the motley multitude of the gold-seekers. He had been the champion of oppressed peoples—the Southern Confederacy, the native American tribes, the Jews of Russia and Palestine, the Cubans, the Boers, the yellow men and the Mexicans in California. And then, to widen his horizon at sunset, he had threaded the golden straits and had sailed "on and on" to the Arctic Seas, to Hawaii, to the Orient, chanting as he sailed, every ready for fresh adventure, ever in love with light, color, and movement, ever himself the romantic troubadour, the picturesque incarnation of the spirit which pervades his poems.

CHAPTER VIII

A NOTE ON CARL SANDBURG

Many of the things which Carl Sandburg relishes I relish: the jingle of the "American language" in the making; the Great Lakes, prairies, mountains, and the diurnal and seasonal scene-shifting of the elements; all kinds of workmen with their tools in city and country, and the "feel" of an axe or shovel in my own hands; the thunder of overland trains and the cross-fire of banter in a barber shop; eating ham-and-eggs with a Chinese chemist at a wayside lunch-counter at four o'clock in the morning, suntime; the mixed human contacts to be had, for example, in a "common" up-country smoker, where black men, Italians, Poles, Swedes, Japanese, Indians, and Germans commune happily in a thick blue mist, and a fluent young travelling man "making" the resort towns drops into the seat beside me and asks what "line" I am carrying, and I exchange matches and crackers with a Dutchman from Java in blue overalls moving from the sugar-beet fields of Wisconsin to the raspberry district of Michigan, accounting spontaneously for the "yoost" and the "yob" in his vocabulary by his long contact with the North Germanic people.

All these things I relish and am familiar with; and yet, as I study my fourth volume of Mr. Sandburg's poems, I wonder why Mr. Untermeyer and the other fugelmen of the "movement" congratulate the public on the ease with which they may read and enjoy poetry, now that classical allusions and the traditional poetic diction have been banished. It is a sham and a delusion. Mr. Sandburg is not easy to read. He is as difficult in his own fashion as John Donne or Browning. If any of the men in my common smoker should glance over my shoulder at the pages before me, they would see abundance of familiar words: "taxi-drivers," "window-washers," "booze-runners," hat-cleaners," "delicatessen clerks." Perhaps also "shovel-stiffs," "work-plugs," "hoosegow," and "exhausted egg-heads" would be familiar to them. But I think they would gasp and stare at "sneaking scar-faced Nemesis," "miasmic" women, and "macabre" moons. I think they would meditate a long while before they felt any emotion whatever in the presence of such word patterns as:

Pearl memories in the mist circling the horizon,
Flick me, sting me, hold me even and smooth.

And I believe they might read the long title-poem, "Slabs of the Sunburnt West," twenty times without suspecting for a moment that it is a meditation on God, civilization, and immortality, conceived on the brink of the Grand Canyon of the Colorado.

Now, the considerable obscurity in Mr. Sandburg's work may be accounted for in two ways.

In the first place, his literary allegiance is mixed. When in his interesting poem on "The Windy City" he begins a lucid paragraph thus: "Mention proud things, catalogue them"—he is writing under the formative influence of Whitman; and both his language and his emotion are straightforward and sincere. But in "Fins," for example, and in "Pearl Horizons," where he asks the "pearl memories" to flick him and hold him even and smooth, he is writing under the deformative influence of the most artificial phase of Imagism; and both his language and his emotion are tortured and insincere.

In the second place, Mr. Sandburg thinks that he is really sympathetic with the "working classes" and with the unloved and not altogether lovely portion of humanity which Mr. Masefield has sung as "the scum of the earth"; and he imagines that he is pretty much out of sympathy with "the great ones of the earth" and with all those who speak complacently of "the established order." Robert Burns sympathized with the Scotch peasant and wrote of him and for him, incidentally pleasing the rest of mankind. The late James Whitcomb Riley sympathized with the farmer's boy and wrote of him and for him; and as there were a great many farmers' boys in the land, he pleased a wide audience. But Mr.

Sandburg, who sympathizes with the taxi-drivers and delicatessen clerks, does not write for them; he writes for the literary smart set, for the readers of *The Freeman, The Liberator, The Dial, Vanity Fair,* etc.

As a consequence of his confronting this audience, Mr. Sandburg appears to me to lack somewhat the courage of his sympathies. He seldom individualizes his working-man; almost never does the imaginative work of penetrating the consciousness of any definite individual and telling his story coherently with the concrete emotion belonging to it. Instead, he presents a rather vague lyrical sense of the surge of but slightly differentiated "masses"; he gives, as the newspaper does, a collection of accidents to undifferentiated children; he is the voice of the abstract city rather than of the citizen. He chants of dreams, violences, toils, cruelties, and despairs. In his long poem, "And So To-day," commemorating the burial of the Unknown Soldier, he finds, however, an appointed theme; he is in the presence of an almost abstract fate, which he renders piteously concrete by a curious parody of Whitman's threnody on Lincoln in a language of vulgar brutality—a language reflecting, it is to be supposed, the vulgarity and brutality of the civilization for which the Unknown Soldier died, as Mr. Sandburg bitterly suggests, in vain. In the short ironical piece, "At the Gate of the Tombs," adopting once more the most biting lingo of the mob, he expresses powerfully the attitude, let us say, of *The New Republic* towards the government's treatment of political prisoners and conscientious objectors—"gag 'em, lock 'em up, get 'em bumped off."

Radical journals, like *The Nation* and *The New Republic,* radical journalists like Mr. Upton Sinclair, and radical poets like Mr. Sandburg, create for themselves purely artistic problems of very great difficulty, of which they do not always find triumphant solutions. When, for instance, Mr. Sinclair presents the entire American press, the churches, and the universities as bought, corrupt conspirators against truth, he creates for himself the pretty problem of showing where truth lodges: it is an artistic necessity—till he has shown that, his great picture of iniquity seems incredible, illusory. When Mr. Sandburg, in his poem, "And So To-day," presents the official pageant of mourning for the Unknown Soldier as a farcical mummery; the President, the commanding officers, the "honorable orators, buttoning their prinz alberts," as empty puppets; and the people from sea to sea as stopping for a moment in their business—"with a silence of eggs laid in a row on a pantry shelf"—when Mr. Sandburg presents a great symbolic act of the nation as vacuous and meaningless, he creates for himself the pretty problem of showing where the meaning of the nation lies: till he has shown that, and with at least equal earnestness and power, he is in danger. He is in grave danger of leaving his readers with a sense either that his conception of the nation is illusory or that both he and they inhabit a world of illusions —a world of dreams, violences, toils, cruelties, and despairs, in which nothing really matters, after all.

Mr. Sandburg is not completely unconscious of the problem which he has created. To take a similar case, even Mr. Oswald Garrison Villard, a man who habitually insists upon the hopeless condition of the Republic and the brainlessness and heartlessness of all our public men—even Mr. Villard, insensitive as he is to the "antique symmetry," is apparently not completely unconscious of the problem which he has created. At least once or twice every year Mr. Villard drops the muck-rake with which he harries Washington, and writes an editorial in behalf of the New Testament and the character of Christ, as if to prove to his anxious readers that he really has a definite standard in mind for the administration of the War Department. Mr. Sandburg does likewise. When he has me all but persuaded that he himself is at heart a barbarian, that he feels a deep and genuine gusto in violence and brutality, that his talk about building a "city beautiful" is for the consumption of ladies who actually bore him, that in fact he chafes at the slight discipline which our civilization as yet imposes, and that we are all callous "galoots" and may as well acknowledge it and act accordingly—then he brings me to a pause by his sympathy for the "insignificant" private life, by the choking pathos of his

epigram on "the boy nobody knows the name of";
then he stuns me by enjoining himself, with a studious nonchalance, to

Write on a pocket pad what a pauper said
To a patch of purple asters at a whitewashed wall:
"Let every man be his own Jesus—that's enough."

IX

ANDREW CARNEGIE

Andrew Carnegie's countrymen felt in his lifetime that $350,000,000 worth of power over them was more than any man ought to hold. Accordingly, except when they were asking him to found a library or to endow a college, they did what they could to keep him humble and to persuade him that no one envied him and that no one would bow an inch lower to him out of reverence for his fabulous wealth. This was no doubt sound democratic discipline. He himself must have applauded the spirit of it. "It was long," he says in commenting on his own radically democratic upbringing, "before I could trust myself to speak respectfully of any privileged class or person who had not distinguished himself in some good way and therefore earned the right to public respect." But he knew all the time, and his countrymen knew at heart, that adding up his stocks and bonds would not summarize his talents and virtues. His gifts made him appear the most magnificent philanthropist that the world had ever seen. And by qualities which remained with him after he had distributed his fortune, he was one of the most original, interesting, and representative men of his generation.

The Iron Master possessed intelligence of the first rank in its kind, an open and free spirit coupled with extraordinary firmness of character, indefatigable energy and initiative and a "creative" benevolence, together with abundant humor, poetic sentiment, and deep feeling with regard to the things that matter. His was, in short, a personality. He appreciated, furthermore, the significant and picturesque aspects of his own career and savored its contrasts like a man of letters. When in his old age, at his retreat on the Scotch moors, he undertook at the insistence of his friends to compose his memoirs, he had the material, the perspective, and the mood for a book fit to stand on the shelf by Franklin's. Following his own precept and Franklin's example, he wrote out his recollections simply, modestly, blithely, like an old gentleman with a good conscience telling the story of his life to his friends and relatives.

The war diverted him from his work before the manuscript was in shape for publication. He wrote on the margin: "Whoever arranges these notes should be careful not to burden the public with too much. A man with a heart as well as a head should be chosen." Professor John C. Van Dyke was selected as an editor possessing both these qualifications. His task, which he says was little more than to arrange the matter in chronological sequence, he

has performed unobtrusively—just a shade too unobtrusively. Carnegie had far more than the ordinary manufacturer's respect for literature, and he
clearly hoped that his autobiography would be considered, in the stricter sense, as "literature." It
contains, however, more instances of the "dangling
participle" than perhaps ever before appeared in a
single volume. There should be nothing sacred, to
one charged with the editing of an unfinished manuscript, about Mr. Carnegie's dangling participles.
Before the book goes into its second edition, these
and such like easily corrigible slips should be silently
amended. Then the really charming spirit which
pervades it—I do not recall a harsh or ill-natured
word from the beginning to the end of it—should
make it a place in the best company, where it
belongs.

Andrew Carnegie was born in 1835 at Dunfermline, Scotland, son of a damask weaver who was
ruined by the introduction of steam looms, and who
in 1848 borrowed twenty pounds to bring his family
to America, where "Andy" made his "start in life"
at the age of thirteen as a bobbin boy in a cotton
factory at a dollar and twenty cents a week. A
second-rate "self-made man" might have attributed
his success to the change of environment and to his
own industry. It is a characteristic and attractive
trait in Carnegie, creditable to both his heart and
his head, that he recognizes and handsomely acknowledges his obligations not merely to his em-

ployers and employees and partners, but to a multitude of benign forces cooperating in his success.

Though he had, for example, but a few years of common schooling, he makes it beautifully clear that he received from various directions the incentives of an excellent education. He declares that he was fortunate in his ancestors and supremely fortunate in his birthplace. He is proud of a grandfather on one side who was familiarly known as "the professor," of a grandfather on the other side who was a friend of Cobbett, of an uncle who went to jail to vindicate the right of public assembly, of a father who was one of five weavers that founded the first library in Dunfermline, and of a mother capable of binding shoes to help support the family, in her morality an unconscious follower of Confucius, in her religion consciously a disciple of Channing. As for the town, it had the reputation of being the most radical in the kingdom: the stimulus of political and philosophic ideas was in the air; the editorials of the London *Times* were read from the pulpit; "the names of Hume, Cobden, and Bright were upon everyone's tongue." Dunfermline was radical, but with a radicalism nourished on history and inclined to hero-worship; for, in the midst of her, Abbey and ruined tower fired the young heart with remembrance of King Malcom and Wallace and Bruce. "It is a tower of strength for a boy," says the old man, "to have a hero." The thought of Wallace made him face whatever he was afraid of, and remained "a real force in his life to the very end."

When the Carnegie family settled in America, their capital was brains, pluck, honesty, willingness to work, and loyalty to one another. The early stages in their pecuniary progress were marked first by payment of their debts, then by purchase of their first little house, and later by their first investment, in five shares of the Adams Express Company. "Andy" did not long remain a telegraph messenger, because he promptly developed his faculty for doing "something beyond the sphere of his duties," which attracted the attention of those over him. He picked up telegraphy while waiting for messages; he learned to receive by ear while others used the paper slip; he mastered the duties of a train-dispatching superintendent of division while sending the messages of his superior. When his chief's arrival at the office was delayed one morning and the division was in confusion, he assumed responsibility and sent out the orders in the superintendent's name, saying to himself "death or Westminster Abbey." The union of special knowledge with courage, which made "the little white-haired Scotch devil" a first-rate assistant at the age of eighteen, promoted him in six years to the superintendency of the Pittsburgh Division. "I was only twenty-four years old," he says, "but my model then was Lord John Russell." Two years later he was assistant director of telegraphs and military railroads for the government. After the Civil War, by swift combinations of his forces and rapid marches into new fields he established his position at the centre of the industries on which the internal development of the country most directly depended. At the age of thirty-three, he had an annual income of fifty thousand dollars; its subsequent expansion there is not space to recite.

That the son of an impecunious weaver should, while acting as telegraph operator in Pennsylvania, have taken Lord John Russell as his model strikes one as astonishing—till one studies the portrait of this young man at sixteen. The bearing and the features—the full brow, the clear penetrating eyes, the firm but sensitive mouth, are those of a well-bred, even of a high-bred youth, quite the stuff, one should say, to develop into a Lord Rector of St. Andrews University, laird of Skibo Castle, and conspirator with Lords Morley and Bryce and Grey for the world's welfare. The record of his early life bears out the impression given by the photograph. It shows a boy grounded by family discipline in self-respect, moral purity, and intellectual ambition. It indicates that the wide beneficence of his later years was not the mere after thought and diversion of a satiated money-getter, but the object towards which his efforts tended from the start.

As a messenger boy he was reading Macaulay, Bancroft, and Shakespeare, and was learning the oratorios of Handel. His first note to the press, written at the same period, was a plea to have a certain small library opened to working boys of his class. The 7,689 organs that he afterwards gave to churches and the 2,800 libraries that he founded were his acknowledgment to society for the impulse it had given him. He had worshipped a popular hero, Wallace, from the Dunfermline days; and the hero funds that he established throughout the world were tokens of his lifelong hero-worship. By the school of thought in which he was nourished, war among civilized nations was reckoned an obsolescent and absurd instrument of statecraft; his Palace of Peace commemorated the aspirations of a genuine friend of all the people.

In 1868 he had made a memorandum, indicating it as his intention to retire in two years and to "settle in Oxford and *get a thorough education*," and then to "take part in public affairs, especially those connected with education and improvement of the lower classes." Like another famous man of our time, he discovered that it is not easy for a leader in the fullness of his power to retire—"he had come to the ring and now he must hop." But he continued his education and his educating, when he could, by reading Plato, Confucius, and Buddha, by travelling in various lands, and by earnestly advising and taking the advice of philosophers, presidents, kaisers, prime ministers, secretaries of state, and other experts. He acknowledged the impulse to intellectual growth that society had given him by gifts of buildings or endowment funds to five hundred educational institutions at home and abroad and by his great central foundation with its liberal charter for "the advancement and diffusion of knowledge and understanding among the people of the United States."

Some of us criticized him because he did not give away his three hundred and fifty millions stealthily and secretly, as we slip a quarter into the collection box, God alone being aware of our munificence. But he knew that one of the most important of his benefactions was precisely the publicity with which he restored his vast accumulations to the people and put them at the service of the upward-striving members of society. It was for him to declare conspicuously and with magnificent and unmistakable emphasis what money is good for; to promote science and literature and music and peace and heroism. He owed the friendship, he tells us, of Earl Grey, who later became a trustee of the ten-million-dollar fund for the United Kingdom, to the publication in the *Times* of these sentences from his instructions to the trustees of his gifts to Dunfermline:

To bring into the monotonous lives of the toiling masses of Dunfermline more "of sweetness and light," to give them—especially the young—some charm, some happiness, some elevating conditions of life which residence elsewhere would have denied, that the child of my native town, looking back in after years, however far from home it may have

roamed, will feel that simply by virtue of being
such, life has been made happier and better. If this
be the fruit of your labors, you will have succeeded;
if not, you will have failed.

Large-scale beneficence—doing good to towns
and entire classes of society and nations—establishes one as a member of a privileged order, which
the average man regards with a certain uneasy
envy. If Carnegie had not taken from us that
$350,000,000 we might all and each have had the
credit of contributing to the purchase of those
organs, the foundation of those libraries, the establishment of those hero funds, the building of that
Palace of Peace, the pensioning of those employees,
the endowment of those universities, that great
fund for the advancement of knowledge. True, we
might have contributed. We might have taxed ourselves at that rate. We might have made similar
investments in human progress. But we know pretty
well that we wouldn't have done so. After we had
taxed ourselves for the necessary upkeep and expansion of our army and navy, we should have felt
too poor, even had steel sold for some dollars a
ton less,—we should still have felt too poor to bear
an additional tax for such remote objects as the
promotion of heroism or science. We should have
felt that we owed it to ourselves and to our families to apportion our little "surplus" to our tobacco
funds and our soft-drink funds for the tranquillizing
of our nerves and the alleviation of our thirst, or

perhaps, if we were a notch above such sensual indulgence, to our fund for the collection of cancelled postage stamps.

In the age of individualism which produced Andrew Carnegie, society had scarcely begun to "tap the resources" of collective effort for any genuine amelioration of common conditions. The people "perished" because they had no vision of powers united. In this present hour, clamoring for a high leadership which fails to appear, we average men may look back a little regretfully at our Carnegies, shrewd and level-headed in their means but wholeheartedly and aspiringly democratic in their ends, being fain to confess, we average men, that it is the pressure of the "hero's" exaction, the spur of high example, a vision not our own, a power not ourselves, that we must depend upon, if we are ever, in Pindar's great phrase, "to become what we are."

X

ROOSEVELT AND THE NATIONAL PSYCHOLOGY

I

Mr. Roosevelt's great and fascinating personality is part of the national wealth, and it should, so far as possible, be preserved undiminished. Since his death those who have spoken of him have observed somewhat too sedulously the questionable maxim, *De mortuis nihil nisi bonum.* To say nothing but good of a great man is generally fatal alike to biographical vivacity and to truth. In this case it is a serious detraction from that versatile and inexhaustible energy which Lord Morley admired when he declared that the two most extraordinary works of nature in America were Niagara Falls and the President in the White House. "He made," says William Hard with the intensity of one catching breath after the close passage of a thunderbolt, "he made Theodore Roosevelt the most interesting thing in the world," and he made "the world itself momentarily immortally interesting." That touches the heart of the matter: it explains comprehensively why his friends loved and his enemies admired him. It leaves him with his aggressive definiteness, his color, and his tang. Mr. Roosevelt, as he proudly insisted and as he admirably painted himself in many a capital chapter of his *Rough Riders* and his hunting and exploring books, was stained with the blood and sweat and dust of conflict. No image presents him whole that lacks a dash of the recklessness which appears in Frederick Macmonnies' vaulting trooper and a touch of the ruthlessness hinted by the fiercely clenched fist in a well-known photograph of him pacing the deck of the flagship with "Fighting Bob" Evans. He lived and died fighting, and he gave a thousand proofs that the keenest joy he knew was the joy of battle. No memorial so little preserves him as a whitewashed plaster bust. Better than all the eulogies pronounced in public places I suspect he would have relished the tribute paid to him in private conversation by one of our distinguished visitors from abroad. "It may be," he said, "that Mr. Wilson possesses all the virtues in the calendar; but for my part I had rather go to hell with Theodore Roosevelt." Mr. Wilson, he implied, might get off in a corner somewhere with Saint Peter and Colonel House, and arrange something of the highest importance to the heavenly host; but all the cherubim and seraphim of healthy curiosity would be leaning over the impassable gulf to see what Mr. Roosevelt would do next.

It is because such notes as these recall the most interesting man of our times, "the great Achilles whom we knew," that I have heard and read with a certain languor the conventional tributes evoked by his death, and, more recently, have gone through the posthumous biographies without entire satisfaction. Excepting Mr. G. S. Viereck's saucy apology for being a pro-German, the cue of recent writers has been canonization. Mr. MacIntire, for example, prefaced by General Wood, has written a purely "inspirational" narrative with a conquering hero ready for the moving-picture screen or a Henty novel or a place on the juvenile bookshelf beside "The Boys' King Arthur." As a specimen of its critical quality, I select the following passage, with the suggestion that it be read in connection with the report of the Federal Commission on the Packers: "One shudders to think of what fate would have befallen the United States if the monopolies which Roosevelt curbed while he was President had been allowed to flourish until this era of revolution." The first three volumes of "Roosevelt, His Life, Meaning, and Messages," is a collection of important speeches, articles, and messages arranged by William Griffith; the fourth volume by Eugene Thwing is a rapid biographical compilation, journalistic, readable, and concluding with the happy thought that if the meaning of Roosevelt's life is fully appreciated we shall find in the next generation of Americans "a veritable race of moral giants." Mr. Lewis's book, for which Mr. Taft supplies an introduction, is, of course, a work of quite another order. For the earlier period it is almost as entertaining as the Autobiography, and for the latter years, particularly for the history of the Progressive movement, in which the author was an important participant, it is an independent authority and an animated and agreeable one with many small intimate strokes of appreciation. Mr. Lewis candidly announces that he considers his subject too near for "impartial judgment," and he lives up to his declaration most loyally, contending that practically everything Roosevelt said and did was exactly the right thing to say and do.

The eulogists and biographers claim rather too much, and one could wish that they would take a little more pains to harmonize their favorite facts. In order to illustrate the power of mind over matter, they all foster the tradition of Roosevelt's sickly youth. But Mr. MacIntire speaks of him in the New York Assembly as "this puny young chap" at just the period in which Mr. Thwing, after a reference to his "puny voice and puny hand," exhibits him knocking out the slugger Stubby Collins and mopping up the floor with "several" others. There is a similar discrepancy with regard to his linguistic attainments. Roosevelt himself testified that he was "lamentably weak in Latin and Greek"; but Mr. Thwing asserts that he was "a scholar of the first rank in the classics." One observer describes his conversational French at a luncheon in the White House as voluble, but regardless of accent and grammar; but Mr. Thwing says that "the savants of the Sorbonne heard him address them in as flawless French as they themselves could employ." Mr. MacIntire credits Roosevelt with the message ordering Dewey to sail into the port of Manila; Mr. Lewis says it has been established that Secretary Long sent it. Mr. Thwing makes him the discoverer and namer of the River of Doubt; Mr. Lewis represents him as only the explorer of that river which in his honor was renamed Teodoro by the Brazilian Government. When there is a difference with regard to verifiable facts, Mr. Lewis appears generally to be right. In the total estimates, however, there is no significant difference; the biographers agree that Roosevelt was "our typical American," and possessed every important virtue that we admire.

When the critical biographer arrives he will re-examine this total estimate. Perhaps he will be challenged to re-examination by a certain passage towards the end of Mr. Lewis's book: "In the year 1918, a friend referred to the year 1921 as the year when he (Roosevelt) would again enter the White House. He had been in one of his jocular moods, but he immediately became very serious. 'No,' he said, 'not I. I don't want it, and I don't think I am the man to be nominated. I made too many enemies, and the people are tired of my candidacy'."

Mr. Roosevelt knew "the people." When he said, "I made too many enemies, and the people are tired of my candidacy," he admitted what none of the biographers concedes, the waning of his star, his perception that he could no longer, as in 1904, say "We believe" with strong confidence that he was uttering the convictions of the overwhelming majority of his countrymen. Both he and "the people" had changed, but the people had changed more profoundly than he in ways which I shall attempt to indicate by sketching an answer to three questions: First, what were the dominant aspects of the national character at about the time of Mr. Roosevelt's advent in public life? Second, what significant alterations in the national psychology did he produce in the period during which his personality was most heartily accepted as an incarnation of the national character? Third, how and to what extent has his national representativeness diminished?

II

Mr. Roosevelt did not emerge conspicuously on the national horizon till late in the nineties. The preceding decade appears to have contained extraordinarily little to kindle the imaginations of spirited and public-minded young men. There had been no war since the youth of their fathers. The Government pursued a policy of sombre rather than "splendid" isolation. The country offered its imposing attractions chiefly to the big business men. Captains of industry flourished like the green bay tree. For diversion there was riotous striking in the Carnegie Steel Works at Homestead; but the State militia put it down. In 1893 there was a financial panic; but it blew over. In 1894 Coxey led an army of the unemployed to Washington; but it dispersed like the chorus of a musical comedy amid general laughter. The Columbian Exposition, at the opening of which Chauncey Depew assisted, was on the whole a symbol of a period of unexampled material prosperity in commerce, agriculture, and manufactures. In 1896 William McKinley, son of an iron manufacturer and author of a tariff bill designed to protect the farmers from the plain people as the manufacturers had already been protected, was elected President under the skilful management of Mark Hanna, wholesale grocer, coal and iron merchant, later United States Senator. Mr. Roscoe Thayer remarks in his life of Hay that the most representative American in the third quarter of the century was P. T. Barnum; and the methods and ideals of Mark Hanna as political manager he compares to the methods and ideals of Barnum. From the popular magazines, reflecting current standards of success, the aspiring youth learned that by frugality and industry he might become as rich as Andrew Carnegie or John D. Rockefeller or as noble and distinguished as Chauncey Depew.

The Plutocratic era lacked—outside the field of business—ideas, imagination, animating purpose.

Mark Twain, in some ways a singularly sensitive person, curiously illustrates the point. He possessed ambition and a restless energy which should, of course, have found satisfaction and ample reward in the production of literature; but in this decade he seems to have been irresistibly driven by the time-spirit to compete with the acknowledged leaders of American life in their own field. He spent himself trying to get rich and live in the grand style like his friend Carnegie and his friend Henry Rogers. Feverishly pushing his publishing house, his type-setting machine, and a half dozen projects for rolling up a fortune, he began to use literature as a mere handmaid to finance and to regard himself as a financier. He felt himself daily on the brink of immense wealth while he was actually headed for bankruptcy. His recently published letters give the emotional reaction. Reading the morning papers, he says, makes him spend the rest of the day "pleading for the damnation of the human race." "Man is not to me the respect-worthy person he was before; and so I have lost my pride in him, and can't write praisefully about him any more." He thinks that he detects in Howells something of his own ennui: "indifference to sights and sounds once brisk with interest; tasteless stale stuff which used to be champagne; the boredom of travel; the secret sigh

behind the public smile; the private What-in-hell-
did-I-come-for."

With less bitterness Mr. Dooley—in 1897, the
year of Queen Victoria's jubilee—testifies to the
same effect in summarizing the achievements of his
own time in America:

> While she was lookin' on in England, I was look-
> in' on in this counthry. I have seen America spread
> out fr'm th' Atlantic to th' Pacific, with a branch
> office iv th' Standard Ile Comp'ny in ivry hamlet.
> I've seen th' shackles dropped fr'm th' slave, so's he
> cud be lynched in Ohio. . . . an' Corbett beat
> Sullivan, an' Fitz beat Corbett . . . An' th'
> invintions . . . th' cotton gin an' th' gin sour
> an' th' bicycle an' th' flying machine an' th' nickle-
> in-th'-slot machine an' th' Croker machine an' th'
> sody fountain an'—crownin' wurruk iv our civiliza-
> tion—th' cash raygister.

It would be easy to multiply illustrations of the
effect of this busy but mercenary and humdrum national mind upon the finer spirits in the political
arena. John Hay, for example, as Secretary of
State under McKinley, seems to have gone earnestly
about his work, suppressing now a yawn of disgust,
now a sigh of despair. "Office holding *per se*,"
he writes in 1900, "has no attraction for me." He
has some far-sighted policies for his department, but
he can't put them through, for "there will always be
34 per cent of the Senate on the blackguard side of
every question that comes before them." Even
more of this quiet disgust with American public

life appears in the now celebrated diary of Henry Adams, a man who "had everything," born into the governing class yet holding no higher office than that of private secretary to his father, unless it was the position of assistant professor of history at Harvard. When the latter position was offered to him, he remarked in a *blasé* tone which would have thunderstruck his great-grandfather: "It could not much affect the sum of solar energies whether one went on dancing with girls in Washington, or began talking to boys in Cambridge." Still more striking is Adams' analysis of the American character in government circles. It might be true, he said, in New York or Chicago, that the American was "a pushing, energetic, ingenious person, always awake and trying to get ahead of his neighbors;" but it was not true in Washington. "There the American showed himself, four times in five, as a quiet, peaceful, shy figure, rather in the mould of Abraham Lincoln, somewhat sad, sometimes pathetic, once tragic; or like Grant, as inarticulate, uncertain, distrustful of himself, still more distrustful of others, and awed by money. That the American by temperament worked to excess, was true; work and whiskey were his stimulants; work was a form of vice; but *he never cared much for money or power after he earned them.* The amusement of the pursuit was all the amusement he got from it; he had no use for wealth."

While the national mind was absorbed in business

why should young men born to wealth and social position strive to thrust themselves in between the captains of industry and their political representatives? Possessing at the start the objects of the race, why should they contend? Politics was generally described as dirty and uninspiring; why should they subject themselves to its soil and fatigue? How some of them were answering such questions, Jacob Riis revealed in his life of Roosevelt:

They were having a reunion of his [Roosevelt's] class when he was Police Commissioner, and he was there. One of the professors told of a student coming that day to bid him good-bye. He asked him what was to be his work in the world.

"Oh!" he said, with a little yawn, "really do you know, professor, it does not seem to me that there is anything that is much worth while."

III

Then came the impact upon the national character of the Rooseveltian personality, persuaded that there are a hundred more interesting things than making money, all "worth while:" hunting grizzlies, reforming, exploring, writing history, traveling, fighting Spaniards, developing a navy, governing men, reading Irish epics, building canals, swimming the Potomac with ambassadors, shooting lions, swapping views with kaisers, organizing new parties, and so on forever. Under the influence of this masterful force the unimaginative plutocratic psychology was steadily metamorphosed into the psychology of efficient, militant, imperialistic nationalism. When Roosevelt heard of the young man to whom nothing seemed much worth while, he is said to have struck the table a blow with his fist, exclaiming: "That fellow ought to have been knocked in the head. I would rather take my chances with a blackmailing policeman than with such as he." Mr. Riis remarks, "This is what Roosevelt got out of Harvard." But clearly he didn't get it out of Harvard. He found it—this wrath at the sluggard—in his own exuberant temperament. Most of his biographers foolishly insist that he had no extraordinary natural endowment. The evidence is all otherwise, indicating a marvellous physical and mental energy and blood beating so hot and fast through brain and sinew that he was never bored in his life. He never felt the ennui or the horrid languor of men like Hay and Henry Adams. He had such excess of animal spirits that, as every one knows, he was accustomed, after battling with assemblymen or Senators, to have in a prizefighter to knock him down.

Whatever delighted him he sought to inculcate upon the American people so that Rooseveltism should be recognized as synonymous with Americanism. Mr. Lewis is at some pains to point out that in his private life he was an old-fashioned gentleman and invariably dressed for dinner. The fact is mildly interesting, but its public influence

was absolutely negligible.   Rooseveltism can never
be interpreted to mean dressing for dinner.   Practically he was a powerful aider and abettor of
the movement to banish the word "gentleman" from
the American vocabulary, except as a term of contempt.   He was ostentatious about his friendships
with Mike Donovan, Fitzsimmons, Sullivan, and
Battling Nelson, just as he was about his pursuit
of the big game of North America, because he
loved the larger vertebrates and wished to implant
an affection for them in the national mind.   In his
sports he can hardly be called a typical American;
the typical American cannot employ the champion
pugilists, nor follow the Meadowbrook hounds, nor
hunt elephants with a regiment of bearers.   These
are the sports of emperors and rajahs and the sporting sons of multimillionaires.   Still Mr. Roosevelt
took them up and journalized them in behalf of a
strenuous athletic ideal for the nation.   A powerful
animal himself, he gloried, day in and day out, in
the fundamental animal instincts and activities, re-
productive and combative, the big family and the
big stick, the "full baby carriage" and "hitting hard
and hitting first;" and he preached them in season
and out of season.

I will give two illustrations.   On his return from
slaughtering elephants in Africa, he stopped off in
Berlin to tell the Germans about the world-movement.   That was in 1910; and perhaps the Germans
were then almost as well informed with regard to

the world-movement as Mr. Roosevelt. But in those days his exuberance was very great; for it had been two years since he had sent a message to Congress, and he found relief for his pent-up energies in bestowing advice all the way around the European circuit. Accordingly he solemnly warned the Germans that one of "the prime dangers of civilization has always been its tendency to cause the loss of virile fighting virtues, of the fighting edge." At the same time he marked it as a reassuring sign of our modern period that there were then larger standing armies than ever before in the world. These words seemed to his German hearers so fitly spoken that they then and there made Mr. Roosevelt a doctor of philosophy. He lectured also at the Sorbonne, finding a text in a novel of Daudet's in which the author speaks of "the fear of maternity which haunts the young mother." The country in which that is generally true, cried Roosevelt to that country of declining birth-rate, is "rotten to the core." "No refinement of life," he continued, "can in any way compensate for the loss of the great fundamental virtues; and of these great fundamental virtues the greatest is the race's power to perpetuate the race."

Roosevelt's mental exuberance may be suggestively measured in this fashion. Mark Twain, when he got under way, was a fairly voluble talker. But Mark Twain was silent and overwhelmed in the presence of Rudyard Kipling. Kipling, then, had a certain flow of ideas. But Kipling was silent and overwhelmed in the presence of Roosevelt. Again I quote Mr. Thayer:

I have heard Mr. Rudyard Kipling tell how he used to drop in at the Cosmos Club at half past ten or so in the evening, and presently young Roosevelt would come and pour out projects, discussions of men and politics, criticisms of books, in a swift and full-volumed stream, tremendously emphatic and enlivened by bursts of humor. "I curled up on the seat opposite," said Kipling, "and listened and wondered, until the universe seemed to be spinning round and Theodore was the spinner.' '

IV

Roosevelt quickened the pace of national life by his own mental and physical speed. His special contribution, however, was not the discovery but the direction of strenuousness. The captains of industry had been strenuous enough. He found a new object for physical and mental energy on the grand scale. More than any other man of his time he made political eminence a prize of the first order by his own unequivocal preference of public service and glory to private opulence and ease. The exigencies of his later political life associated him indeed with what a western humorist has described as the "high-low-brows;" he consorted with publicans and sinners; he broke bread with bosses and malefactors of great wealth; he played up the prize-fighters and the cowboys; he hurled epithets at Byzantine logothetes and college professors: so that one almost forgets that he began his career distinctly on the "high-brow" side as a "silk-stocking" reformer, supported by the vote of the "brownstone fronts," foremost of the pure-principled purposeful young "college men in politics" in an era of sordid greed and corruption. But in the days when he was assemblyman at Albany, police commissioner, and civil service reformer, men did not speak of him nor did he speak of himself as a "practical politician." In those days there was a certain bloom on the fruit that he reached for; and he did not disdain to speak of himself as a "practical idealist." In that rôle he delighted even fastidious disciples of Charles Eliot Norton's fastidious school; and he exercised a wonderfully tonic influence upon well-bred young men of his generation.

His first great service was to his own prosperous class, to young men of means in college, to the "intellectuals" generally. He did not preach against wealth. He held, like the philosopher Frank Crane, that "men who get $20,000 a year and up are the most valuable citizens of the nation." On the other hand, he maintained, like that journalistic sage, that the man who inherits a million and spends his days playing bridge and changing his trousers is "a cootie on the body politic." To fortune's favored sons he declared the responsibilities of wealth and he taught the right uses of leisure. In the vein of

Carlyle and Kipling he preached against an idle, pleasure-seeking life as not merely undesirable, but contemptible. He preached the gospel of work for every man that comes into the world, work to the uttermost of his capacity; responsibility for every advantage and every talent; ignominy and derision for the coward and the shirker and the soft-handed over-fastidious person who thinks public life too rough and dirty for his participation. Writing of machine politics in 1886, he said, rather fatalistically: "If steady work and much attention to detail are required, ordinary citizens, to whom participation in politics is merely a disagreeable duty, will always be beaten by the organized army of politicians to whom it is both duty, business, and pleasure, and who are knit together and to outsiders by their social relations." But in 1894 he put the bugle to his lips and summoned the more intelligent class of "ordinary citizens" to arms:

The enormous majority of our educated men have to make their own living. . . . Nevertheless, the man of business and the man of science, the doctor of divinity and the doctor of law, the architect, the engineer and the writer, all alike owe a *positive duty* to the community, the neglect of which they cannot excuse on any plea of their private affairs. They are bound to follow understandingly the course of public events; they are bound to try to estimate and form judgments upon public men; and they are bound to act intelligently and effectively in support of the principles which they deem

to be right and for the best interests of the country. . . . If our educated men as a whole become incapable of playing their full part in our life,
if they cease doing their share of the rough, hard
work which must be done, and grow to take a position of mere dilettanteism in our public affairs, they
will speedily sink in relation to their fellows who
really do the work of governing, until they stand
toward them as *a cultivated, ineffective man with
a taste for bric-à-brac* stands toward a great artist.
When once a body of citizens becomes thoroughly
out of touch and out of temper with the national
life, its usefulness is gone, and *its power of leaving
its mark on the times is gone also.*

I have italicized in this passage the characteristic
three-fold appeal: the straightforward statement
of duty, the craftily constructed contemptuous
phrase for the dilettante, the quiet but significant
reference to the rewards of virtue. In Roosevelt's
heart there sang lifelong the refrain of Tennyson's
ode on the Duke of Wellington, "The path of duty
is the way to glory;" and he made it sing in the
ears of his contemporaries until the blasé young
man of the Yellow Nineties became unfashionable,
yielding his place to the Man Who Does Things.
This alteration of the national psychology was of
profound importance. It marked the difference between a nation headed for decadence and a nation
entering upon a renaissance; and Roosevelt's service
in bringing it about can hardly be overvalued. Some
appraisers of his merits say that his most notable

achievement was building the Panama Canal. I should say that his most notable achievement was creating for the nation the atmosphere in which valor and high seriousness live, by clearing the air of the poisonous emanations of "superior" people:

Let the man of learning, the man of lettered leisure, beware of that queer and cheap temptation to pose to himself and to others as the cynic, as the man who has outgrown emotions and beliefs, the man to whom good and evil are as one. The poorest way to face life is to face it with a sneer. . . . There is no more unhealthy being, no man less worthy of respect, than he who either really holds, or feigns to hold, an attitude of sneering contempt toward all that is great and lofty, whether in achievement or in that noble effort which, even if it fails, comes second to achievement. . . . The man who does nothing cuts the same sordid figure in the pages of history, whether he be cynic, fop, or voluptuary.

Preaching duty and meditating on glory, Roosevelt came up through the dull nineties as the apostle of "applied idealism;" and all good men spoke well of him. He seemed to be striking out a new and admirable type of public man: well bred but strenuous, ambitious but public-spirited, upright but practical and efficient—the idealist who gets things done which everyone agrees ought to be done. But few men guessed the height and depth of desire in this fighter of legislative crooks, this reformer of metropolitan police, this advocate of the merit system;

and no one knew what his ideas and temperament would do to the national life if he became its acknowledged leader. In 1898 came the Spanish War, then the governorship of New York, the vice-presidency in 1900, and a year later Roosevelt was in the saddle. These events swiftly disclosed the wider horizon of his mind and the scope of his ambition for himself and for America. The war with Spain brought him forward as the Seminole War brought forward Andrew Jackson; and his personality was immensely responsible for the effect of that "incident" upon the national character.

V

Mr. Roosevelt was an admirer of Thucydides, but he was a much less philosophical historian; for he says that the war with Spain was "inevitable," and leaves his readers to explain why. The small jingo class whose veins perennially throb with red blood and national honor fought, of course, to avenge the blowing-up of the Maine. The mass of the plain people with their perennial simple-hearted idealism were persuaded that they were going in to set Cuba free, even after they discovered that they had also gone in to subjugate the Philippine Islands. Mr. J. A. Hobson, the English economist, says:

Not merely do the trusts and other manufacturing trades that restrict their output for the home market more urgently require foreign markets, but they are also more anxious to secure protected markets, and this can only be achieved by extending the area of political rule. This is the essential significance of the recent change in American foreign policy as illustrated by the Spanish War, the Philippine annexation, the Panama policy, and the new application of the Monroe doctrine to the South American States. South America is needed as a preferential market for investment of trust "profits" and surplus trust products: if in time these States can be brought within a Zollverein under the suzerainty of the United States, the financial area of operations receives a notable accession.

There is an absence of rose-pink altruism from this last explanation which should commend it to *The Chicago Tribune;* but Roosevelt, though the *Tribune's* chief hero, would certainly have rejected it for an interpretation at once more personal and more political.

It is fairly plain that this war, which he had done his utmost to prepare for and to bring about, was first of all an opportunity for a man of his strenuous leisure class with fighting blood and fighting edge to win personal distinction. He himself speaks of his baptism of fire as his "crowded hour of glorious life;" and throughout his narrative of the exploits of his regiment—"My men were children of the dragon's blood"—he exhibits a delight in fighting that reminds one of the exuberant praise of "glorious battle" uttered early in the late war by the Colonel of the Death's Head Hussars. He

is as proud of personally bringing down his Span-
iard as of slaying his first lion. He played his
daring and picturesque part in a way to rehabilitate
military glory in the national mind. But for the
astonishing skill with which he wrung the last drop
of dramatic interest from his troop of college men
and cowboys the reverberations of the affair would
soon have died away in the popular consciousness.
He made the deeds of the Rough Riders a popular
classic like Lexington and Bunker Hill. His little
war did as much to kindle as Mr. Wilson's big war
did to quench the military spirit; for Mr. Wilson
went in with the grim determination of a chief of
police, and Mr. Roosevelt with the infinite gusto
of a big game hunter. His little war, as he himself declared, made him President.

In office, he did not sicken of power as did the
Washingtonians of whom Henry Adams speaks.
With the vast influence of his position he sought to
mould the national mind and feelings into the like-
ness of his own. He sought to make the national
mind virile, daring, imaginative, aggressive, and
eager for distinction in the world. He preached
to the nation as if it were a rich man of leisure with
a splendid opening, made by his war, for the practice
of the strenuous life. He set the example by magnifying his own office, concentrating power, teaching
the public to look to the Federal Government as
the controlling, dynamic, and creative center of
American life. His measure for the regulation of

monopolies, his seizure of the canal zone, his irrigation acts, his reservation of public lands all exemplify in one way and another his aversion from the spirit of *laissez-faire*, his passion for identifying the state with the man who does things. In domestic affairs this policy generally estranged the "big interests" and won the support of the "plain people." In foreign affairs the big interests supported him, but the plain people were first dazzled, and then astonished, and then a little perplexed. The plain people do not understand foreign affairs.

President McKinley, by instinct and upbringing a domestically-minded statesman, had indeed begun to speak in a resigned way of manifest destiny with regard to our newly acquired island possessions. He could hardly do otherwise, for this was the midsummer time of the imperial enthusiasm of the "Anglo-Saxons." These were the days of Rhodesian dreamers; Kitchener was fighting in Egypt; Roberts was fighting in South Africa; and in 1899 Mr. Kipling struck up his famous chant: "Take up the white man's burden, send forth the best ye breed." And so McKinley gravely recognized our manifest destiny in the Far East. Yet John Hay says that he was called in by McKinley to discuss foreign affairs not more than once a month, but that as soon as Roosevelt was in office he was called upon every day. It was Roosevelt first who embraced manifest destiny with the joy of an enkindled political imagination. It was he that resolutely sought to waken the expansive energies of the nation and to give it the fighting edge and the will to prevail in the impending conflicts of the powers. It was he that tirelessly went up and down the land declaring that the imperialistic tendencies developed by the Spanish War were tokens of national virility and that the responsibilities of the new foreign policy were glorious opportunities for men of the heroic mood imbued with the new Rooseveltian Americanism.

If we are to mark his place in the spiritual history of the times, we must clearly understand the temper which, at the turn of the century, he brought into our era of atrocious international conflicts. Nowhere, perhaps, did he declare more eloquently the gospel of militant imperialistic nationalism than in his address on The Strenuous Life, delivered before the Hamilton Club of Chicago in 1899:

The timid man, the lazy man, the man who distrusts his country, the over-civilized man who has lost the great fighting virtues, the ignorant man and the man of dull mind, whose soul is incapable of feeling the mighty lift that thrills "stern men with empires in their brains"—all these, of course, shrink from seeing the nation undertake its new duties. . . . The army and navy are the sword and shield which the nation must carry if she is to do her duty among the nations of the earth. . . . The twentieth century looms before us big with the fate of many nations. If we stand idly by, if we seek merely swollen slothful ease and ignoble peace, if we shrink from the hard contests where men must win at hazard of their lives and at the risk of all they hold dear, then the bolder and stronger peoples will pass us by, and will win for themselves the · domination of the world. Let us, therefore, boldly face the life of strife. . . . Above all, let us shrink from no strife, moral or physical, within or without the nation—for it is only through strife, through hard and dangerous endeavors, that we shall ultimately win the goal of true national greatness.

That the sentiments and principles here expressed sound very familiar to us today is not, I fancy, because most of us have been reading Roosevelt's addresses of the Spanish War period, but because we have been reading the utterances of the Pan-Germans whom Roosevelt himself in 1910 was adjuring not to lose the fighting edge and whom he was congratulating on the size of European military establishments as a sign of health and virility. Retrospectively considered, his solicitude for the fighting edge of the Germans reminds one of the matador in Blasco Ibáñez's *Blood and Sand*, who, it will be remembered, prays for a "good bull." With the essentials in the religion of the militarists of Germany, Roosevelt was utterly in sympathy. He believed that if you kept your fighting edge keen enough no one would seriously question your righteousness. The only significant difference in objects was that while they invoked the blessing of Jehovah upon Pan-Germany he invoked it upon Pan-

America, meaning the United States and her dependencies, protectorates, and spheres of influence—and the Pan-America of his dream made Mittel-Europa look like a postage-stamp. The highest point of his working upon the national mind, the point at which his powerful personality most nearly succeeded in transforming the national character from its original bias, was that in which he made it half in love with military glory, half in love with empire-building, half in love with the sort of struggle which was preparing in Europe for the domination of the world.

VI

The American leader of militant imperialistic nationalism fell at the end of his last great fight, a fight which, it may be soberly said, he had done his utmost both immediately and remotely to prepare for and to bring about. All his friends and many who were not his friends give him credit for the immediate preparation. But few of his friends claim or admit his profounder part in the preparation of the stage for the conflict, the will of the combatants, the conditions of the struggle, the prizes of victory. The preparation runs far back to the days when he began to preach the strenuous life in the flush of the Spanish War, to the days when he dangled before our eyes "those fair tropic islands," to the days when he boasted that he had taken

Panama and let Congress debate after the act. In
the stunning clash of militant imperialistic nations,
a clash which was the "inevitable" goal of his lifelong policy, as it is that of every imperialist, he
towered above his fellow-citizens, constantly and
heroically calling to arms. His countrymen rose,
but not for his battle. They fought, but not for his
victory. Time and events with remorseless irony
made him the standard-bearer and rallying point for
an American host dedicated to the destruction of
his policy of militant imperialistic nationalism
abroad and at home. He said "Belgium," he mentioned Germany's transgressions of law; and his
countrymen cheered and buckled on their armor.
But if, during the war, he had dared to exhort them,
as in the earlier time, "to face the life of strife
for the domination of the world," they were in a
mood to have torn him in pieces. In that mood
they fought and won their war. Highly as they
valued his instrumental services, the principles on
which they waged it and the objects which they
sought drew them away from Roosevelt and towards Lincoln and Washington.

At the present time it is obvious to everyone that
a faction of his old friends, incorrigibly born and
bred in militant imperialistic nationalism, are making a fight over his body to wrest from the simple-
hearted idealistic plain people the fruits of victory.
Gloomy observers—too gloomy, I think—declare
that the fruits are already gone. The exponents of

nationalistic egoism and selfishness will win some partial and temporary triumphs in this as in other countries. In the immediate future the memory of Roosevelt will be the most animating force among our American Junkers. There will be an attempt to repopularize just those Bismarckian characteristics of their hero which made him so utterly unlike Lincoln—his moral hardness, his two-fistedness, the symbolic big stick. But his commanding force as chief moulder of the national mind is over. He must take his rank somewhere among the kings and kaisers in competition with whom he made his place in the spiritual history of his times. He can never again greatly inspire the popular liberal movement in America. The World War has too profoundly discredited the masters of *Weltpolitik* in his epoch. It has too tragically illuminated the connections between the cataclysm and the statecraft and militaristic psychology behind it. He was a realist with no nonsense about him; but all the realists of the period are now under suspicion of being unrealistic in that they ignored the almost universal diffusion of "nonsense" or idealism among mankind. When Mr. Roosevelt fell out with "practical" men, he almost invariably strengthened his position with the plain people. It was when he offended their "nonsense"—as in his vindictive and ruthless onslaughts upon his successor and upon his great rival, and in his conduct of the Panama affair—that they began to doubt whether he had the magnanimity, the fairness of mind, the love of civil ways requisite to guide them towards the fulfillment of their historic destiny. He developed a habit of speaking so scornfully of "over-civilization" and so praisefully of mere breeding and fighting as to raise the question that he himself raised about Cromwell, whether he had an adequate "theory of ends," and whether he did not become so fascinated with his means as frequently to forget his ends altogether.

Take the ever-burning matter of militarism. His apologists, like those of the Kaiser, all declare that he loved peace; and one can quote passages to prove it. I will quote a beautiful passage from his speech in Berlin in 1910: "We must remember that it is only by working along the lines laid down by the philanthropists, by the lovers of mankind, that we can be sure of lifting our civilization to a higher and more permanent plane of well-being than ever was attained by any preceding civilization. Unjust war is to be abhorred——." I pause to ask whether any one thinks this remark about working on the lines of philanthropists and lovers of mankind is characteristic Rooseveltian doctrine. I now quote the rest of the passage: "But woe to the nation that does not make ready to hold its own in time of need against all who would harm it. And woe thrice over to the nation in which the average man loses the fighting edge." I stop again and ask whether any one thinks that is *not* characteristic Rooseveltian doctrine? Why does the second of these sentences sound perfectly Rooseveltian and the first absolutely not? Because into the first he put a stroke of the pen; into the second the whole emphasis of his character. The first is his verbal sop to the idealist; the second is his impassioned message to his generation. By his use of rhetorical balance he gives a superficial appearance of the mental equivalent; but by his violent and infallible emphasis he becomes the greatest concocter of "weasel" paragraphs on record. In time his hearers learned to distinguish what he said from what he stood for, the part of his speech which was official rhetoric from the part that quivered with personal force.

He said, it is true, that "mere fervor for excellence in the abstract is a great mainspring for good work;" but in practice he night and day denounced in the most intolerant language those who exhibited mere fervor for excellence in the abstract, and even those who sought excellence by other ways than his. He professed love for the plain people; but the Progressive episode looks today, so far as he was concerned, like a momentary hot fit and political aberration of a confirmed Hamiltonian, regarding the plain people not so much socially as politically, not so much as individuals as a massive instrument for the uses of the state and the governing class. He said that he had a regard for peace but he made plain that he loved and valued war; and he denounced every one else who said a good word for peace, he reviled every type of pacifist so mercilessly as to rouse suspicion as to whether he really cared a rap for the *object* of the pacifists. He expressed approval of arbitration; but he invariably followed up such expressions with an assertion that the only effective arbitrator is a man in shining armor. He avowed a desire for international order; but his imagination and his faith did not rise to a vision of other ways of attaining it than the ways of Alexander and Caesar—by the imperial dominion of armed power; and he denounced other modes of working for international order so bitterly as to raise a doubt as to his regard for the object. He admitted, like many of his followers, a faint and eleventh-hour respect for the abstract idea of a league of nations; but he led in raising such a thunder of opposition to the only league within sight and reach that he weakened the hands of the American framers, and he raised a question as to what he meant in the old days by his fiery declamation against those who "make the impossible better forever the enemy of the possible good."

Mr. Roosevelt has attained satisfactions which he thought should console fallen empires: he has left heirs and a glorious memory. How much more glorious it might have been if in his great personality there had been planted a spark of magnanimity. If, after he had drunk of personal glory like a Scandinavian giant, he had lent his giant strength to a cause of the plain people not of his contriving nor under his leadership. If in addition to helping win the war he had identified himself with the attainment of its one grand popular object. From performing this supreme service he was prevented by defects of temper which he condemned in Cromwell, a hero whom he admired and in some respects strikingly resembled. Cromwell's desire, he says,

was to remedy specific evils. He was too impatient to found the kind of legal and constitutional system which would prevent the recurrence of such evils. Cromwell's extreme admirers treat his impatience of the delays and shortcoming of ordinary constitutional and legal proceedings as a sign of his greatness. It was just the reverse. . . . His strength, his intensity of conviction, his delight in exercising powers for what he conceived to be good ends; his dislike for speculative reforms and his inability to appreciate the necessity of theories to a practical man who wishes to do good work . . . all these tendencies worked together to unfit him for the task of helping a liberty-loving people on the road to freedom.

XI

EVOLUTION IN THE ADAMS FAMILY

Mr. Brooks Adams apologizes for the inadequacy of his introduction to his brother's philosophical remains on the ground that the publishers hurried him, saying that if he did not get the book out within the year it would have lost its interest. Of course the readers who take up *The Education of Henry Adams* because it is the sensation of the hour will soon drop away, perhaps have already done so; but interest in the Adamses, so long quiescent, so piquantly reawakened at the end of the fourth eminent generation, is likely to hold more serious readers for some time to come. Henry Adams has thrown out challenges which the reviewer cannot lightly answer nor easily ignore. What shall be done with that profoundly pessimistic theory of the "degradation of energy"—a degradation alleged to be discoverable in the universe, in democracy, and even in that incorruptible stronghold of pure virtue, the Adams family? Every one who has sat blithely down to read *The Education,* much more to review it, must have discovered that it is only the last or the latest chapter of a "continued story."

It is a lure leading into a vast literary edifice, built by successive generations, which one must at least casually explore before one can conceive what was the heritage of Henry Adams, or can guess whether the family's energy suffered degradation when it produced him.

One who wishes to measure the decline from the source must begin with *The Works* of John Adams in ten volumes, edited by his grandson Charles Francis Adams I, and including a diary so fascinating and so important that one marvels that American students of letters are not occasionally sent to it rather than to Pepys or Evelyn. One should follow this up with the charming letters of John's wife, Abigail, also edited by Charles Francis I, in 1841—a classic which would be in the American Everyman if our publishers fostered American as carefully as they foster English traditions. For John Quincy Adams, we have his own *Memoirs* in twelve volumes, being portions of that famous diary of which he said: "There has perhaps not been another individual of the human race whose daily existence from early childhood to fourscore years has been noted down with his own hand so minutely as mine;" also a separate volume called *Life in a New England Town,* being his diary while a student in the office of Theophilus Parsons at Newburyport. One may perhaps pass Charles Francis I with his life by Charles Francis II. Then one descends to the fourth generation, and reads the *Autobiography* of

Charles Francis II, published in 1916, a notable book with interest not at all dependent upon reflected glory. Of Brooks Adams one must read at least *The Emancipation of Massachusetts* and the introduction to *The Degradation of Democratic Dogma;* and then one is tantalized on into *The Law of Civilization and Decay, America's Economic Supremacy,* and *The Theory of Social Revolutions.* Finally one approaches Henry's *Education* not quite unprepared and not overlooking the fact that, besides biographies of Gallatin and Randolph, he wrote what has been called "incomparably the best" history of the administrations of Jefferson and Madison, in nine volumes distinguished by lucid impartiality, and *Mont Saint Michel and Chartres,* an interpretation of the twelfth century as impressive in height and span as the great cathedral which Adams takes as the symbol of his thought.

Historians, of course, are familiar with all these paths. I should like, however, to commend them a little to gentler and less learned readers. Taken not as material for history but as the story of four generations of great personalities, living always near the center of American life, the Adams annals surpass anything we have produced in fiction. One may plunge into them as into the Comédie Humaine of Balzac or Zola's Rougon-Macquart series and happily lose contact with the world, which, if we may believe Brooks Adams, *ultimus Romanorum,* is going so fatally to the dogs. Perhaps an Adams of the present day must come forth from the study of his heredity, environment, and education with a conviction that he is an automaton, moved forward by the convergence of "lines of force," and that he is a poorer automaton than his grandfather. But for my part, I have emerged from these narratives much braced by contact with the stout, proud, purposeful Adams will, and with an impression that their latest pessimistic theories are poorly supported by their facts.

The Adams pessimism has a certain tonic quality due to its origin in the Adams sense for standards. The three Adonises, Charles Francis, Brooks, and Henry, have humiliated themselves all their lives by walking back and forth before the portraits of their statesmen ancestors and measuring their own altitude against that of "the friends of Washington." An Adams should always be in the grand style. So history presents them to the young imagination: Plutarchan heroes, august republicans, ever engaged in some public act or gesture such as Benjamin West liked to spread on his canvases—drafting the Declaration of Independence, presenting credentials to George III, signing the Monroe doctrine, fulminating in Congress against the annexation of Texas, or penning the famous dispatch to Lord Russell: "It would be superfluous to point out to your lordship that this is war." In a nation which has endured for a hundred and fifty years, it ought not to be easy to equal the elevation of character, or to attain the heights of achievement reached by the most eminent men. There should be in every old national gallery certain figures unassailably great to rebuke the natural insolence of younger generations and silently to remind a young man that he must have a strong heart and almost wear it out before he can hope to deserve what these worthies have made the proudest of rewards, the thanks and the remembrance of the Republic.

For an Adams, who needs a bit of humility, it no doubt is wholesome to dwell on the superiority of his forefathers; but for the average man who needs a bit of encouragement, it is equally wholesome to reflect that John Adams represents a distinct "variation" of species. The family had been in America a hundred years before the grand style began to develop. In the words of Charles Francis I, "Three long successive generations and more than a century of time passed away, during which Gray's elegy in the country churchyard relates the whole substance of their history." If we can only understand the processes by which John was transformed from a small farmer's son to President of the United States, the evolution of the rest of the family will be as easy to follow as the transmission of wealth. Now, John's emergence is singularly devoid of miraculous aspects, and it is therefore of practical interest to the democrat.

John abandoned the pitchfork and varied his species by taking two steps which in those days were calculated to put him in the governing class. He went to Harvard—a course which may still be imitated, but which in 1755, when the total population of the colonies only equalled that of one of our great cities, set a man far more distinctly in a class by himself than it does today, and marked him for a professional career. Second, after an insignificant interval of school teaching, he studied law in the office of Rufus Putnam, and thus entered a still smaller class, carefully restricted by limitation of the number of apprentices who could be taken in any office.

At the same time he began keeping a diary, a habit which it is now the custom to ridicule. What strikes one about John's diary in his years of adolescence is that he uses it as an instrument for marking his intellectual progress and getting himself in hand, neither of which is a morbid activity. He notes that he is of an amorous temperament and that his thoughts are liable to be "called off from law by a girl, a pipe, a poem, a love-letter, a Spectator, a play, etc., etc." But *studia in mores abeunt;* and year after year he is digging away tenaciously and purposefully at studies which communicate a masculine vigor to the mind; and he is reading, with instant application to his own future, authors that are still capable of putting a flame of ambition in a young man's vitals.

The breadth and humanity of the old-fashioned

program of reading for the bar may be suggested by one of his entries at the age of twenty-three:

Labor to get distinct ideas of law, right, wrong, justice, equity; search for them in your own mind, in Roman, Grecian, French, English treatises of natural, civil, common, statute law; aim at an exact knowledge of the nature, end, and means of government; compare the different forms of it with each other, and each of them with their effects on public and private happiness. Study Seneca, Cicero, and all other good moral writers; study Montesquieu, Bolingbroke, Vinnius, etc., and all other good civil writers.

He enjoins it upon himself to observe the arts of popularity in the tavern, town-meeting, the training field, and the meeting-house, though it must be added that none of his line mastered these arts. He frequents the courts, converses with successful men, records a public-spirited act of Franklin's, and surmises after an hour's talk at Mayor Gardener's that "the design of Christianity was not to make men good riddle-solvers or good mystery-mongers but good men, good magistrates." After a bit of dawdling, he tells himself that "twenty-five years of the animal life is a great proportion to be spent to so little purpose." He vows to read twelve hours a day. He cries to himself: "Let love and vanity be extinguished, and the great passions of ambition, patriotism, break out and burn. Let little objects be neglected and forgot, and great ones engross, arouse, and exalt my soul." Such temper issued from that diet of lion's marrow, that energetic digestion of law and classical literature!

II

The only remarkable aspect of the variation effected in this generation was that such a man as John Adams should have found such a wife as Abigail Smith, a woman descended from the religious aristocrats of New England, and her husband's equal in heart and mind. Her descendants of the present day would say that predetermined lines of force—theological and legal—converged here to strengthen the social position of John and to insure the production of John Quincy; but that is not the way most men think of their wooing. Abigail had no formal schooling; yet, as "female" education went in those days, it mattered little. She was obviously the "product" of that family culture and social discipline which, at their best, render formal schooling almost superfluous. She had the gaiety of good breeding, the effusion of quick emotions, and that fundamental firmness of character which are developed by a consciousness that one was born in the right class. From books, from table-talk, from the men and women who frequented her home, not least from her lover, she had derived the views of the classical mid-eighteenth century, with just a premonitory flush of romantic enthusiasm; she had become familiar with public affairs; she had acquired the tone and carriage, she had breathed in the great spirit, of such a woman as Cato would have a Roman wife and mother.

Emerson cherished the thought of writing an American Plutarch. In such a book we should have a picture of Abigail managing her husband's estate in Braintree while he is at the Congress in Philadelphia—through pestilence, siege, battles, and famine-prices not venturing to ask a word of his return, lest she perturb a mind occupied with public business. We should have her reply at a later period to one who asked whether she would have consented to her husband's going to France, had she known that he was to be absent so long:

> I recollected myself a moment, and then spoke the real dictates of my heart. "If I had known, sir, that Mr. Adams could have effected what he has done, I would not only have submitted to the absence I have endured, painful as it has been, but I would not have opposed it, even though three years should be added to the number (which Heaven avert). I find a pleasure in being able to sacrifice my selfish passions to the general good and in imitating the example which has taught me to consider myself and family but as the small dust of the scale when compared with the great community.

We should see her called from her farm to be the first American lady at the English Court. We should remark that she finds the best manners in England in the home of the Bishop of St. Asaph, old friend of her adored Franklin, where, by the way, she meets those dangerous English radicals Priestley and Price. And with the warmth of fond native prejudice, we should adore her for writing home:

Do you know that European birds have not half the melody of ours? Nor is their fruit half so sweet, nor their flowers half so fragrant, nor their manners half so pure, nor their people half so virtuous; but keep this to yourself, or I shall be thought more than half deficient in understanding and taste.

III

In the jargon of Brooks and Henry Adams, as I have remarked, irresistible "lines of force" converge for the education of the second generation. More humanly speaking, the ambition of John, the tenderness and pride of Abigail, unite above the cradle of John Quincy, and most intelligently conspire to give him what he later was to recognize as "an unparalleled education." "It should be your care and mine," John writes to his wife, "to elevate the minds of our children, and exalt their courage, to accelerate and animate their industry and activity." It is the fashion nowadays to assert, against the evidence of history, that great men in their critical hours are unconscious of their greatness; but these Adamses assuredly knew what they were about. With the fullest recognition that her boy's father and his friends are living classics, Abigail writes:

Glory, my son, in a country which has given birth to characters, both in the civil and military depart-

ments, which may vie with the wisdom and valor of antiquity. As an immediate descendant of one of these characters, may you be led to that disinterested patriotism and that noble love of country which will teach you to despise wealth, pomp, and equipage as mere external advantages, which cannot add to the internal excellence of your mind, or compensate for the want of integrity and virtue.

Of course John Quincy was to use the "external advantages" which his mother a little hastily urged him to despise. By working twelve hours a day at the law, John Adams had raised the family from the ground up to a point at which he could give to the educational processes of his son a tremendous expansion and acceleration. At an age when John had been helping his father on the farm, from eleven to fourteen, John Quincy, son of the peace commissioner, was studying in Paris or Leyden, or travelling in Russia as private secretary to the American Envoy. He acquired history, diplomacy, geography as he acquired his French—by what we call in the case of the last, "the natural method." It cannot be too much emphasized that in the second, third, and fourth generations the family and its connections were in position to provide a liberal education without resort to a university. Before John Quincy went to Harvard he had assisted in negotiating the treaty of peace between his country and Great Britain. The whole matter of external advantages may be summed up in a picture of the boy, at the age of eleven, returning from France in a ship with the French Ambassador, the Chevalier de la Luzerne, and his secretary M. Marbois, the three lying side by side on their cots and thus portrayed by the boy's proud father:

The Ambassador reading out loud, in Blackstone's Discourse at his entrance on his Professorship of the Common Law at the University, and my son correcting the pronunciation of every word and syllable and letter. The Ambassador said he was astonished at my son's knowledge; that he was a master of his own tongue, like a professor. M. Marbois said, Your son teaches us more than you; he has *point de graces, point d'éloges.*

Charles Francis II, who knew his grandfather only in his old age, says that he was not of a "holiday temperament;" but the diary of John Quincy Adams's early life in Newburyport shows a fairly festive young Puritan, tempted, like his father before him, to frequent truancies from the law, reading *Tom Jones* and Rousseau's *Confessions,* shooting, playing the flute, visiting, frequently dancing till three, occasionally drinking till dawn, and regretting it for three days afterward. His social position was secure, his experience and attainments already notable, his career marked out, the reflected glamour of paternal glory gratifying; perhaps he asked himself why he should not rest on his oars while his contemporaries were catching up. Such considerations may occur to an Adams, but they do not remain with him. His ambition widens with his culture. He begins on the verge of manhood to pant for distinction, bids farewell to the revellers, girds up his loins, and strikes into his pace.

John Quincy Adams had found his stride when he wrote to his father from London, December 29, 1795:

When I am clearly convinced that my duty commands me to act, if the love of ease, or the love of life, or the love of fame itself, dear as it is, could arrest my hand, or give me a moment's hesitation in the choice, I should certainly be fit for no situation of public trust whatever. . . . So much for the principle. But I may go a little further. The struggle against a popular clamor is not without its charms in my mind.

In the next year, following the example of John Wesley, he began rising at four o'clock; and so eager was his mind, so tireless his industry, so completely had he taken himself in hand, that he rose not later than four-thirty for the next fifty years— fifty years spent almost without interruption in public service, fighting the Jacksonian democrats, fighting for internal improvements, fighting the extension of slavery, fighting for free speech, till he sank in harness in his eighty-first year on the floor of the House of Representatives.

His training in law and diplomacy had fitted him for statesmanship, and as a statesman chiefly he lives. But Brooks Adams makes much of his philosophical temper and of his talent for scientific investigation. For our purposes it is important also to note that he had a marked taste for literature, as the vast memoirs bear witness. In his old age he spoke of the "ecstasy of delight" with which he had heard a choir singing his version of the 65th Psalm as surpassing all the pleasure he had received in the whole course of his life from the praise of mortal men. His literary and his political aspirations were intimately associated. He had hoped that his diary would rank next to the Holy Scriptures as the record of one who "by the irresistible power of genius and the irrepressible energy of will and the favor of Almighty God" had "banished war and slavery from the face of the earth forever."

IV

Charles Francis Adams I, perhaps not the most ambitious of John Quincy's children, was the only one that survived him; he must therefore be our representative of the third generation. We may, however, pass lightly over him, because, though an eminent, sturdy, and capable man, he repeats in general the formative processes and the careers of his predecessors without any singular distinction or deviation from type. His richness of educational opportunity may be summarized by saying that he learned French at St. Petersburg, where his father was minister, spent several years at a school in England, passed through the Boston Latin School and

Harvard, and studied law and observed public men from the White House in the administration of his father and in the palmy days of Jackson, Clay, and Webster. Possibly if the father had retired after his defeat for reëlection in 1828, Charles Francis might have felt more distinctly called to advance the Adams banner; but the almost immediate return of the ex-president, plunging into his long Congressional career, preëmpted the field. Charles went to Boston, engaged in business, served for several years in the legislature, was elected to Congress in 1859, and crowned his achievements in the period of the Civil War by staunchly and successfully representing the Union in his ministry to Great Britain.

V

Coming now to the representatives of the fourth generation, who made their careers after the Civil War, we confront once more the three Adonises who more or less darkly despair of the Republic and of the future of the Adams line—Henry, Brooks, and Charles Francis II. All three were bred in the traditions of the great family, inherited its culture and social advantages, became conscious of an obligation to distinguish themselves, strove to keep pace with the new nation which the war had created, and all three, rendering an account of their adventures, intimate a degree of failure and rail at their education as inadequately adapting them to their circumstances. As a matter of fact they did fall short of the glory of their ancestors in that no one of them held public office of first-rate national importance. But, on the other hand, none of them really competed with his illustrious predecessors. Each of them developed marked variations from the ante-bellum type, in one case so marked as to constitute a new species. If the ancestral energy is degraded, it is none the less abundantly present in them all.

Charles Francis II, the least highly individualized of the trio, was the one who most conspicuously fell into the stride of the new industrial, expansive America. At his graduation from Harvard in 1856 he had discovered no remarkable aptitude—for which he blames his teachers—and so gravitated into a law office. At the outbreak of the war, it slowly occurred to him to enlist; but, once in, he enjoyed the hard athletic life, and developed a drill-master's pride in his company and in his regiment, at the head of which he rode into burning Richmond. His military duties disclosed to him his talent for organization, and also the disquieting fact that famous fighters and great organizers were frequently beneath his standard for gentlemen; Grant, for example, "was a man of coarse fibre, and did not impress with a sense of character."

But the war had toughened his own fibre and had opened his eyes to new careers for talents. When it was over, he turned to the study of railroads as the biggest enterprise of the new era, wrote his *Chapters of Erie,* became a member of the Massachusetts Board of Railroad Commissioners, which was created largely through his instrumentality, and crowned his professional career with the presidency of the Union Pacific. He was perhaps the first Adams who looked west with any special interest. His flash of genius was divining the future importance of Kansas City. The business success on which he plumes himself is his organization of the Kansas City Stock Yards Company, which, under his forty-year headship, increased its capitalization from $100,000 to over ten millions, and earned annually above $1,200,000. He does not blush to declare that he also organized in Kansas City another enterprise which made in one year "twelve dividends of ten per cent each."

The big business men, however, like the big generals, disappointed him socially: "Not one that I have ever known would I care to meet again, either in this world or the next." Having made, as the vulgar say, his "pile," this well-bred, energetic Massachusetts business man withdrew from the ungentlemanly world of business, moved from Quincy, the home of his ancestors, to Lincoln, because the former residence had become too "suburban," and devoted his leisure to writing his memoirs, criticizing Harvard, and composing communications to the Massachusetts Historical Soci-

ety. At the age of fifty-five he burned his diary,
full till then with the expectation that he might
accomplish something notable; and in his Autobiography, with the tang of the new Adams humility,
he declares: "I now humbly thank fortune that I
have almost got through life without making a conspicuous ass of myself."

Brooks Adams also set out as a lawyer, but he
seems to have retired much earlier into authorship.
His writing is less perspicuous and well-ordered
than that of his brother Charles; but that is partly
because he has more ideas and more difficult ones.
Brooks is a restless-minded lawyer of a not unfamiliar type, who turns here and there for something
"craggy" upon which to wreak his excess of mental
energy; and so he becomes amateur-historian, ama-
teur-economist, amateur-philosopher. The antiqua-
rianism of historical societies is a bit too tame for
his temper. Like his brother Henry, and indeed
in collaboration with him, he seeks a law connecting
phenomena, and in search of it he ransacks history.
He imagines and declares that he has made his mind
passive to the lessons of facts and that his results
are scientific; but the truth is that he is a dogmatic
materialist, an infatuated mechanist, who, when he
has formulated an hypothesis, sees nothing between
earth and heaven and the first Adam and the last
Adams but the proof of it.

Like his grandfather, he finds a certain charm in

an unpopular position. Sitting in the neighborhood of Plymouth Rock, he discovers that the scutcheon of his Puritan forefathers blushes with the blood of Quakers and Anabaptists; and in his *Emancipation of Massachusetts,* Puritan as he is, he remorselessly prosecutes them as selfish and bloodthirsty hypocrites. Looking further into history, he concludes that the same indictment can be brought against all religious societies and organizations from the time of Moses down; for the facts constrain him to believe that the two master passions of man are Fear and Greed. If he refrains from censure, it is because he holds that mental as well as physical phenomena are determined as fatally as the earth moves round the sun. The examination of long periods of history impresses him with "the exceedingly small part played by conscious thought in moulding the fates of men." He applies the doctrine of manifest destiny in the most fatalistic sense to the Philippine Islands and to capitalistic society, which, however, seems to him on the point of disintegration into a condition from which it can only be revivified by an "infusion of barbarian blood."

Brooks attributes many of his views to Henry and undertakes to interpret him; but temperamentally he is not qualified to understand him. He admits, indeed, that there were crypts in his brother which he had never entered. Chief of these was the unfathomable crypt of his skepticism. By con-

tact with Mill, Comte, Darwin, Spencer, all the
Adamses of the fourth generation had been emancipated from their attenuated hereditary belief in
a beneficent overruling Providence. But Charles
Francis II and Brooks recommitted themselves
without reservation to the overweening posivitism
of mid-century "scientific" philosophy. Henry alone
refuses to surrender. A wily, experienced wrestler,
returning again and again to grapple with the Time-
Spirit, at the end of each bout he eludes the adver-
sary; and at the moment one expects to see him
thrown, suddenly he has vanished, he has fled
through centuries falling about him like autumn
leaves, and from somewhere in the Middle Ages,
near some old shrine of the Virgin, one hears the
sound of mocking laughter. It is the free spirit,
eternally seeking.

Henry was, I think, a great man and the only
great Adams of his generation. All the other
Adamses had been men of action tinctured with
letters. Henry alone definitely renounced action
and turned the full current of the ancestral energy
to letters. By so doing he established a new
standard of achievement for the Adams line; and
in consequence, of course, for the rest of us. Up
to the time of the Civil War there had been for
them but one field of glory, the political arena, and
but one standard of achievement, national administration. After the war Charles Francis II tried
to be great in "big business," but in the Adams sense

"failed" because his culture was of no use there. Brooks tried for greatness in naturalistic philosophy, but found that his creed ignobly reduced all heroes to automata. But Henry, without otherwise committing himself, sought to comprehend and to represent his world, and he achieved greatness. Like yet unlike his ancestors who were painted by Copley and Stuart, he is in the grand style.

The Education of Henry Adams marks with precision the hour when its author became conscious of his variation. It was in England, towards the close of the war, where as secretary to his father he had exhausted all the excitements of the diplomatic "game," and London society had begun to pall, and loitering in Italy had ceased to charm, yet he was collecting bric-à-brac and sketches by the old masters and becoming attached to his habits and his hansom cabs, and was in a fair way to become one of those dilettantish, blasé young Americans of the period, whom Henry James has preserved like pressed flowers for posterity. It was after Sir Charles Lyell and the evolutionists had set him off on a new quest for a "father"—it mattered not, he said, "whether the father breathed through lungs, or walked on fins, or on feet." It was in that summer hour, characteristically marked by him with its picturesque accessories, when he had wandered to Wenlock Edge in Shropshire, and, throwing himself on the grass where he could look across the Marches to the mountains of Wales, thus meditated on the new theory:

Natural selection seemed a dogma to be put in the place of the Athanasian creed; it was a form of religious hope; a promise of ultimate perfection. Adams wished no better; he warmly sympathized in the object; but when he came to ask himself what he truly thought, he felt that he had no Faith; that whenever the next new hobby should be brought out, he should surely drop off Darwinism like a monkey from a perch; that the idea of one Form, Law, Order, or Sequence had no more value for him than the idea of none; that what he valued most was Motion, and that what attracted his mind was Change. . . . Henry Adams was the first in an infinite series to discover and admit to himself that he really did not care that it should be proved true, unless the process were new and amusing. He was a Darwinian for fun.

From that moment, literature was the one career for Henry, and all his overtures were failures till he discovered it. He returned to America, indeed, with the Emersonian resolution that "the current of his time was to be his current, lead where it might." He went to Washington, as a member of the governing class should do, and while waiting for an opportunity to serve the incoming administration of Grant, offered himself on long argumentative walks as the anvil for Sumner's hammer. The announcement of Grant's cabinet, however, as he explains the matter, closed for him the door of political opportunity. A revolution had taken place which had made him appear "an estray of the fifties, a belated reveller, a scholar-gipsy." Coal, iron, and steam had supplanted agriculture, handwork, and learning. "His world was dead. Not a Polish Jew fresh from Warsaw or Cracow—not a furtive Yaccob or Ysaac—but had a keener instinct, an intenser energy and a freer hand than he— American of Americans, with Heaven knew how many Puritans and Patriots behind him, and an education that had cost a civil war." And so Henry drifted into his antiquarian professorship at Harvard, cut loose from that and wrote his great history of Jefferson and Madison, and only returned to Washington to watch the spectacle, and to sit in his windows with John Hay, laughing at Presidents, and mocking the runner's heat.

Where was the bold energy of the first and second Adams that broke down barred doors of opportunity and found a "charm" in contending against a powerful opposition? Transmuted by the accumulated culture of the Adams family education —not wasted. The mockery and the pervasive irony, so seductive in *The Education,* spring from no sense of essentially depleted energy in the author; on the contrary, they have their origin in a really exuberant sense of spiritual superiority. Adams after Adams has seen himself outshone, in the popular estimate, by vulgar "democratical" men,

by rising men of the "people," whom he has half
or wholly despised—by Franklin, by Paine, by Jefferson, by Jackson, by Lincoln, by Grant.   But
when John Quincy was defeated by Jackson, though
he thought God had abandoned America, he felt
himself still high priest.   And though Henry thought
the progress of evolution from Washington to
Grant sufficient to upset Darwin, and though he
regarded Grant as a man who should have lived in
a cave and worn skins, he reinstated Darwin in the
next breath; for Henry Adams would not have
changed places with Washington; he regarded
Washington himself as but a cave man in comparison with Henry Adams!

In revulsion from a world bent on making twelve
dividends of ten per cent in a year and spending
them for it knew not what, the Adams energy in
him had been diverted to the production of a human
measure of civilization; to a register of the value
of art and social life and manners and those other
by-products of coal and iron which the Philistines
of every age rate as superfluous things; to a search,
finally, to an inquiry all the way from Kelvin to the
Virgin of Chartres, for some principle of Unity, for
some overarching splendor to illumine the gray twi-
light of an industrial democracy.   He did not find
it, but the quest was glorious.

Henry Adams was an egotist.   Granted.   But
what an egotist!   Not since Byron

                                                                bore
With haughty scorn which mock'd the smart
Through Europe to the Aetolian shore
The pageant of his bleeding heart—

not since the days of "Childe Harold" have we had
so superb an egotist in literature, so splendidly in
revolt, so masterly in self-portraiture, so romantically posed among the lights and shadows of history, against the ruins of time. Let us forget and
forgive the unfeeling cynic who inquired, "If a
Congressman is a hog, what is a Senator?" Let
us remember the poet who felt the "overpowering
beauty and sweetness of the Maryland autumn" and
the "intermixture of delicate grace and passionate
depravity that marked the Maryland May." Let
us fix our gaze on the Pilgrim receiving the news
of the blowing up of the *Maine* as he watches the
sun set across the Nile at Assouan:

One leant on a fragment of column in the great
hall at Karnak and watched a jackal creep down
the débris of ruin. The jackal's ancestors had
surely crept up the same wall when it was building.
What was his view about the value of silence? One
lay in the sands and watched the expression of the
Sphinx. Brooks Adams had taught him that the
relation between civilizations was that of trade.
Henry wandered, or was storm-driven, down the
coast. He tried to trace out the ancient harbor of
Ephesus. He went over to Athens, picked up Rock-
hill, and searched for the harbor of Tiryns; together
they went on to Constantinople and studied the
great walls of Constantine and the greater domes

of Justinian. *His hobby had turned into a camel, and he hoped, if he rode long enough in silence, that at last he might come on a city of thought along the great highways of exchange.*

Though Henry Adams was "a Darwinian for fun," in his search for God he was as much in earnest as a man can be who sets out for a far country which he knows that he shall never reach. To him, as to his great-grandfather and his grandfather before him, the tribal Jehovah created by the ancient Semitic imagination, the competitor of Baal and Astoreth, was a mythological abomination, surviving in the minds of those early New England pedants who had instigated the hanging of witches in Salem and the persecution of Quakers and Anabaptists. His ancestors, John and Abigail and John Quincy Adams, had entered into the religious enlightenment of the eighteenth century. But to him, a son of the mid-nineteenth century, the improved God of the Deists and the Unitarians—the bland, just, and benevolent Providence of Franklin, Jefferson and John Quincy Adams—had become as obsolete and incredible as the more markedly vertebrate deity of Increase Mather's time.

Those who read Henry Adams with inadequate sense of his irony may feel that the God whose laws he attempted to discover in his quest through contemporary science is not more real than the Providence of the Deists nor less dreadful than the Jehovah of the old theologians. That all-pervading Power, blind but physically omnipotent, which attracted his mind, that Power which moves in thunder and earthquake, in the growth and decay of living forms, in the dynamo, the gun, the man-of-war, that Power worshipped by Carlyle and Bismarck and Disraeli and Roosevelt and all the "strong men" of recent history—has neither feet to bring good tidings, nor bowels of compassion, nor countenance divine; and knees that have bowed at the foot of the Cross, hands that have clutched the robe of the Virgin, hearts that have cried out of their depths to a heavenly Father, turn uncomforted from Motion and Change enshrined, turn dismayed from the roaring whirlwinds of physical power as from an altar to an obscene Thing.

But Henry Adams turned away, also—and this is the mark of his greatness—murmuring disdainfully, partly to himself and partly to the age which was soon to make ten millions of its sons pass through the fire to its Moloch: "Him whom ye ignorantly worship, the same declare I unto you. Your God himself, in the lapse of ages, has suffered a degradation of energy." Henry Adams turned away from the shrine of the obscene Thing with a jest of invincible skepticism, and went on a long holiday through the Middle Ages, "wooing" the Virgin, incredulous to the end that the divine love should have been transformed and annihilated in the abysses of energy, seeking to the end for a clue to "a world that sensitive and timid natures could regard without a shudder."

The bronze statue by St. Gaudens which in 1887 Henry Adams caused to be erected, without inscription, upon the grave of his wife in the Rock Creek Cemetery, in Washington, seems curiously to symbolize the spirit and the fruit of his own pilgrimage. The strangely haunting figure, enveloped in heavy drapery, sits on a rough-hewn block of granite against a granite wall, the great limbs in repose, the right hand supporting the face, shadowed and almost invisible. Here at sunset, after long wandering, the Pilgrim comes at last to the place where no answers are given; at the gateless wall ponders the mysteries, silent, passive, thinking without hope yet without despair: "Here restless minds and limbs of divine mold rest at last. This is the place of dust and shadow and the dispersion of all that was sweet and fair into the devouring tides of energy. This may be the end of all, forever and ever. If so, so be it."

Thus that sombre figure appears to commune with itself; but so much will is manifest even in its repose, it seems so undefeated even in defeat, that the visitor departs saying to himself: "Man is the animal that destiny cannot break."

XII

AN IMAGINARY CONVERSATION WITH MR. P. E. MORE

American criticism, as I think Mr. Bliss Perry remarked a few years ago, has been singularly unsociable, reserved, and poor in personality. The academic critic delivers his discourse to his audience of ten or a hundred thousand people in the style of a surpliced clergyman reading a presidential proclamation in a great cathedral. Consequently he is not much impressed by them nor they by him. How to get the audience and the speaker in touch with one another is a question that needs to be treated; for the solitude which many of our most serious men of letters inhabit, their remoteness from stimulating living companionship, is like that of the inter-stellar spaces explored by the astronomer's telescope. Lately some of the young people have attempted a solution, which is not, I think, wholly satisfactory. In order to provoke some one to notice them, to speak to them, if only to expose and flagellate them, they have banded themselves, like the Grub Street wits of old, into a league against virtue and decorum and even against the grammar and idiom of English speech.

Impudence is one mode of familiarity, and its vogue is increasing. But there are other ways to make literature affable and engaging which may be recommended to those whose talent for impudence is imperfectly developed. On my desk lies a tattered volume of selections, six hundred pages of the *Causeries du Lundi,* which is like a circle of charming people conversing. It is intimate: many of the writers introduced in these delightful pages were contemporaries and personal friends of the author. Frequently Sainte-Beuve presents no formal treatment of their works. He does something for you which quickens your literary sensibilities as no formal analysis does: he admits you to the inner circle. He makes his writer live for you by dissolving his books and ideas back into the character and personality which they imperfectly expressed, and by then presenting you a speaking portrait, executed with the appreciativeness, the gentle firmness, the candor, the affectionate malice of a friend who, from looking into your eyes year after year, has come to love the crow's feet that time and thought have etched around them.

Mr. More, our American Sainte-Beuve, has painted an abundance of such portraits of celebrities who are dead. But, like the students in the Royal Academy of Art in Sir Joshua's day, he has given little attention to drawing from the life. He has never, like Rossetti, gone to market before breakfast to paint a calf in a farmer's cart. In the hundred and sixteen Shelburne essays, there are only a dozen American subjects; and of these only four or five at the most can be called in any sense "contemporary." This proves, I think, a partial retrogression from the purpose indicated by the epigraph of his First Series: "Before we have an American literature, we must have an American criticism." Mr. More has written distinguished and important criticism in America for Americans apropos of English themes. But he has done too little to meet his poor living fellow-countrymen half way; and to give and to receive the recognitions which are among the functions and the rewards of letters. He has not done as much as he might have done to establish a place for easy colloquial intercourse at some point between the news-papering reading public and that hermit's retreat of his with the Sanskrit inscription above the door.

For this reason, I welcome, as a token of amendment, his preface to his recent volume on *The Wits*. Mr. More has not the prefatory habit. It is his custom to plunge *in medias res*, like an epic poet or a member of the Modern Language Association. But here, like a man of this world, he begins with a preface, affable, familiar, charming, provocative. He chats about the way he composed these essays— that was before he withdrew from New York to Princeton in order that his children might grow up

among the English-speaking peoples—through the
strenuous years in New York, when a Sunday dinner
broke up his one precious day of "scholarly leisure,"
and, when, as critic, he wrote for immortality with
one hand what, as editor of *The Nation*, he ruth-
lssly abridged with the other. He pleasantly dis-
cusses the vices and foibles of reviewers; and so by
insensible degrees he passes to the prevailing foibles
and vices of man; and thence to the present and
perennial need for satire.

If I understand him aright, he intimates that the
unifying spirit of this book is a hope that it will
"vex somebody." It has vexed me sharply at some
points and pleased me much at others, as everything
that he writes does. I shall explain my pleasure
and my vexation with that freedom which I learned
from him and from his equally independent predecessor, Hammond Lamont, two editors, who taught
their reviewers to fear nothing but deviations from
the truth and the insidious vices of puffery and log-
rolling. Of the terrible integrity of that office I
fondly cherish one recollection. I had sent in—it
was long ago—a very "pleasant" review of an
amusing novel by an author who, as I happened to
know, was an old friend of the editor; and I added
a note to the effect that, though the book had some
defects, it seemed not worth while to speak of them
in so brief a notice. Back came the proof, inscribed
in Mr. Lamont's bold hand, with the only suggestion
that he ever made for an alteration in my copy.

"You had better give it," he said, "the full measure of damnation." Mr. More, as all contributors and authors know, sustained the great tradition.

An inheritor of the high mission of damnation does not fluently mix with the various literary adulation societies of the metropolis. To a man of Mr. More's internal preoccupations the great city offers in vain that life which impresses the eye of a Maupassant from Texas as so rich and various. Her highway pageantry, her chirping slopes of Helicon, her "colorful" coast of Bohemia, her swarming literary proletariat, leave him as cold as Nineveh and Babylon. And so Mr. More does not conceal from us that he is happier since he left New York. There are more days in a Princeton week. There is more leisure in a Princeton chair. A man of immense intellectual possessions, he has from the outset manifested a marked predilection for literary society in the grand style; to have much of which, one must choose one's avenue and residence. I conceive the Shelburne essays, to which he adds a wing year after year, as a many-chambered mansion, conspicuously withdrawn from the public highway, built and maintained for the reception of Indian sages, Greek philosophers, great poets, moralists, scholars, statesmen, and other guests from the Elysian Fields, who, but for his lordly pleasure-house, would be hard put to it for a resting place when, of a week-end, they revisit the glimpses of the moon. Let us be thankful—we

academic cottagers, we journalistic occupants of
three-rooms-and-a-bath—let us be thankful for an
intellectual capitalist or so with means and inclination to entertain these shadowy ambassadors from
other ages, and so to establish for our undistin-
guished democratic society fruitful and inspiring
relations with the deathless *grand monde* of antiquity.

If W. D. Howells was the dean of our fiction,
Mr. More is the bishop of our criticism. His classical and Oriental scholarship, his reverence for tradition, his reasoned conservatism, his manner, a
little austere at first contact, and his style, pure and
severely decorous, all become the office. By the
serenity of his pleasure in letters and the life of the
mind he recalls those substantially happy old church-
men-scholars of the eighteenth century, Warton and
Percy and Warburton; by the range of his deep and
difficult reading he suggests Coleridge, to whose
intellectual dissoluteness, however, his intellectual
organization and concentration are antithetical; by
his aloofness from the spirit of the hour and its
controversies he reminds one of Landor, striving
with none, because none is worth his strife; by his
touch of mystic ardor and his sustained moral intensity and philosophic seriousness, he belongs with
Savonarola and the great French ecclesiastics of the
seventeenth century. One may visualize him in
these later years, since his retirement from editorial
duties, as sitting in external and internal placidity

under a pallid bust of Pallas in a commodious
library, learnedly annotating in fine small hand an
interleaved edition of Plato, or poring with a reading glass over the Greek folio of Origen, or perhaps
quite lost to the world in the wide wilderness of
Leo XIII's Aquinas.

Men with such companions are less solitary than
they seem. Upon a scholarly leisure so austerely
industrious, you and I would not lightly venture to
intrude, even though we had heard that after a week
with St. Augustine Mr. More enjoys a Saturday
evening with a tale of Anna Katherine Green; or
will good-humoredly meet the Princeton pundits and
Bluestockings at a rubber of bridge, bringing to the
solution of its problems the logical rigor of Duns
Scotus and the transcendental insight of Plotinus.
On another night, at tea-time or after, Samuel Johnson would not hesitate to stumble in, and, stretching
his great legs towards the fire, challenge Mr. Henry
Holt's views of Patience Worth and the ouija
board, or summon Mr. More to a defence of the
thesis, somewhat wearily stoical, which he has
carved in tall Greek letters across the wide face of
his mantel shelf—a thesis of which this is the gist:
"Man's affairs are really of small consequence, but
one must act as if they were, and this is a burden."
Later in the evening one can imagine that saturated
student of Queen Anne's time, Professor Trent,
completing the semi-circle; and then the three of
them, confirmed Tories all three, joining in an ami-

able but heated altercation on the merits of Milton
and Defoe, or more harmoniously discussing, judg-
ing, and gossiping over the "wits" of tavern and
coffee-house whom Mr. More has gathered into his
latest volume: first, Beaumont and Fletcher, Hali-
fax, Mrs. Behn, Swift, Pope, Lady Mary, Berkeley,
the Duke of Wharton, Gray; and then, more sum-
marily, those golden bugs, those "decadent" fellows
who wore the green carnation and sipped absinthe
for coffee between the reign of Wilde and the reign
of G. B. Shaw.

It is good literary talk—better is not to be heard
in these degenerate days. It is talk now grave, now
gay, richly allusive and erudite and deliciously sea-
soned with malice—"at every word a reputation
dies." For the host, quoting Samuel Butler, has
given his guests this note: "There is nothing that
provokes and sharpens wit like malice." What a
lurking whig or a modern Democrat or a Romanti-
cist would miss, if he were eavesdropping there, is
a clash of fundamental belief and theory. Professor
Trent may differ tenaciously on a nice point, such
as the circumstantial evidence in the case of Lady
Mary's virtue. But as to the *apriori* evidence they
are all in substantial agreement; they accept with
a dreadful Calvinistic accord man's natural predis-
position to evil. They all applaud the wits for saying so sovereignly well those infamous things about
human nature, which, alas, every now and then,
human nature deserves to hear. They all speak sus-

piciously and derogatively of the *mobile vulgus*.
And they fail, as nearly every militant classicist
does, to recognize the "grand style" in Shakespeare,
though, as Mr. More's favorite abomination, Professor Saintsbury truly says, the heretic has but to
open the plays anywhere and read fifty lines, and
the grand style will smite him in the face, "as God's
glory smote Saint Stephen." Mr. More, receding
from the position taken in the second series, now
admits, indeed, that the greater plays are in their
substance "profoundly classic," which is as much
as one ever extorts from a defender of the Acropo-
lis; but he clings to his heresy in the case of *Romeo
and Juliet,* ranking its exquisite symphonies of meaning and music below the ethical plain-song of the
Hippolytus.

We are interrupting better talk than our own.
"Stay, stay," as the German visitor exclaimed on
another occasion, "Toctor Shonson is going to say
something."

"Sir," cries the Doctor, dashing at "P. E. M."
with brutal downrightness, "in your essay on a Blue-
stocking of the Restoration, you have applied a vile
phrase to Congreve. You have done an injustice to
Congreve by coupling him with Wycherley and Mrs.
Behn as 'wallowing contentedly in nastiness.' A
critic should exert himself to distinguish the colors
and shades of iniquity. Wycherley splashed through
the filth of his time like a gross wit. Mrs. Behn
dabbled in it like a prurient and truckling wit. Swift,

indeed, wallowed in it, not contentedly but morosely, truculently, like a mad wit. But Congreve picked his way through it disdainfully, like a fastidious wit."

"But did you not," inquires Mr. More, "in your *Lives of the Poets*, remark that the perusal of Congreve's works will make no man better?"

"True," retorts the Doctor, "but I acknowledged that I knew nothing of Congreve's plays. Years had passed since I had read them. I am better acquainted with them now. Sir, in the Elysian Fields, Hazlitt, Thackeray, and Meredith, your best judges of wit and the beauties of English prose, converse with the members of my Literary Club in the language of Congreve. Conversational English reached its height in Congreve. In my days of nature, I did him at least the justice of recording that he could name among his friends every man of his times, Whig and Tory alike, whom wit and elegance had raised to reputation. A man who wallows in filth does not win universal esteem. No, sir, Congreve was an acute critic, a man of taste, and a fine gentleman, a very fine gentleman. In your next edition you must retrieve your blunder of representing the patrician wit of the Restoration as wallowing in nastiness."

"I will make a note of it," says Mr. More with an audible sigh of regret. For, to tell the plain truth, Mr. More values the writers of the Restoration chiefly for their wickedness. It is such good ammunition to use on the humanitarian enthusiasts and the whitewashers of human nature. He can forgive Pope his virulent personal satire, but not his deistic optimism. He praises Swift above Pope for his consistent adherence to the representation of his fellows as "the most pernicious race of little odious vermin ever suffered to crawl upon the face of the earth." He requires, or thinks he requires, the Yahoos as hideous caryatydes to uphold the towering superstructure of his aristocratic political and social philosophy.

"Cheer up, More," interposes Professor Trent jocosely; "don't let the loss of Congreve shake your beautiful faith in human depravity. The Doctor allows that Congreve was a rare bird, a very phœnix. I'll tell you a Yahoo friend of Defoe's that you can put in his place. Swift knew his English people. For my part, give me the Turks."

A belief in the baseness of average human nature is, as I have said, something that Mr. More requires as a builder requires a basement, not expecting to live in it. Despite his profession of love for Pope, I suspect he has little more fellow-feeling for the sad wags of Anne's time or of Victoria's than Milton had for his kitchen-folk. When Professor Trent and Doctor Johnson grow weary of impaling ghosts on epigrams and are packed off to a nightcap and to bed, one can fancy P. E. M. returning to the library to recover possession of his soul. Extinguishing the lights, he sinks into his easy chair,

and watches for a time the flickers of his expiring
fire, fingering the dusky folios, while the Princeton
chimes announce the midnight, and silence envelops
that quaint little imitation English city, striving so
bravely amid the New Jersey oil refineries to be a
home of lost causes and to dream, under the Cleve-
land memorial tower, like the Oxford of 1830. As
he meditates there in the fitful gloaming by the
hearthside—Mr. More is one of the last of the
meditative men—the gossip and scandal of the evening's talk rise from his mind like a phantasmal
smoke, in which the huge illusory bulk of Johnson
appears but a whirling eddy in knee-buckles and the
slighter form of Professor Trent but a momentary
shape in frock coat, floating wisp-like heavenwards.

From his mood of recreative dissipation "P. E.
M." passes into his mood of critical self-collection;
thence, into his mood of philosophic contemplation;
and so to his mood of mystical insight, in which
space and time, like insubstantial figments of the
imagination, dissolve and mingle with the smoke
and the Professor and the Doctor, and drift up the
flue into night and nothingness. "Such stuff as
dreams are made of," murmurs the mystic, in a
mood like that in which Carlyle saw through the
transparent body of Louis XVI the Merovingian
kings wending on their ox-carts into eternity. A
chill pervades the still air of the study. Into the
vacant chairs glide one by one the quiet ghosts
of Henry More, the Platonist, and Sir Thomas

Browne, for whom Oblivion scattered her poppy in vain, and Cudworth rising from his tomb in *The True Intellectual System of the Universe,* and pale John Norris of Bemerton, wafted thither by a passion of loneliness from his dim prison in *The Theory of an Ideal World.* There is no sound of greeting; but the five silent figures commune together in perfect felicity on *That Which Endureth Forever.* They speak not a word, yet they understand one another by a mere interpenetration of their beings. . . . And when the Northern Waggoner has set his sevenfold team behind the steadfast star, and Chaunticlere warns erring spirits to their confines, "P. E. M." rouses himself from his deep trance, and says to himself, softly under his breath, *"Hodie vixi—*to-day I have *lived!"*

After two cups of coffee and a bit of toast, he goes to his desk and, without haste or rest, sets to work upon—what? A man who keeps such company and lives such an internal life should write his memoirs, a new *Biographia Literaria,* a philosophical autobiography. Such a book from Mr. More, delivering in his pure grave style a continuous narrative of the travels and voyages of his spirit from Shelburne, New Hampshire, by way of India to ancient Athens, making all ports which for storm-tossed sailors trim their lamps,—such a narrative, plangent through all its reserves with nostalgia for the infinite, would be of unique interest and value to us, complementing the spiritual adventures of

Henry Adams, and deepening the resonance of American letters.

But Mr. More, returning to his desk, either continues his history of Neo-Platonism, which I wish he could leave to a scholar with no autobiography to write, or else—which fills me with "malice"—he supplants that great work by a Shelburne essay on Aphra Behn. This "pilgrim of the infinite"—what has Aphra to do with him, or he with Aphra? But what is a Shelburne essay? It is generally an imperfect, fragmentary cross-section, sometimes only the outer bark of a cross-section, of the character and personality which I have been sketching. It is criticism, it is history, it is philosophy, it is morality, it is religion, it is, above all, a singularly moving poetry, gushing up from deep intellectual and moral substrata, pure, cold, and refreshing, as water of a spring from the rocks in some high mountain hollow. This poetry of ideas was abundant in the first and the sixth series of the Shelburne essays and was nearly continuous in some of the single essays like *The Quest of a Century* in the third and *Victorian Literature* in the seventh. By its compression of serious thought and deep feeling it produces an effect as of one speaking between life and death, as the *Apology* of Socrates does. There is a pulse in the still flow of it, as if it had been stirred once and forever at the bottom of the human heart. It is for this poetry that we love Mr. More. But one has to go so far for it! In the long series, it is so intermittent! There is so much territory through which it does not flow.

A young friend of mine who takes his world through his pores, little experienced in literary exploration, unable to discover the spring, announced to me, after a brush with the "wits," that the essays are "dry." He is mistaken. A Shelburne essay is not infrequently, however, astonishingly difficult. Mr. More has not attended to the technique of ingratiation by which a master of popularity plays upon an unready public with his personality, flattering, cajoling, seducing it to accept his shadow before his substance arrives. He takes so little pains, I will not say to be liked but to be comprehended, that I sometimes wonder whether he has ever broadly considered the function of criticism—in a democracy as different as ours is from that in Athens. He writes as if unaware that our General Reading Public is innocent of all knowledge of the best that has been said and thought in the world. He writes at least half the time as if he contemplated an audience of Trents, Coleridges, Johnsons, and Casaubons.

Let me illustrate. Occasionally he will give you some paragraph of literary history as plain as a biographical dictionary and as dry as, let us say in deference to Mr. Mencken, as dry as a professor of English. But of a sudden, in a harmless-looking essay, say that on the eighteenth century dilettante, William Beckford, you, if a plain man, stumble and lose your footing over "the law of *autarkeia*, the perception of the veritable infinite within harmonious self-completeness which was the great gift of the Greeks to civilization"; and down you go whirling headlong into the bottomless pitfall and abyss of a discussion of the difference between the Oriental and the Occidental sentiment towards the infinite and towards personality, while Hinduism, Semitism, Alexandrianism, Platonism, and the Gnostic and Manichean heresies rush past you with the flash and roar of the wheels within wheels that dazzled Ezekiel when the heavens were opened and he saw "visions of God"—and "my word," as Mr. Drinkwater's Lincoln would say, what a God! You are, it is true, brought out of that headlong plunge into the unfathomable, as a skilful sky-pilot brings you out of a "nose spin," or as a dentist brings you out of the gyrations of a nitrous oxid trance; and you hear Mr. More at your side quietly, suavely assuring you that now you understand "why Goethe curtly called romanticism disease and classicism health." Maybe you do; but it is not by reason of your ride behind him on the Gnostic nightmare. What passed in that flight is only a shade more intelligible to you than a Chinese incantation. Your education was imperfect: you are neither a Coleridge nor a Cudworth.

"Perverse as it seems to say so," remarked Matthew Arnold in reply to Professor Newman's charge that he was ignorant, "I sometimes find myself wishing, when dealing with these matters of poetical criticism, that my ignorance were even greater than it is." How often one wishes that Mr. More would steal an hour from the study of Neo-Platonism to meditate on that paradoxical utterance! How often one wishes that Mr. More's ignorance were far, far greater than it is. With many of Arnold's fundamental intentions in criticism he is profoundly sympathetic; but he has never, as it appears to me, felt in a compelling way the Englishman's passion for diffusing his ideas, for making them "prevail," for carrying them from one end of society to the other. He has never taken adequately to heart Arnold's true and memorable description of the "great men of culture." They are those, Arnold declares, "who have labored to divest knowledge of all that was harsh, uncouth, difficult, abstract, professional, exclusive; to humanise it, to make it efficient outside the clique of the cultivated and learned, yet still remaining the *best* knowledge and thought of the time, and a true source, therefore, of sweetness and light."

When I ask myself why "P. E. M." has not taken these words more obviously home, why he writes so exclusively for the "clique of the cultivated and learned," I come invariably to one conclusion, namely, that his interest in the uncultivated and unlearned is horribly chilly, is not much livelier, in fact, than his master Plato's concern for the Helots, who are silently to bear on their shoulders the burden and splendor of the Athenian Republic; is not much warmer than his master Burke's concern for the driver of oxen, the carpenter, and work-master, who are not to be sought for in counsel, but are "to maintain the state of the world." When I consider how rich "P. E. M." is in the very wisdom which our democratic populace needs and vaguely desires, and when I observe how persistently he repels the advances of the vulgar by flinging a handful of political and social icicles in their faces, I wish from the bottom of my heart that he had loved the exclusive, metaphysical, aristocratic Plato less and the hobnobbing, inquisitive, realistic, democratic Socrates more.

If Socrates were among us to-day, I am convinced that he would be leader of the Democrats in the House; but Plato, I suspect, would be a member of the Senate from Massachusetts. Having Plato as his monitor, Mr. More sides politically and socially with the little group of Americans who hold that there are only half a dozen great families, all in the Republican party, capable of governing and guiding the destinies of the United States. Though they may pass without question for "good" citizens, distinguished and patriotic, they have never accepted one characteristic word that Jefferson wrote into the political Scriptures of the American nation; they have never felt one generous throb of the faith, regenerative and sustaining and uniting, which Jefferson poured broadcast upon the spirit of the

American people—faith in the sense and virtue of the community and in the sense and virtue of the majority of its components.

With Socrates as his guide through the modern world, "P. E. M." might have left his library and have broken from the circle of his Immortals, to stand on one leg and grow wise in the market-place. He might have suppled and vulgarized his tongue to chat with the work-master and carpenter and the driver of oxen who have had an American education and have fought under the American flag from Verdun to Archangel for, as they thought or hoped, an American democratic faith. He might have fallen in with the young carpenter, cited for gallantry in the Argonne, who is repairing my roof; or with another, concealing a Carnegie medal, who built me a tolerable bookcase after saving, single-handed, seventeen lives in a fire. He might have met with a Northern peasant farmer of my acquaintance who, after recounting the hardships of his winter work in the absence of his eldest son, said to me, with a smile as profoundly philosophical as anything in Epictetus: "Well, I suppose that is what we are here for." He might have read the halting, ill-spelled letters of that stalwart eldest son who, while breaking mules for the Expeditionary Force in France, wrote to his old mother with a filial piety as beautiful as anything that Mr. More commends in Pope.

If he had enjoyed opportunities such as these—

somehow he seems always to have evaded them—he
would have recognized with dismay that Swift and
the wits have coarsely libeled the *mobile vulgus* and
have deceived him about its capacities and tendencies. He would have discovered in the average man
—along with healthy self-interest, petty vices, and
envy enough to keep him stirring—courage, forti-
tude, sobriety, kindness, honesty, and sound practical intelligence. If he could have pressed critically
into the matter, he would have discovered something even more surprising. He would have learned
that the average man is, like himself, at heart a
mystic, vaguely hungering for a peace that diplomats cannot give, obscurely seeking the permanent
amid the transitory; a poor swimmer struggling for
a rock amid the flux of waters, a lonely pilgrim
longing for the shadow of a mighty rock in a weary
land. And if "P. E. M." had a bit more of that
natural sympathy of which he is so distrustful, he
would have perceived that what more than anything
else to-day keeps the average man from lapsing into
Yahooism is the *religion of democracy,* consisting
of a little bundle of general principles which make
him respect himself and his neighbor; a bundle of
principles kindled in crucial times by an intense emotion, in which his self-interest, his petty vices, and
his envy are consumed as with fire; and he sees the
common weal as the mighty rock in the shadow of
which his little life and personality are to be sur-

rendered, if need be, as things negligible and transitory.

I am speaking of the average man and traits of his which I can never contemplate, being one myself, without a lift of the heart; and I frankly avow that it vexes me to hear this emotion which does so much to keep us average men from weariness, and from the devastating cynicism of the wits, and the horrid ennuis of the great, and from their sense that the affairs of men are really of small consequence— it vexes me to hear this emotion dismissed as fatuous democratic self-complacency.

But even as I write these words, I seem to hear Mr. More, in an accent slightly eighteenth century, exclaiming, not without asperity, yet rather in pity than in anger: "Sir, I perceive that you are a vile Whig!"

To which I reply, not without animation, yet more in affection than in malice: "Sir, I perceive that you are a stubborn Tory!"

"Sir," says Mr. More, "I am obliged to lean a bit backward to counterbalance the vileness of your Whiggery."

"And, sir," I conclude, "I am obliged to lean a bit forward to counterbalance the stubbornness of your Toryism."